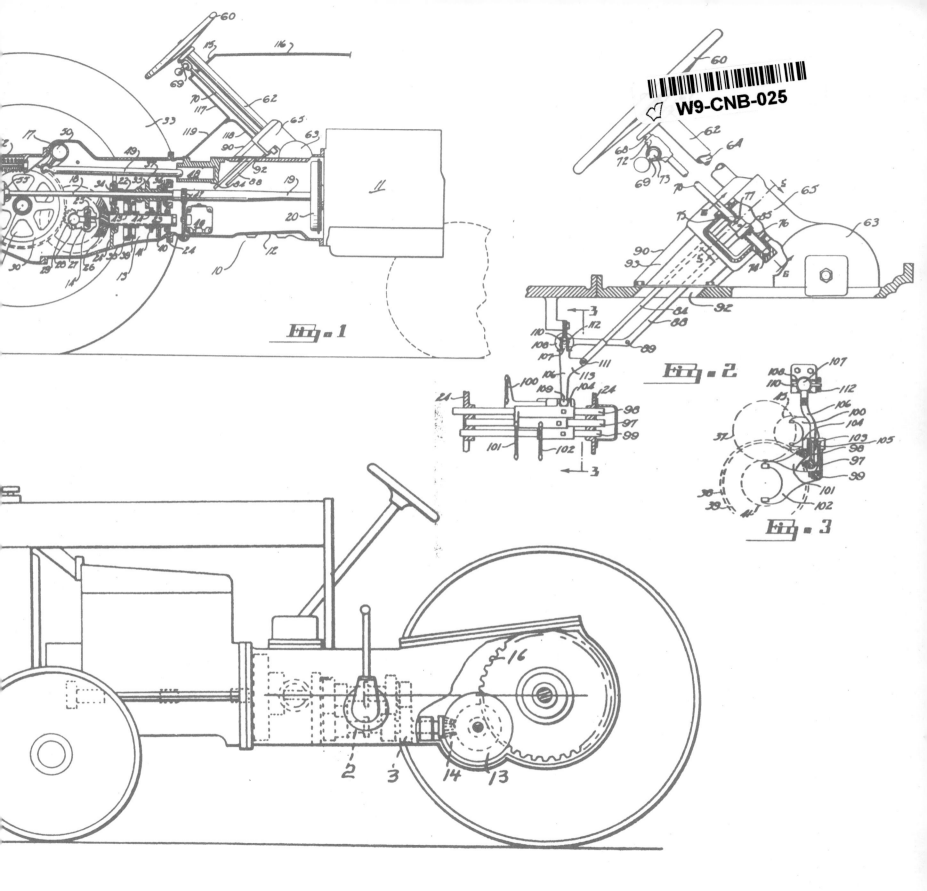

$Fig.1$

$Fig.2$

$Fig.3$

$FIG.1$

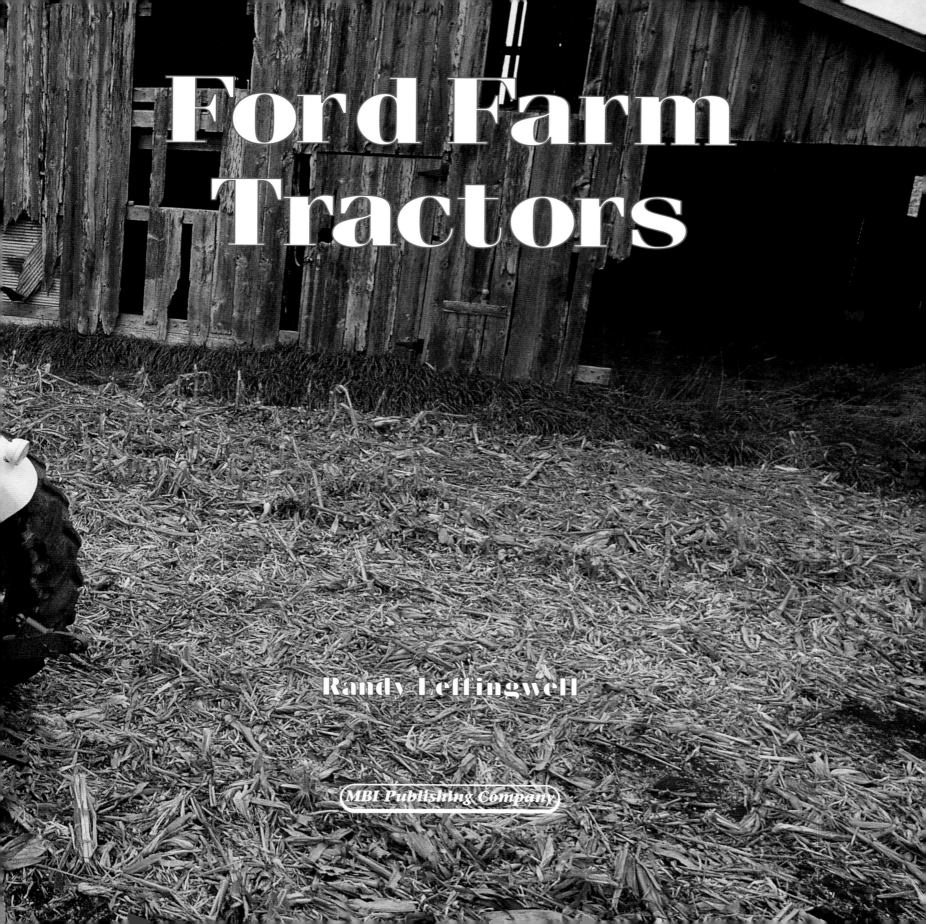

Ford Farm Tractors

Randy Leffingwell

MBI Publishing Company

Dedication

This book is dedicated to Lester Larsen,
director emeritus of the University of Nebraska Tractor Test facility
(from 1946 through 1975).

On the front cover: Ford consolidated their tractor operations in the early 1960s, creating a line of tractors produced worldwide. The red paint formerly used for domestic machines was replaced with Dagenham blue. This model is a 1963 Model 2000.
—*Randy Leffingwell*

On the frontispiece: This early Ford tractor was not actually built by Henry Ford. It was a tractor of questionable quality built in limited numbers by the Ford Tractor Company, a firm that saw fit to name itself that after a single employee, Paul B. Ford.—*Randy Leffingwell*

On the title page: This 1967 Ford 6000 LPG with Select-O-Speed transmission, full hydraulics, PTO, and the LPG fuel system, weighed in at nearly 7,000 pounds and sold for almost $5,600. Ford's Model 6000 tractors were plagued with problems from their introduction in 1961, ultimately causing Ford to replace them under warranty.—*Randy Leffingwell*

On the back cover: Top: This Ford N-series tractor was owned by the late Albert Dunning. —*Randy Leffingwell*
Bottom: The Automobile Plow towing an early type of road grader. Considering automotive development in 1907, the Automobile Plow was a fairly sophisticated machine. A transverse spring supported the front axle below the fuel tank. *Henry Ford Museum and Greenfield Village*

First published in 1998 by MBI Publishing Company, 729 Prospect Avenue, PO Box 1, Osceola, WI 54020-0001 USA

© Randy Leffingwell, 1998

MBI Publishing Company books are also available at discounts in bulk quantity for industrial or sales-promotional use. For details write to Special Sales Manager at Motorbooks International Wholesalers & Distributors, 729 Prospect Avenue, PO Box 1, Osceola, WI 54020-0001 USA

Library of Congress Cataloging-in-Publication Data

Leffingwell, Randy
Ford tractors / Randy Leffingwell.
p.   cm.
Includes index.
ISBN 0-7603-0337-1 (hardback : alk. paper)
1. Ford tractors—History.   2. Title. Ford Motor Company—History.
I. Title.
TL233.6.F66L44   1998
629.225'2—dc21   97-52220

Edited by: Lee Klancher

Designed by: Amy T. Huberty

Printed in Hong Kong through World Print, Ltd.

CONTENTS

ACKNOWLEDGMENTS

I am most grateful to the staff of the Research Center at the Henry Ford Museum and Greenfield Village, Dearborn, Michigan, for kind permission to quote extensively from materials within their archives. The Ford Museum and its Research Center are an engrossing and entertaining place to visit and work, offering abundant information on U.S. history. For their generous cooperation and assistance to us throughout this project, I am particularly grateful to Terry Hoover, archivist; Charles Hanson, head of research/access services, and Benson and Edith Ford Librarian; and to Leo Landis, curator of agriculture. In addition, I must thank Cathleen LaTendresse, access coordinator, Research Center; Linda Skolarus, access services coordinator, Historical Resources; and John Bowditch, curator of steam power. These kind, patient individuals served up thousands of pieces of paper and photographs pulled from hundreds of boxes of archives and accessions to which they steered us and discovered with us. I appreciate perhaps most of all their encouragement and enthusiasm.

No less generous, encouraging, and enthusiastic were Darleen Flaherty, assistant corporate archivist, and Pamela Przywara, project archivist, Ford Motor Company Archives, Ford Motor Company, Dearborn, Michigan. They graciously made available to us voluminous and significant information that is otherwise unavailable. Further, I thank Elizabeth W. Adkins, C.A., manager, archives services, Ford History Department, for her cooperation and advice.

I am extremely grateful to Harold and Kathleen Brock, Waterloo, Iowa, for their time, cooperation, recollections, and encouragement; and to Joe Funk, Coffeyville, Kansas; Delbert and Bernice Heusinkveldt, Sioux Center, Iowa; Edward and Jeannine Pinardi, Dearborn, Michigan; and Bruce H. Simpson, Dearborn, Michigan, for their huge contributions to this history.

Furthermore, I appreciate the detailed and fundamental education I received from Gerard Rinaldi, Chelsea, Vermont, publisher of the N-Newsletter, and from former Ford tractor dealers Don Horner, Geneva, Ohio, and Harold Ypma, Ladysmith, Wisconsin. They also provided most enjoyable and enlightening reminiscences and recollections.

I also thank Jack Heald, Cave Junction, Oregon, for his exceptional research, wisdom, and insight into the earliest days of Ford tractors through the Fordsons.

My thanks go also to Gregory J. Plunges, archivist, National Archives Northeast Region, New York, New York, for his fine judgment and ready assistance in pursuing and sorting through information about William Baer Ewing, et al., and the entire Minneapolis Ford Tractor escapade.

I want to thank Glenn Heim, Lockport, Illinois, for generously opening his extraordinary collection of Model T and Model A tractor conversion kits to me. He tracked down more than 125 such manufacturers and owns more than 50 different kits. Even as he prepares his own book on this subject, he, his wife, Mary, daughters, Katie and Annie, and son, John, worked frantically to prepare the machines for this book.

So many tractor collectors opened their shed doors and willingly provided their machinery and time for photography. I give my heartfelt thanks:

Jack Bernal, Art and Lillian Bright: 1958 Fordson Power Major on Leeford Rotaped tracks, p. 158-9; Duane Chamberlain: 1995 Ford New Holland Versatile 9280 with 24ft disk, p.190; Wayne Coffman: 1938 Ford air-cooled prototype, p. 122-3; Dick Cummings: 1937 Ford prototype with flathead V-8, p. 94, 100-103; Don and Patty Dougherty: 1926 Model T Roadster Pickup with Fond du Lac conversion, p. 42; the late Albert Dunning: 1949 Ford 8N with Wood Bros. Dearborn Harvester, p. 169; Roger and Jane Elwood: 1953 Ford Jubilee NAA with Ford 101 2-bottom plow, p. 172. 1959 Ford 841 Powermaster with ELENCO Front Wheel Drive assist, p.183. 1959 Ford 871 Gold Select-O-Speed dealer demonstration tractor, p. 183. 1959 Ford 971 Select-O-Speed High Crop, p. 184. 1961 Ford 741 Workmaster, p. 185; Dwight and Katy Emstrom: 1939 Ford-Ferguson 9N (#16), p 130-1. 1951 Ford 8N high crop, p. 170. 1952 Ford 8N Meili-Blumberg Road Maintainer, p.171. 1956 Ford 950 High Crop, p. 178. 1957 Ford 840 Sherman Forklift, p. 179. 1967 Ford 6000 Commander (liquid propane gas), p. 189; Tim Farnham; Palmer Fossum: 1926 Fordson F "potato-masher" Horseshoe Lug wheels, p. 76. 1941 Ford-Ferguson 9N with Swan Rapiddiger, p. 136. 1952 Ford 8N with Funk V-8 conversion with low pipes, p. 144. 1952 Ford 8NAN Kerosene, p. 171. 1953 Ford NAA Jubilee with Funk six-cylinder conversion, p. 144; Rocky Fowler: 1938 Prototype with English Ford truck engine, p 122-3; Jack Fuhs and his family: 1925 Five-eighths scale Fordson, p. 79; Rudy and Carol George; Edith Heidrick: 1921 Fordson with 1925 Gleaner Universal Harvester Thresher, p. 61. 1924 Fordson F Trackson Model D Full Crawler, p. 68; Fred Heidrick: 1922 Model T with Shaw conversion, p. 49. 1920s Fordson F Snow-Motor conversion, p. 51; Glenn Heim: 1914 Model T with Geneva Adapto-Tractor conversion, p. 47. 1918 Model T Roadster with Knickerbocker Forma-Tractor conversion, p. 44-5. 1922 Model T Pickup with Pullford conversion, p.48-9; Duane and Carolyn Helman: 1917 Ford prototype 9X, p.32, 38-41 1918 Fordson F, p. 54-5. 1923 Fordson F, Hamilton transmission, Waukesha/Ricardo head, p. 67; Delbert Heusinkveldt: 1948 Ford 8N-V8 Number 3, p. 146-7 1963 Ford 2000, p. 186; Ed and Jeri Huisman: 1938 Ferguson Type A, p. 110-13. 1947 Ferguson TE-20, p. 165; Ralph and Marion Johnson: 1922 Fordson F Trackson Model F Full

INTRODUCTION

Crawler, p. 64. 1923 Fordson Industrial, p. 68. 1944 Ford-Ferguson 2N with Sherman two-way plow; Paul and Lorene Jonas; Ron and Linda Lamoly: 1948 Ford 8N, p 168; David and Suella Lory: 1951 Ferguson-Reekie raspberry/cane tractor, Ferguson sprayer, p.166. 1956 Ferguson TO-35 Diesel, p. 167. 1956 Ferguson 40 Hi-Arch, p. 168; William and Treva Lucabough: 1918 Fordson with Moline 2-row cultivator, p. 56-7 1923 Fordson F on lawn wheels, p.6, 66. 1936 Fordson All-Around, p. 88-9. 1940 Fordson N Standard Agricultural, p.92-3. 1959 Ford 961 Row Crop, p. 185; Paul and Dorothy Martin: 1926 Fordson F one-row Nichols & Shepard Corn Picker-Husker, p.70. 1938 Fordson All-Around, p. 90-1. 1950 Fordson E27N, p. 152, 156, 157; Doug and Margaret Norman: 1940 Ford-Ferguson 9N, p. 133-5. 1943 Ford-Ferguson 2N on steel, p.140. 1949 Ford 8N Hi-crop, p.170. 1953 Ford NAA Jubilee, p. 173. 1955 Ford 660, p.177. 1955 Ford 740 with over-under transmission, p. 174. 1958 Ford 841 with model 711 "side-arm" Front Loader, p. 180 1959 Ford 541 Offset, p.181. 1959 Ford 621 Workmaster, p.182. 1966 Ford 4000 standard Educational Unit, p. 188; Rufus and Dorothy Roberts: 1939 Ford-Ferguson 9N, (#504), p. 132. 1943 Ford-Ferguson 2N on steel, p. 141. 1944 Ford-Ferguson 2N High Crop, p. 120, 142-3. 1947 Ford-Ferguson 2N (left, cast 6-6-47) and 1947 Ford 8N (#637, right, cast 6-6-7), p. 169. 1952 Ford 8N with Funk six-cylinder conversion, Dearborn One-Way plow, p. 148-9. 1952 Ford 8N with Funk V-8 conversion, p.150; Gene Runkle: 1922 Fordson F on Hadfield-Penfield Rigid Rail Model X tracks, p.65 1925 Fordson F on Hadfield Penfield Rigid Rail Model X tracks, p.65: 1936 Fordson N, p. 80, 86-7; Carlton Sather: 1953 Fordson Power Major, p. 157; Bob Scott; the late Roland Spenst and family: 1915 Minneapolis Ford, p. 24, 26-8; Chuck Walkemeier: 1927 Fordson F Wehr One-Man Road Grader, Trackson Model D p. 77; Richard and JoAnn Stout; Lloyd Westerlind: 1969 Fordson County Super Six, p. 161; Chuck Walkemeier; Lloyd Westerlind; Kermit Wilke: 1922 Fordson F with 1928 Belle City Corn Picker, p. 60; Dan Zilm: 1918 Fordson F, p. 52.

I am grateful to my editor, Lee Klancher. He didn't just push me, he shoved me. This book is much better because of it.

Last, but certainly not least, I give heartfelt thanks to Lorry Dunning, historical consultant, Davis, California, and Guy Fay, Madison, Wisconsin, for their extraordinary—and relentless—efforts in research for this book. These two gentlemen are the rest of the "us" to whom Ford Motor Company Archives and the Henry Ford Museum Research Center were so very helpful. These two worked tirelessly to do this book right. Their insights, imaginations, and senses of humor were critical to the completion of this book.

In the past two decades, research on Fordson and Ford tractors has been eye-opening and surprising. Following Alan Condie's first publications, Oregonian Jack Heald, co-founder of the National Fordson Tractor Club, dug into numerous resources to produce his insightful, informative "The Real Fordson Story", which ran in five parts between July 1985 and November 1988 in Gas Engine Magazine. Heald set the standard for Fordson and Ford research, and he excited a lot of interest in Ford's tractors because of what he wrote.

Others followed, enlarging the body of knowledge and folklore along through the Ford-Ferguson tractors and up into the 1960s.

Ford tractor enthusiasts are fortunate that a great deal of the history is safeguarded at the Henry Ford Museum & Greenfield Village. More recent records and documents are held in Ford Motor Company's own corporate archives. While Ford Tractor and Implement Division seemed to not record data that some enthusiasts desire—production numbers for given dates, initial delivery records and the like—even some of that can be deduced from what is still available.

The approach I took was to expand on stories and facts already known and to include first-hand tales of the triumphs and trials of Henry Ford and his engineers. After reading thousands of documents during nearly two months in the Ford Museum and Ford Archives, I realized that there was a wealth of untold history about Ford tractors. I believe this book takes the next step in developing the Ford story.

If you know Ford's tractors, you may enjoy what you read here.

Randy Leffingwell
September 1997

One

HENRY FORD'S EARLY EXPERIMENTS

T is for Tractor

When young Henry Ford first saw a Nichols and Shepard steam traction engine chuffing along, it was too much for the intrepid 12-year-old to ignore. This was early 1876, and it was the first time he'd ever seen something move that wasn't led by horses. Henry had heard of these machines; now, no longer forced to imagine what they looked like, he flagged down the operator, Fred Reden, and put him through an inquisition. Reden told Henry about the steamer and workings. Through the next year he taught Henry to fire and operate it, letting the boy learn its capabilities and peculiarities himself.

Ford was born on his parents' farm in Dearborn on July 30, 1863, during the endless days of the Civil War. He was the second of William and Mary's seven children and their first son. William, primarily a farmer, worked for the railroads as a carpenter when he could. Henry disliked the drudgery of farming and was intrigued by machines.

He left home in 1879, the year his mother died. He lasted only six days on his first job at the Michigan Car Company, 6 miles from home. Michigan Car produced railroad cars with 1,900 employees on an early assembly line. He was fired for impertinence, for fixing something in 30 minutes that others, older than he, had not repaired after five hours of trying.

Henry Ford quickly found work at James Flowers and Brothers Machine Shop in Detroit. He

Henry Ford completed his Automobile Plow in 1905, using a Ford Model B automobile four-cylinder engine and planetary transmission. Ford's chief engineer, Joe Galamb, heavily modified a Dodge Brothers frame, bringing it to a point in front for maneuverability. *Henry Ford Museum and Greenfield Village*

During the summer of 1905, an operator identified as F. Fukalek drove Ford's Automobile Plow while W. W. Case rode the binder. The heavy exhaust smoke was produced by the typically heavy oil consumption of turn-of-the-century gas engines. *Henry Ford Museum and Greenfield Village*

Joe Galamb improved the Automobile Plow in 1907, replacing the cylindrical convection radiator with one from Ford's luxurious Model K automobile. He relocated the fuel tank above the front axle to improve traction. He installed a coil box (above Henry Ford's feet in this photo). This photo was made at Ford Farms; Rufus Bannister Sr. sat on the disk harrow. *Henry Ford Museum and Greenfield Village*

learned blueprints and pattern making, and he produced molds and cast pieces and finished and installed them. He repaired time pieces at night for nearby McGill Jewelry.

Nine months later, he joined Detroit Dry Dock Company at age 17. This was a shipyard and repair shop for steamships, schooners, ferries, and barges built of wood, iron, or steel. It made steam engines from 600 to 3,500 horsepower. On his time off he built his first crude steam traction engine, which lumbered just 40 feet and broke. Before Ford left the

shipyard, he finished his second machine, which performed reliably.

Ford quit at age 20, lured home by the promise of an adjacent 80-acre farm if he would give up machines. With 40 of those acres wooded, Henry saw a chance to keep his hand in machines for the two years it might take to clear the land. He knew he would never farm. He found John Gleason, a neighbor with a Westinghouse portable steam engine, and Ford threshed grain for him for 83 days straight that summer. This impressed John Cheney, Westing-

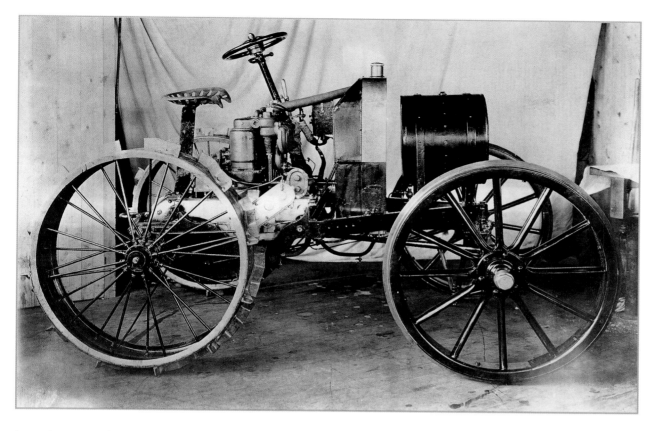

Henry Ford completed his Automobile Plow in 1905, using a Ford Model B automobile four-cylinder engine and planetary transmission. Ford's chief engineer, Joe Galamb, heavily modified a Dodge Brothers frame, bringing it to a point in front for maneuverability. Rear wheels for the machine came from a ground-powered corn binder. The 1907 configuration showed the 20-horsepower Model B engine transversely mounted behind the Model K radiator. The coil box is visible just below the radiator hose. Wheel hubs, steering gear, and other pieces came from the Model K as well. Front wheels were called "artillery wheels." Rear wheels came from a corn binder. *Henry Ford Museum and Greenfield Village*

house's regional distributor, who hired Ford to deliver and set up steam traction engines for customers around southern Michigan.

Ford met 19-year-old Clara Jane Bryant, the oldest of 10 children who lived with her parents a few miles north of his father's farm. They married in April 1888, and for the next three-and-a-half years he milled lumber, keeping some to build their home. In late September 1891, they moved to Detroit. Ford's job with the Edison Illuminating Company would teach him electricity, an element in gasoline engines he hadn't mastered.

He completed his first automobile in 1896 as chief engineer at Edison. His Quadricycle was simple, small, and light, running on a horizontal, two-cylinder engine. It was a perpetual work-in-progress as Ford learned the intricacies of brakes, electricity, chassis, transmissions, and cooling. He sold it for just $200, but not before he drove it extensively, improved it greatly, and showed it widely.

He started on his second automobile at the end of 1897. By July 1899, this larger two-seater was running. When it was reliable, Ford picked up William Murphy, a successful lumber merchant. Murphy ear-

lier had told Ford he would back him if Ford could give him a trouble-free ride to Pontiac, Michigan, and back. Both men were good to their word. With Murphy and others, including a Scottish coal merchant, Alexander Malcomson, Ford founded the Detroit Automobile Company on August 5, 1899. Quitting Edison, he became a full-time auto maker.

Detroit Auto produced only 18 or 19 vehicles. Ford, a perfectionist, wanted to improve the automobile; his backers wanted production and profit. Detroit Automobile came apart in 1901. (Murphy remained, reorganizing it in 1902 with Henry M. Leland. They renamed it the Cadillac Automobile Company, after Detroit's founder.) Malcomson stayed with Ford, and in late 1902, with additional backing, they formed Ford and Malcomson.

Ford's investors directed what he built. The cars Ford and Malcomson made were not simple, widely affordable machines Henry Ford desired. Automobiles were playthings of the rich. His backers, torn between desire for exclusively prepared diversions or larger profit from Ford's automobiles, continued to interfere. Henry was 39 and wiser: he had held onto a greater share of the partnership.

Rufus Bannister rode the self-binding reaper while Burt W. Scott operated Joe Galamb's 1907 version of the Automobile Plow, Henry Ford's "second" tractor. C. J. "Jimmy" Smith sat on the fuel tank, posing with Bannister and Scott for a photo during a break from harvesting wheat on the Ford Farm. Henry Ford Museum and Greenfield Village

Ford already had gathered some mechanics, engineers, tinkerers, and visionaries who would provide years of loyalty and hard work. One of these, C. (Childe) Harold Wills, helped design and fabricate the "999," one of Ford's two race cars. Wills designed the Ford script logo.

By Christmas 1902, Ford, Wills, and others completed Ford's newest design. With funds scarce, Malcomson and James Couzens, his cautious business adviser, sought additional investors. Certain he must move forward, Ford ordered 650 engines, transmissions, axles, and chassis at $250 each from John and Horace Dodge, irascible, inseparable brothers who operated one of America's best machine shops. The Dodges used Ford's blueprints, and cast and assembled the engines and other parts. With all parts coming from outside sources, Ford and Malcomson were essentially car *assemblers*, similar to many hundred others struggling to get started. Between 1900 and 1910, some 500 auto makers opened their doors; 300 failed. This kind of performance frightened investors away from the auto industry.

Once they completed their first car, designated the Model A, in early 1903, Couzens secured several Malcomson business associates and friends. On June 16, 1903, they changed the name to Ford Motor Company. Impressed by Henry Ford's engine and his personal drive, John and Horace Dodge contributed 28 complete running chassis, worth $7,000 and $3,000 cash, giving them 10 percent interest.

Ford Motor Company began on a shoestring. For the first six weeks there were no orders. The company turned out one Model A each day. It still was not perfect in Ford's eyes; yet James Couzens became iron-willed in his determination to deliver products and start cash flowing. Problems came not from Ford's design but from the Dodge's manufacture. Couzens argued for and got deep discounts on faulty pieces, but Ford's name was on the car. John and Horace promised better work; the Model As—substantially revised from early ones in 1903—improved, and sales increased. Couzens developed dealer organizations nationwide, and a service staff from Detroit went out to repair faults and calm angry owners.

By mid-1905, production outgrew Ford's first factory on Mack Street in Detroit. He opened new facilities on Piquette Street. Assembly still was disorganized; outside-manufactured pieces were gathered together, then attacked by a dozen or so men. A completed car emerged a couple of hours later. Ford and Harold Wills both knew this system needed organization: perhaps, like Michigan Car, it could run down a line where subassemblies were attached in a logical sequence.

During 1905, several significant individuals appeared. Charles J. "Jimmy" Smith, young and sharp-witted, worked for Wills as mechanic, innovator, and test driver. Charles E. Sorensen, with movie-star looks but an explosive temper, came in as assistant to the chief pattern maker. A Hungarian-born, German-educated engineer, Joseph Galamb, who had trained at Westinghouse, went to Ford's new Experimental Room. Frank Klingensmith, a bookkeeper and clerk, worked for Couzens keeping a handle on income, expenses, and Ford's mounting correspondence. Each of them, and about 300 other individuals working by mid-1904, was often transferred to one or another of Ford's experiments.

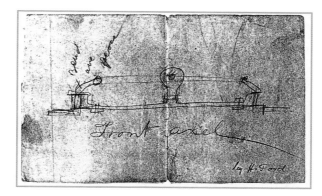

Henry's First Tractor

When the Fords returned to their Dearborn farm in early 1905, Henry meant to begin farming. He began adapting automobile engines to farm implements. He developed his "Automobile Plow," as he called it, from pieces of production cars, taking the planetary transmission from the Model B and the vertical four-cylinder engine from his Model F. Joe Galamb heavily modified a Dodge Brothers' frame, tapering it to a point at the nose to accommodate a pivoting front axle he devised from Henry's sketches. A large cylindrical radiator provided convection cooling. They took wheels from a corn binder; rears were ground-power-type with grousers that turned as the binder crossed the land. Through the fall, Jimmy Smith and Henry himself ran the machine at Ford's farm, mowing and binding. For this it was acceptable, but when plowing came, the machine overheated and never provided enough traction.

Through the winter of 1905 and 1906, Ford directed revisions to the machine, replacing the ineffective cooling system with a Model B radiator. The gas tank was moved out front, isolating it from engine heat and sparks. With the tank full, the weight improved traction, but this benefit decreased as the tank emptied. Galamb fitted the more powerful Model B engine, and he made another planetary transmission. Ford approved of this tractor's light weight (just less than 2,000 pounds), but he was disappointed by its lack of strength. Other tractors available weighed up to 10 times his Automobile Plow. This skewed his thinking. As Allan Nevins reported in his *Ford: the Times, the Man, the Company* (McMillan, 1976), when Henry made up his mind, he wasted no time: " 'Joe,' Ford said to Galamb, seeing him for the first time one morning in the spring in 1907, 'we have to build a tractor in three days.' "

Galamb later recalled that it took them a week. Jimmy Smith explained what happened next, speaking to Ford Motor Company interviewer Owen Bombard in 1951. "We went out on the farm on Ford Road to develop the tractor," Smith told Bombard. "We used to work on it out there, and then Mr. Ford got the idea of making another one . . . a bigger tractor. In order to make that, he wanted to get a place to work where nobody would know about it. So we found a place at 1302 Woodward Avenue [in Detroit]. It was a large old house with a big barn where they used to keep their buggies and horses.

"We got the house and set up a shop in the barn [renting it all for $40 a month]. We made our own patterns there, got the chassis. . . . Then we assembled it all there. That's where we built the first big tractor. . . ."

Richard Kroll, another mechanic with Galamb and Smith, also spoke with Bombard in 1953. These and the other oral reminiscences in this book are part of the vast collections of the Henry Ford Museum.

"There was a barn at 1302 Woodward, which was part of a church. That's where we built that big horizontal type tractor at that time. That was the tractor that had the big water tank on the front. The water inlet was about ten inches in diameter. The reason I remember that so well was because they sent word that they had trouble with the tractor. At that time the tractor was moved out to what they called the Black Farm, where Fair Lane is now. . . .

"When I got there it was about noontime. We went out into the field. Jimmy Smith was running the tractor with Frank McCormick. I asked what was wrong, and he said, 'Nothing.'

"It was running and I said, 'Well, you're not using it. Why don't you shut it off?'

"He said, 'Wait a minute.'

"He goes up to that top opening there and pulls out a sack with eight eggs in it. They were boiling their eggs in there. After he took them out, he shut it off." Kroll recalled this as the heaviest tractor Ford built. The Automobile Plows used stock Model B engines and had been assembled at the Piquette plant. They tested those and the larger tractor at the farm under working conditions.

Ford had an insatiable curiosity and while he could imagine things, he liked seeing them in metal, watching them work in a field or on the road. He might already sense impracticality, or in the case of a large cast-iron tractor, a direction away from smaller size and lighter weight. But failed or discontinued projects yielded developments or ideas of use later. It was Henry Ford's adherence to something historian Allan Nevins characterized as "John Fritz's principle: 'Let's start it up and see why it doesn't work.' "

News of the large tractor spread. L. W. Gunby, a hardware and machinery manufacturer and dealer in Salisbury, Maryland, wrote Ford on February 24, 1910, asking his plans. Frank Klingensmith replied

In spring 1907, Henry Ford assigned Joe Galamb to build a new, much larger tractor. Galamb, Jimmy Smith, and Richard Kroll built it in about a week in a spacious barn rented in Detroit. The tractor was powered by a four-cylinder gasoline engine: Note the spark plug visible beneath the diagonal supports for the front steering column. *Henry Ford Museum and Greenfield Village*

*R*ichard McCormick ran Ford's unit-frame tractor, pulling a two-bottom plow at Ford Farm. The cylinder head supported front wheel framework while cylinders and crankcase carried the rest of the tractor. Due to the huge tank that housed the gas tank, water tank, and radiator, cylinder led many to call it a steamer. McCormick and Jimmy Smith occasionally boiled eggs for lunch in the 10-inch water inlet tube. *Henry Ford Museum and Greenfield Village*

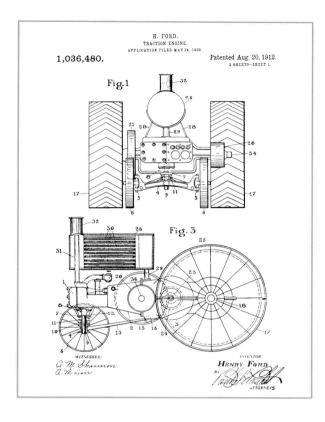

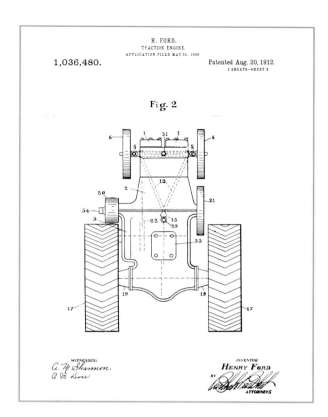

"What I claim as my invention," Henry Ford wrote in his May 24, 1909, patent application, "is . . . a tractor comprising an internal combustion motor with a crank and gearcase extending horizontally from the motor and forming therewith the frame of the tractor, and traction and pilot bearing wheels carrying the frame." In other words, Ford sought to patent a unit-frame tractor in mid-1909. *Henry Ford Museum and Greenfield Village*

While it resembled a steam traction engine, Ford patented this unit-frame internal combustion engine in 1912, a year before Clarence Eason and Robert Hendrickson announced their unit-frame Wallis Cub. The end view shows combustion cylinders below the tubular fuel and water tank. The side view shows the load-bearing structure of the cylinder head and crankcase. *Henry Ford Museum and Greenfield Village*

Once Ford abandoned his 5,000-pound four-cylinder unitized tractor, he asked Galamb to create a new lightweight. Galamb assigned his new assistant Eugene Farkas and Richard Kroll to create a cultivating tractor. Farkas executed an early high-crop Model T, replacing the artillery wheels previously used on Ford's Model T prototypes with these which probably came from hay rakes. Rear wheels were grain harvester bull wheels. *Henry Ford Museum and Greenfield Village*

15

In 1913, Galamb's new assistant, Eugene Farkas, quickly began to work with Model T engines. He carried over little from Ford's Automobile Plow to develop a high-clearance cultivator. In mid-1914, Farkas lowered the machine for plowing, modifying a frame provided by John and Horace Dodge. The early bucket seat was rigidly mounted to the frame, creating a brutal ride. *Henry Ford Museum and Greenfield Village*

Farkas, Kroll, and Smith built four of the Model T prototypes at Henry Ford's Experimental Engineering shops. Here, Farkas drooped the frame rear while using a higher arched front spring to improve ground clearance. Ford had begun casting 10-spoke wheels. Farkas mounted the operator's seat on a spring. Twin tanks were even more heavily reinforced. *Henry Ford Museum and Greenfield Village*

16

for Henry Ford on the 28th: "Mr. Ford has been experimenting for three or four years with Farm Tractors, and is now working on a new one which will be completed this season, which he will put on the market next season.

"This is a four-cylinder machine of 50 horse-power, and will handle a gang of four plows in any soil, throwing 12-inch furrows 8 inches deep, draw any kind of agricultural implements and has pulley for driving any kind of farm machinery.

"There has been no price established as yet, but it will be under a thousand dollars. The fact that Mr. Ford has been experimenting for about four years with this tractor on his own farm, under all kinds of conditions, makes it a sure fact that when this machine is finished, it will be properly presented. The machine will weigh about 5,000 pounds."

This machine was a radical departure from Ford's previous experiments. Joe Galamb used a large four-cycle, four-cylinder engine acquired from the Dodges, mounted transversely and laid over on its side. The engine crankcase and enclosed cast-iron gear transmission housing supported the cast-iron front steering gear and radiator of the tractor. Ford sought a patent.

"In the drawings," he wrote in its application filed May 24, 1909, "an explosive engine of any suitable standard design is disposed with its . . . cylinders (1) horizontally arranged with crank case (2) formed or secured on the inner ends thereof, and a closed transmission gear housing (3) extending therefrom, the cylinders, casing and housing constituting a very rigid, horizontal, substantially integral or one-piece frame."

Henry Ford received his patent, number 1,036,480, granted August 20, 1912, for a unit-frame tractor a year before Clarence Eason and Robert Hendrickson announced their landmark unit-frame "Cub" for the Wallis Tractor Company (and two years before they received their patent).

"Mr. Ford couldn't see the big tractor after that." Jimmy Smith told Owen Bombard. "He wanted something small, like the low priced car was, so he [gave] up the big tractor idea [to] work on a small one."

Adapting the Model T

Ford wanted to reduce the prices. He needed to cut his costs to do it. He and Harold Wills concluded that making parts identical and interchangeable would accomplish this. In the factory, pieces no longer would require painstaking laborious matching of one to the next during assembly. This would benefit customers because any replacement would fit, even engine camshafts or crankshafts. His new Ford Manufacturing Company already provided an

increasing number of parts that the Dodge Brothers had previously produced.

Conflicting philosophies forced a showdown between Henry and Alex Malcomson. Malcomson sold his stock back to Ford Motor Company for $175,000, a grand profit on his initial investment. In the next year, three more investors sold their stock back to Ford, giving him control with 58.5 percent of his company. He could follow his own inclinations, free from interference from others who believed they knew better. One of Henry's goals was to produce products that his own workers could buy. This allowed him to approach another goal of producing several vehicles—automobile, tractor, or truck—on one chassis. To Ford, an altruist and pacifist, a simple vehicle sold worldwide might be the one thing peo-

Two tanks, not headlights, straddled the Model T radiator. The left carried gasoline while the right supplemented the radiator, which required 15 gallons of water daily to cool the engine. With the higher ground clearance, vibration increased. Farkas fitted two straps across the tanks to anchor them. Kroll and Farkas nicknamed this machine "The Bug." Henry Ford Museum and Greenfield Village

reflect the logic necessary for economical and efficient production. The company was building a new plant at Highland Park.

Now Ford would begin tractor experiments from his new car. It offered him an affordable platform on which to make an inexpensive, popular tractor. The 5,000-pound, 50-horsepower four-cylinder was no longer a consideration.

The Model T introduced removable cylinder heads to the scorn of his competitors who assured him they would leak. Ford suggested Joe Galamb set 16 magnets into the flywheel to supply current for the ignition and lights. Once he perfected this magneto system, there was little room for improvement until generators appeared. George Holley, a Bradford, Pennsylvania, machinist who devised carburetors for the Model A, proposed one in solid brass for the Model T; but production costs were too high. He developed a lighter, cheaper, more reliable ironbodied version, which could be adjusted from the instrument panel. The cooling fan was gear-driven. A mechanism within the engine splashed the oil up, letting gravity bring it down to lubricate moving parts. Each of these features made the car suitable to other applications.

Ford cars already were accepted in England. In 1904, a 26-year-old former law student named Percival Lea Dewhurst Perry was co-founder of the American Motor Car Company. In 1908, Perry, as managing director, established the Ford Motor Company branch in London, to import and distribute Model Ts throughout the United Kingdom.

Introduced on October 1, 1908, the car had few problems, and by large measure, these were easily remedied. Within a few years, they resolved production variables and manufacturing glitches. Ford's new plant at Highland Park, occupied in 1909, was as smoothly run an example of mass production as Henry Ford could dream. He nearly had completed acquisition of almost 6,000 acres for his own farm that he and Clara would name Fair Lane. After such preoccupations, he began thinking about farm tractors, anxious to try again.

Joe Galamb, Jimmy Smith, and an engineer named Frank Kratz produced the first tractor based on the production Model T. Kratz, working for Galamb, used a Model T engine and transmission with a dual-reduction rear axle. Then Kratz, tired of automobiles, quit Ford Motor Company to become

Before tractors, Farkas worked on final drive reduction gears for an electric car project. When that project was dropped, Ford asked Farkas to apply the experiences to tractors, resulting in the worm-and-sector final drive. Initially, Farkas placed the worm on top, its shaft housing discernible just to the right of the right-hand plow lift lever. Henry Ford Museum and Greenfield Village

ple everywhere could have in common. The night he reacquired Malcomson's stock, Henry rode home with Fred Rockelman, one of his mechanics.

Allan Nevins quoted Ford: "If you get people together so they get acquainted with one another, and get an idea of neighborliness, the car will have a universal effect. We won't have any more strikes or wars." This optimist's view of human nature energized Ford and directed his company.

By early 1907, Ford knew his next car—the Model T already on the drawing boards in the Experimental Room under care and feeding from Galamb, Smith, and Wills—would be that chassis. They, along with Charles Sorensen and James Couzens, shepherded it from Henry's imagination into production. One last critical element required completion: orderly assembly. Its effects would allow Ford Motor Company economy of production for automobiles and farm tractors. Henry Ford would set up and lay out foundries, machine shops, and assembly areas to

5676-5-26-16

The unit-frame tractor first ran in the winter of 1915–1916, plowing in snow. Once it proved itself, Farkas, Jimmy Smith, and Richard Kroll began a series of prototypes. By late May, they had a more polished unit-frame prototype plowing at Ford's Farm. This tractor with its overhead worm-gear final drive easily pulled two Oliver plows through Dearborn's soil. Farkas moved seating to the center from the Model T's left-side position for better plowing visibility. *Henry Ford Museum and Greenfield Village*

In mid-1914, Galamb learned that Wallis Tractor Company would introduce a new unit-frame tractor later that year, similar to Henry Ford's 5,000-pound tractor five years earlier. Galamb and Ford jettisoned Model T ideas. They roughed out a concept full-size, in chalk on a black cloth board. Later transferring everything to blueprints, they created their own unit-frame tractor using Farkas' overhead worm final drive. *Henry Ford Museum and Greenfield Village*

a home builder, and Galamb brought Gene Farkas into the project.

"That was the Model T tractor," Farkas recalled. "I never knew they built more than 12. They were built at the Highland Park plant. I've seen two or three, maybe more, plowing on the farm."

Fordson historian Jack Heald learned about variations Farkas saw, describing them in his series, "The Real Fordson Story," in *Gas Engine Magazine*. Farkas, Smith, and Richard Kroll, the engineer working for Galamb in the Experimental Department, revised and modified several Model T tractors. They developed a "bent frame" that allowed greater crop clearance. They experimented with a number of wheel sizes and types, with flat spokes, settling on angled spokes for greater strength. Kroll and Smith placed two equal-sized tanks out above the radiator. One held fuel, the other was a water reservoir because

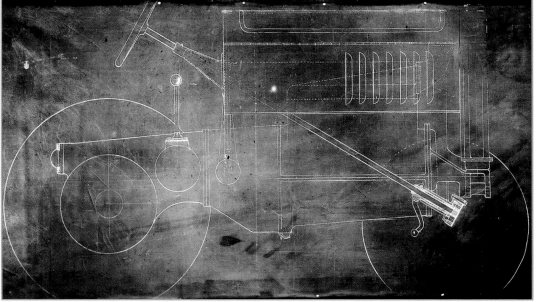

Farkas replaced the previous 10-spoke wheels with new ones with 8 inner and 8 outer spokes. The unit frame, broken into three pieces in this prototype, consisted of engine, flywheel, and clutch housing, and transmission with worm-gear final drive. Several prototypes were completed by late May. The radiator circular badge identified the machine's maker as Henry Ford & Son. *Henry Ford Museum and Greenfield Village*

Model T engines used 15 gallons of water daily. Their bucket seat, first mounted rigidly to the frame, was a brutal ride. Farkas and Smith improved later versions by mounting it on a bent spring. They replaced a hard tube leading from the water reservoir to the radiator with a flexible hose. They developed "Industrial" versions to use as Highland Park shop tugs, but, according to Heald, these were just shortened Model Ts using solid rubber tires all around.

Richard Kroll, working for Galamb in the Experimental Department, told Owen Bombard about a unique tractor he developed at Highland Park.

"This was a high one . . . more of a cultivator. It had high wheels and a seat in the center. Everything was built light. It had to have high wheels for cultivating so it wouldn't knock the crops over. There was a Model T engine in it." It was nicknamed "The Bug."

The May 11, 1915, issue of *The Automobile* magazine published two photos and a story about the Model T-based tractors, announcing that Ford would place on the market later that fall a lightweight machine intended to sell for $200.

The tractor, they reported, "will have much of the familiar Ford car appearance. It will have the same motor, front axle and radiator, but a much stronger and shorter frame. . . . The rear wheels will be 12 inches wide. . . . The weight now is 1,600

pounds but this will be reduced to 1,500 pounds. The tractor will be able to do easily the work of six horses, and it is expected [to] revolutionize farming methods, just as the passenger car has so changed traveling on the road."

This tractor had no name. The Ford moniker was taken by a small operation in Minneapolis that employed a man named Ford so its backers could use his name on the tractor they introduced about this time. Confusion was widespread, as was hoped. Henry Ford puzzled over what to call his machine, hinting in print at the "Auto Plow" and later, the "Agrimotor," a name coincidentally used by a new publication that announced Ford's choice with pride.

As word of Henry Ford's developments spread, Klingensmith fielded requests for information and orders for tractors. Yet Ford, ever the perfectionist, delayed the production start date. Jimmy Smith and Frank McCormick spent hours operating Model T tractors out on the farm. Smith remembered Henry Ford out there as well.

"Mr. Ford tested the Model T himself. He went out with us many a time. Mr. Ford wouldn't let anything go out of the shop unless he was satisfied that it was as nearly perfect as you could make it. . . . He wouldn't sell the tractor developed from the Model T parts because it wasn't right yet."

Further Experimental Work

As Ford's experiments with Model T conversions progressed, he came to believe that an all-new tractor design was the only way to meet his expectations. Design and development of this new machine were done exclusively through Joe Galamb's Experimental Department. Gene Farkas worked under Galamb's and Henry Ford's direction.

These plans, however, made John and Horace Dodge nervous. They had grown wealthy off Ford contracts producing chassis and running gear, but they were also earning big stock dividends from their 10 percent interest in the company. Ford's stated objectives for his new foundry and plant, located east of the Dearborn plant along the Rouge River, would decrease their business. In their view, Ford's expensive tractor experiments, Model T or otherwise, diminished their dividends, costing them money. They wanted tractors stopped.

Eventually, they filed suit to restrain Ford from expanding into any business other than automobiles.

Ford, angered, announced he would pour earnings back into the company to fund expansion. The Dodges panicked. It was partially to satisfy the Dodges that he took his tractor operations out of mainstream company production and accounting, establishing Henry Ford and Son to do so. This gave him independence from outside influence. (That, plus his belief in the tractors, had led him in late 1914 to authorize a production run of 50 or so Model T tractors for extensive testing, before discontinuing the attempt.)

Ford opened his Dearborn Tractor Plant on October 1, 1915. Charles Sorensen, its manager, brought in Gene Farkas immediately. Farkas, along with two other draftsmen, Rene de Lauzaingheim, a Frenchman, and Harold Blair, worked in the experimental drafting room at Fair Lane, a small office the size of a bedroom with a large blackboard and three flat tables. At Dearborn, Farkas said in company archives, they had another little room squeezed in between the new Pattern Shop and the old Machine Shop.

Jimmy Smith's experimental machine shop repaired the farm implements and machinery. When Farkas arrived, Smith's shop had been in operation at Dearborn for nearly a year. Farkas' work increased. He called de Lauzaingheim over from Highland Park. They laid out and detailed a new tractor, taking their prints around to the pattern shop. Smith and Frank McCormick assembled completed pieces in Smith's shop.

Tractor design at Henry Ford and Son had taken a dramatic turn in mid-1914. Fordson historian Jack Heald reported that during the summer, a parts salesman called on Joe Galamb. While they talked, the salesman showed Galamb pictures of Wallis Tractor Company's new "Cub" with a unit-frame design for which chief engineer Robert Hendrickson and his assistant Clarence Eason had obtained a patent (number 1,205,982, following Ford's patent number 1,036,480, by a year). Ford had used the side of the engine block and transmission housing as the load-bearing member; Hendrickson and Eason used the engine sump, transmission, and final drive for that purpose.

Galamb probably experienced déjà vu seeing Wallis' compact tractor. Not only did it use a unit frame, but also it was closer to Ford's goal for his machine: strong, lightweight, and easy to manufacture. This was evident to Galamb's experienced eyes. Ford abruptly discontinued experiments on the

Model T Tractors

"The first I heard about the design of another tractor was when Mr. Ford told me to design one. The transmission demanded more attention than anything else, because on the Model T tractor we simply used the planetary transmission, but on this new tractor we decided that this new transmission would have to be part of the gear reduction system."

Farkas, hired in 1913, was first assigned to Ford's ill-fated electric car. This was meant as a tribute to Ford's friend Thomas Edison, and it was to use Edison's new steel plate batteries. There were many challenges. Slowing an electric motor to suitable road speeds required a double reduction final drive, introducing too many gears, and too much weight and friction. The prototype would barely move.

One day, watching it struggle, Ford thought out loud about final drive configurations, saying to Galamb and Farkas, "Now, if you make that a single reduction, a worm drive, that would be so much simpler."

"Right away," Farkas told interviewer Owen Bombard, "we started to work on a worm drive. . . . I made everything bronze. But Mr. Ford wanted it cast steel. He wanted to take the last ounce of weight out of anything.

"We finished the job . . . but [we didn't get] the right data about the battery. They had to put in lead batteries which were twice as heavy. It was abandoned. I was put on the tractor job almost immediately.

In August 1916, Jimmy Smith went with Kroll, Galamb, Charles Sorensen, and Henry and Edsel Ford to Fremont, Nebraska, for national tractor demonstrations. They took three tractors, one each running on alcohol, gasoline, and kerosene, and a large static display showing construction and the parts of the new tractor. Jimmy Smith, on number 28, plowed through a huge crowd. *Henry Ford Museum and Greenfield Village*

In late fall 1916, Henry Ford stood on the plow drawbar after dropping a plowshare. Jimmy Smith drove the tractor down a road alongside Fair Lane Farm (on which construction had begun two years earlier). By this time, Ford had authorized assembly of 50 prototypes for rigorous testing in harvesting, plowing, and disking activities. *Henry Ford Museum and Greenfield Village*

Henry Ford's faith in worm gears led him to a different approach to reducing high engine speeds to usable ground speeds for a tractor. He proposed to Galamb and Farkas they take some of the reduction inside the transmission; this reduced the size of the final worm pinion gear. Farkas inverted his original design to better lubricate and cool the spiral worm gear. This full-size paper blueprint reflected changes made in chalk on the drawing. *Henry Ford Museum and Greenfield Village*

"They already had another tractor running around. . . . The original Model T tractor used the planetary transmission, and we just had a bigger reduction on the rear . . . , about thirty-six to one.

"Here was a big problem. To design a worm drive with one reduction, thirty-six to one . . . , it would heat and the efficiency would be low. . . ."

Farkas explained that with this 36:1 ratio, there would be great loss of efficiency due to friction. He calculated actual loss to a 20-horsepower tractor at 20 percent. "That would be four horsepower, and the heat generated that was transmitted with the oil would be terrific. It would be enough to burn itself up." Or fry the backside of an operator seated above it.

Farkas recalled that Ford suggested "we take part

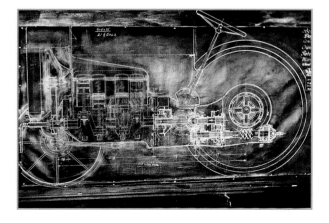

of the reduction in the transmission and the other part in the worm. That's the way we built those tractors that we finally demonstrated on the State Fairgrounds in 1915.

"That entire tractor was laid out on the blackboard but no final details were settled, and the detailed drawings had not been started yet. It was just a preliminary layout . . . full size. Mr. Ford liked to see these right on the wall so he could see exactly what it looked like.

"This new tractor had no frame. There was quite a discussion on that when I first went out there. . . . I convinced Mr. Sorensen that it didn't have to have a frame. He could design the castings so that they will be strong enough to support the entire tractor. I remember he was trying to talk that over with Mr. Ford privately."

Jimmy Smith recalled events during the fall and early winter. "When we were developing the tractor, Mr. Ford bought another tractor made in Europe, a couple of them, and brought them over here. He wanted to find out what they were developing over there. These were gasoline tractors.

"At this plant where the Engineering Building is . . . we had a foundry where they made castings. I remember the time the tractor was first run. We got it put together and ran it inside the foundry building—it was the only place that wasn't frozen."

"The first tractor was completed a little after the first snow fell," Gene Farkas recalled. "I was worried about it and how we were going to try it out if the snow fell because we wouldn't be able to plow. The snow fell all right, but we went ahead and plowed anyway and turned the ground over.

"The first experimental tractor was working all right, it was plowing. It had more power than the Model T, and it was heavier and it held the ground better. My recollection is, outside of a little incident of a front axle failure which we remedied shortly afterwards, we had no trouble with it. That is, we had no trouble at the beginning. We had plenty of trouble later on. Things happened, like dirt getting into the bearings and the sand getting in there. We found out that the tractor had to be protected from dust and sand much better than an automobile."

The October 14, 1915, issue of *The Automobile*, reported, "The building upon the property of Henry Ford in Dearborn, where the first Ford tractors were built, is to be greatly enlarged so that

building of experimental tractors on a large scale may be started. It is said that many changes will be made in the new demonstrators. . . . The demonstrations given by the tractors at the recent Michigan State Fair led to many suggestions for their improvement." Another item one month later described the building as four stories in height and 160 by 800 feet, with several small buildings as well. Price of the addition, the goal of which was to make the factory "the biggest and best equipped tractor plant in the world," was $1 million.

Farkas recalled assembling the tractors one after another, each one slightly different as they learned how different parts functioned. Only five or six were completed before Henry increased the run to fifty.

"Even that first fifty wasn't the final design," Farkas explained. "The final design was entirely different. We had about a year and a half on these experimental tractors before we crystallized one

design. We had the entire farm at our disposal, to plow them up and fit them up."

Three of these 50 were painted white, one each running on alcohol, gasoline, or kerosene. These went to Fremont, Nebraska, for a national plowing demonstration in early August 1916. Jimmy Smith, Richard Kroll (in charge of the experimental machine shop), Galamb, and Sorensen accompanied Henry Ford and his son Edsel. Along with the three tractors, they brought a large display showing parts and construction of the tractor.

"Those fifty were made in 1916, before Sorensen went over to England," Farkas recalled. "The only way I found out that England was interested in these tractors was when the trip was decided upon. I had to get two tractors ready with the latest design and equipment. The decision was made that Bricker and Sorensen should go. Those were the experimental tractors that were shipped January 27, 1917." (Mead L. Bricker at that time was Sorensen's deputy.)

During hay harvest in the fall of 1916, prototype number 16 showed a few of the ongoing improvements. Gene Farkas viewed each tractor as a work-in-progress. Changes appeared on one tractor but not another. Louvered engine side panels and six-spoke rear wheels were obvious. More subtle was the change from round to oval "Henry Ford & Son" badge on the radiator. *Henry Ford Museum and Greenfield Village*

EWING'S FORD TRACTOR

What's In a Name?

Farm tractor manufacturers were more common than perfect weather around 1910. According to historians Glenn Heim and C. H. Wendel, more than 1,000 U.S. companies promised, attempted, or actually produced farm tractors. In 1905, barely a dozen of them made gas-engined machines. By 1915, there were more than 150 doing this. Name repetition was an occupational hazard. There were three Generals, four Uniteds, five Universals, six Westerns, and 10 calling themselves the American Tractor Company. Considering the unregulated nature of these operations, some of this was not coincidence; it was fraud. The first tractor company to call itself Ford was one such case, its only connection being a young employee, Paul Boynton Ford, hired solely for his name.

Within this vast number of tractor companies, a tiny fraternity of talented engineers were responsible for designing many smaller companies' tractors. While the larger manufacturers had the resources to assemble talented in-house staffs, these makers hired independents who never quite connected with the majors, or never wanted to. Robert Stanard Kinkead was one such independent. So was Clarence Eason, as well as D. Maurice Hartsough and Dent Parrett. As designers and consulting engineers, these people were responsible for creating (or avoiding patent infringement for) perhaps 100 tractors during the early days.

*I*n 1915, William Baer Ewing, a San Francisco promoter, appropriated D. Maurice Hartsough's tractor design. Ewing hired another Minneapolis-based designer, Robert Kinkead, to revise it. Ewing paid a shop clerk, Paul B. Ford, to use his name. Kinkead felt the tractor needed work, but Ewing knew Ford's name would sell; he hurried his flawed Ford Tractor into production in 1916.

The engine came from Gile Boat Works, Luddington, Michigan. Rated at 8hp drawbar and 16hp on the belt pulley, the two-cylinder-opposed engine measured 5in bore and 6.5in stroke. In the late 1960s, North Dakotan Roland Spenst found this tractor and restored it, showing it often before his death in 1997. Its original magneto had disappeared but Spenst found it ran well with an International.

The designer whose work eventually led to the creation of Ewing's Ford Tractor, D. Maurice Hartsough, became one of the co-founders of the Bull Tractor Company. Hartsough designed a powerful machine that Patrick Lyons noticed working in North Dakota in 1904. Hartsough improved the machine for Lyons' new operation, the Transit Thresher Company, organized in 1906. Two years later when the "Big 4" 30-horsepower tractor came out, Lyons and Hartsough formed the Gas Traction Company. The Big 4 was powerful and reliable, an

uncommon package in those days. Emerson-Brantingham bought them in 1912 for just those reasons.

Hartsough designed another tractor, and Andrews Heating Company in Minneapolis built prototypes. Named the Little Bull, Lyons showed one in September 1913 at the Minnesota State Fair. Its $355 price and enthusiastic reception accelerated the introduction. With additional backing, Lyons and Hartsough started Bull Tractor Company in 1914.

The Little Bull was insufficiently developed, and its opposed two-cylinder engine lacked power for

The two drive wheels were 54-inch diameter rolled steel, 12 inches wide, with wrought-iron spokes and cast-iron hubs. The rear was 24 by 6 inches. Ground clearance was 11 inches. Ewing had Kinkead and Ford patent the design despite flaws. Kinkead quit in frustration. Ford was made a director of the firm, paid for use of his name, and then given stock in the firm.

The Hartsough-Kinkead design drove off the two large front wheels and steered with the single rear. The tractor was nearly as wide as its wheelbase; with any drawbar load, the tractor wandered from side-to-side, pulled by the plow more than the tractor pulling it. It measured only 11 feet long while it was 6 feet, 5 inches wide and weighed 3,800 pounds.

For $350 the buyer got a Ford Tractor produced in Minneapolis. William Michaels and Sons, agents in Monroe, Indiana, for the Ford tractor, promised, on receipt of a $75 down payment, to arrange delivery, for which the $275 balance plus shipping had to be paid within 48 hours. The warranty, good for parts for one year from purchase, promised free replacement.

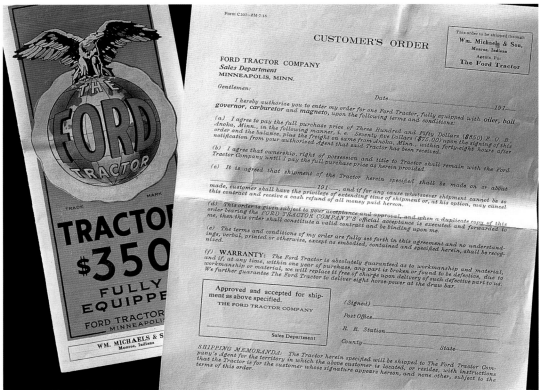

tough work. Still, Bull sold 3,800 machines from April through December 1914, when Hartsough's companion Big Bull appeared. This 4,500-pound, $585 three-wheeler used a stronger, opposed two-cylinder engine produced by Gile Engine Company of Ludington, Michigan. Both Bulls, driven by one of the two rear wheels, were manufactured by Minneapolis Threshing Company. By 1915, these two machines propelled the Bull Tractor Company to becoming the industry's production leader.

In late 1915, the Little Bull's reputation caught up with them. Gile Engine Company had bailed out earlier. Minneapolis Threshing introduced its own tractor, telling Bull plant space was no longer available. Hartsough designed a new tractor and departed, while Bull struggled to stay afloat.

Visiting Chicago, Hartsough met William Baer Ewing, a wealthy San Franciscan who had just arrived. The two men joined forces and convinced Diamond Iron Works in Minneapolis to produce Hartsough's new tractor, based on his reputation and Ewing's assurances of support. They founded Lion Tractor Company. The Lion, a short three-wheeler with rear-wheel steering, used the Gile two-cylinder 8-16 engine promised to Lyons by Gile. When Ewing announced the $565 tractor in early 1915, Patrick Lyons sued. A federal court restrained Lion from manufacture. Ewing urged Hartsough to continue production, saying things would blow over. Taking no chances, Ewing discretely withdrew, removing a set of drawings with him. (Hartsough settled with Bull in 1916, but neither firm recovered; both were out of business before 1920.)

Ewing took Hartsough's drawings and hired a reputable designer, Robert Kinkead, to develop the design for manufacture. As the owner of Kinkead Tractor Company, Kinkead produced his own machine. His three-wheeler used a cross-mounted four-cylinder engine driving a central rear wheel, steering with the two in front. Kinkead judged that Hartsough's machine needed work because, as the story was reported in the August 2, 1917, *New York Times*, "it would not plow to a line." The story went on to say, however, that "the machine turned out to be good enough for Ewing's purposes."

With a semi-workable design in place, Ewing needed a good name for his tractor. He discovered Paul Ford, who was employed by the Andrews Heating Company (Hartsough's prototype builder). He made Ford a director, gave him stock, and incorporated the Ford Tractor Company (in South Dakota), renting a plant in Minneapolis.

The shaky foundations of Ewing's Ford Tractor Company were poorly hidden, at least to those who looked closely. In 1915, General Motors (GM) knew of Henry Ford's plans to build a tractor. GM founder Billy Durant, unfamiliar with tractors, hired Philip Rose, technical editor of *Country Gentleman*, to report on the business. Durant wanted Rose's recommendation on which tractor to acquire to get GM quickly into the business. Rose investigated 98 companies, finding many in Minneapolis. He was unimpressed with Ewing's Ford Tractor.

"This company is another stock selling proposition," Rose wrote. "W. Baer Ewing is president and promoter. He is well known in Minneapolis for . . . a number of other bubbles. . . ." Ewing had a reputation, Rose learned: When dividend payments came due, he discretely withdrew.

"The name Ford is probably assumed for its trade value," Rose reported. "A young man named Paul Ford is manager. Until recently, he worked as a hard-

THE FORD TRACTOR

$350

Fully Equipped, including Magneto, Carburetor, Governor and Oiler.

| Does the work of 6 to 8 horses. Costs less than a good team. | Develops 8 horse power at draw bar and 16 horse power on the belt. |

THE FORD TRACTOR COMPANY
General Offices: 2619-2627 University Ave. S. E.
MINNEAPOLIS, MINN.

ware clerk in one of the city stores.

"The tractor is small and light and does not look to have enough metal to stand up to the work for which it is intended. The workmanship is not good and there are many faults of design."

Ewing funded Ford Tractor Company offices, flyers and advertising, and patents. On October 18, 1915, Kinkead and Ford applied for two patents, with rights assigned to Ewing. One was for an entire tractor, the second for its transmission.

Ewing received patent number 1,243,184, on October 16, 1917. The "variable transmission mech-

How many orders were placed for the Ewing Ford Tractor is unknown. One significant buyer was Nebraska educator and state legislator Wilmot Crozier. His Ford broke before he got it to his farm. He found its warranty worthless. Enraged, Crozier proposed Nebraska permit manufacturers to sell only after thorough evaluations verified the claims. When his law passed, the University of Nebraska began testing tractors in 1920.

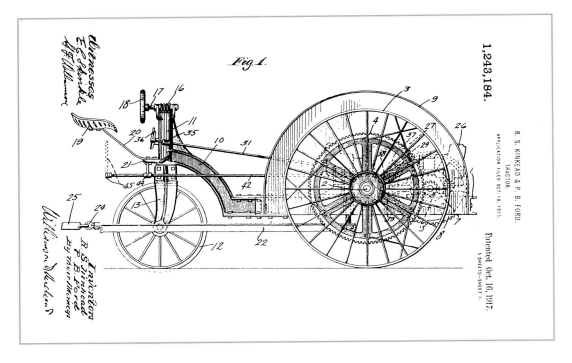

While the tractor measured 11 feet long overall, its wheelbase was barely 5 feet, 6 inches, 1 foot less than its width. With only the operator's weight over that single rear steering wheel, it is no wonder that the tractor "would not plow to a line." Designer Robert Stanard Kinkead wanted to revise the machine, but Ewing refused.

anism" patent had cleared four months earlier. Working toward these patents, Ford and the more experienced Kinkead concluded that, while they strove to produce a reliable, competitive tractor, Ewing had other ideas. He discretely withdrew from Ford Tractor of South Dakota. The *New York Times* continued the story, a history of Ewing's exploits.

"The company ran along for about one year from June 1915. Then Ewing, it was said, got into a wrangle with his associates. Some of those who had bought stock raised a row, and Ewing was on the verge of being forced out when he threw the company into bankruptcy."

Ewing organized Ford Tractor Company Inc. of Delaware. He acquired the "good will and assets of the South Dakota concern [drawings, patents, and Paul Ford's name], and assumed responsibility for $9,000 of its liabilities." The Delaware Ford began business on November 8, 1916. Ewing was listed as president, Paul Ford as a director.

Ewing arranged with Nichols Field Wilson, a broker with Robert P. Matches and Company (whom he had met in San Francisco during a taxicab promotion) to sell stock. At Wilson's suggestion, Ewing increased the capital of Ford Tractor from $1 million to $10 million, because "stock in a big concern sold much more readily than stock in a small concern." Nearly 80,000 shares sold to almost 2,000

investors for between $40 and $50 a share.

The arrangement was questionable. C. H. Wendel reported that "the contract called for a sale of $3 million in stock; $850,000 to go to the Ford Tractor Company, and $2,150,000 to the Matches stockbrokers."

Earlier that year, New York financier Willis George Emerson contacted Matches. Emerson wanted to produce an automobile to rival Henry Ford's Model T. Emerson hired 39-year-old Robert Craig Hupp, creator of the Hupmobile, to design and oversee production of the Emerson. With Theodore A. Campbell, a respected engine designer (co-founder of the Imperial Automobile Company of Michigan) as president, Emerson needed Matches' help. Nichols Wilson became a director, and they incorporated on April 29, 1916.

As the federal indictment quoted, beginning on June 21, 1916, Wilson mailed out stylish, heavily illustrated brochures to potential investors. He claimed that at "Emerson Motors Company . . . work was in progress, assuring the delivery of several hundred cars in the year 1916, and that . . . contracts were being made and material purchased to begin manufacture of one hundred cars a day by January 1, 1917."

The stock proposals, written by Wilson, were pure fiction. Emerson did acquire a factory in November 1916, at Kingston, New York, and through the winter into 1917, Wilson's imagination flowered. "The building of demonstration cars by Emerson . . . had considerable to do with Mr. [Henry] Ford's reducing the price of the automobile manufactured by him." Wilson also wrote that "Robert Craig Hupp was one of the designers of the first Ford Motors," [Hupp worked for Ford for 18 months in sales, service, and shipping]. Hupp resigned immediately.

Wilson and Matches sold $1.5 million in Emerson stock. By April 1, Emerson produced only 69 cars. Wilson, Emerson, Cameron, and Hupp were indicted on 13 counts of mail fraud on June 6, 1917.

On August 1, the U.S. District Court filed suit against Robert P. Matches, the Ford Tractor Company (of South Dakota), and the Ford Tractor Company Inc. (of Delaware), charging them with using "the mails in furtherance of a scheme to defraud. . . . Both offenses involved sale and distribution of the shares of The Ford Tractor Company. . . . The gist of the fraud relates to the financial and business condition of said corporation."

Ewing pleaded not guilty on August 2, posting bail of $5,000. He was ordered to not leave the area. Ewing swore that Matches *asked* him to serve as officer of Ford Tractor Company, that Matches conducted the business of company, and he was merely an *employee*.

M. H. Boutelle, a Minneapolis lawyer, wrote Henry Ford on March 15, 1918. He was Ford Tractor's court-appointed receiver. He wrote that the tractor had continued interest from dealers in the United States and Canada who would take delivery on orders if production resumed: "The mere liquidation of the business . . . would not interest me. That appears relatively easy. Any suggestion that you purchase the 'intangibles', such as the Good Will, Patents, etc., etc., must emanate from someone else other than myself as this would savor too much of the nature of a 'hold up' to appeal to me. Moreover it is doubtful if any fair or reasonable price could be fixed for these items which would make it worthwhile for the stockholders to sell. In the element of establishment, however, they have a relatively valuable asset. . . ."

Boutelle, whose writing skills approached Wilson's, saw commission and consultation dollars spinning in his head. He continued: "I would gladly render my heartiest cooperation.

"The plant could be put into operation inside of five days and could start deliveries within a relatively short time. I am satisfied that [all] stock in the enterprise, which represents absolute control, would be surrendered to the persons who furnished the requisite capital to put the business on its feet."

Ford's new secretary, Ernest G. Liebold, responded three days later.

"As you are perhaps aware, Mr. Ford has spent the greater part of the past five or six years in perfecting [his] tractor and the publicity incident hereto has undoubtedly furnished considerable means of exploitation of the tractor you refer to.

"Our business has reached the point now where we are about to make deliveries and it would therefore be utterly impossible for Mr. Ford to consider any interest in a similar undertaking. It is our opinion, also, that, with the unprecedented demand for farm implements, you should have no difficulty in seeking a market for your tractor if it is what you claim it to be."

Boutelle's assurance of "absolute control" was as fanciful as Wilson's prose. Shares that Matches held were spoken for, as the *New York Times* made clear.

"Following the indictment June 6, of Wilson, Emerson, Cameron, and Hupp, those speaking for Emerson emphasized that the company was solidly backed by a well-funded tractor operation that promised large financial returns, the Ford Tractor Company of Minneapolis. Even if their business of making and marketing automobiles did not enable it to get upon its financial feet, it was said, the tractor business would assure it."

In July 1921, after four years of hearings, trials, and appeals, Wilson was sentenced to seven years in federal prison in Atlanta and was given a $13,000 fine. He jumped bail and was captured in November 1922 and delivered to Atlanta. Matches served three years there with no fine. Emerson died a shattered man in California in December 1918. Hupp returned to Detroit where he did automotive engineering consulting until he died in 1931 at age 53. His, Emerson's, and Cameron's names were all cleared by 1923.

Neither Robert Kinkead nor Paul Ford were charged with anything related to these frauds. Kinkead spent four years in the Army during World War I; his own tractor was carried on by Andrews Tractor Company. Following active duty, he returned to Minneapolis in 1921 and merged with Andrews to form Andrews-Kinkead. They produced a tractor that sold through 1922. Kinkead, Andrews, and Paul Ford all disappeared from the tractor business by 1924.

On September 6, 1928, charges against Ewing were dropped for insufficient evidence. His bail was returned and court orders limiting his travel were removed. Rumor placed him in several discrete withdrawals during that decade, including runs to Canada to organize a new tractor company. Once free, Ewing withdrew from public view.

Final motions from U.S. government and defendants' lawyers were settled on July 17, 1931. Charges were dismissed and indictments vacated against Ford Tractor Company. After 14 years of investigation, prosecution, and appeals, the U.S. attorney concluded this was not prosecutable. The Ford name was no longer associated with any tractor, legal complication, or bad taste. Almost no one noticed.

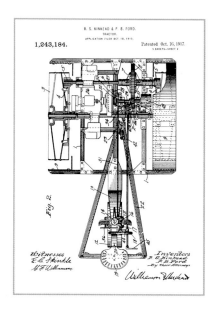

The pivoting drawbar, number 22 in the drawing, was anchored just 6 inches behind the front axle, further hampering the tractor's ability to plow a straight line or to pull a plow around any kind of curve in a field. Ewing was anxious only to patent and control the name of his Ford tractor before Henry Ford had a chance to introduce his own.

Three

BUILDING FOR THE BRITISH

MoM Called

The Model T brought Henry Ford great wealth and worldwide recognition. It changed him little. In his childhood his mother had instilled a trust in humans and a mistrust in wars. His upbringing taught him that any dispute could be settled verbally. His wealth allowed him to try anything, from the efforts to produce tractors to attempts to make peace in Europe. One of Ford's grandest gestures toward peace would, ironically, play a part in landing a contract that greatly accelerated the development of his first commercially available tractor.

Ford did not accept the inevitability of war. He chartered a ship, the *Oscar II*, and, loaded with 158 peace supporters, artists, philosophers, politicians, industrialists, and journalists, he sailed off to encourage nations of Europe to settle their differences with words around a table, not with bullets across a farm field.

This was all organized with Ford's typical zeal and energy. The Peace Ship, as it was dubbed, was conceived in late November 1915, and it sailed December 4. Putting so much personal energy into the mission cost Ford his health. Very ill when the ship reached Oslo, Norway, on December 18 after two rough weeks at sea, he didn't appear in public until December 22 in the smaller port of Christiana. He finally summoned the strength to talk to the press, both Norwegian locals and Americans who had come on the voyage. The group was full of questions about the ship and

This X-series prototype was part of Ford's efforts to quickly design and construct a tractor to meet the growing demand for tractors in Europe during World War I. Because of Ewing's Ford Tractor Company exploits, Henry Ford chose not to name these tractors. Prototypes had a small "Henry Ford & Son" badge, first round and then oval. The X-series bore no identification, as did the first batch of tractors built for the British government.

Ford's mission. To their surprise, he spoke instead about his new tractor.

"The machine and not man," he said, his remarks quoted first in the *Philadelphia Inquirer*, "would now be the drudge. The invention is not patented. Armament makers would realize a greater profit by manufacturing tractors than guns." Some who heard these words thought Ford had gone mad. He simply paraphrased to a world audience the belief he expressed to his mechanic, Fred Rockelman, a few years earlier: If every farmer used one simple tractor, they'd know they had *that* one thing in common. It might lead to greater understanding of their other similarities: "We won't have anymore strikes or wars."

While the voyage did not bring peace, it brought attention to the need to seek peace. War began in Europe in June 1914. A number of mutual support treaties were triggered. England entered the war on August 4. Before the end of the month, most European nations fought their neighbors.

England suffered quickly. Its population of 40 million could never feed itself off its land. England hadn't needed to do so for centuries; industrial wealth allowed it to buy from other European countries food it didn't raise at home. With the war con-

suming European countryside and farmland, England came up hungry.

War forced England's government to prepare and provide food, clothing, shelter, and labor where it was needed; Percival Perry was appointed to the Food Production Board. This group worked closely with the Royal Agricultural Society of England and the British Board of Agriculture. Perry shared Ford's belief that tractors were more efficient than horses. The Ministry of Munitions (MoM) had ordered a prototype tractor built and tested, intending to mass produce and lease these to farmers since all available English men and horses were needed in Europe. Perry had seen Ford's new unit-frame tractors, operating them at Fair Lane. He organized trials where he wanted Ford's machine represented. He asked Henry to send samples. This was the word that went to Farkas: prepare two of the still-experimental tractors, with all the latest engineering and technical developments, for shipment to England.

Battles on the Home Front

As Ford looked for an engine for the tractor he was considering producing, he knew that one of his key suppliers, John and Horace Dodge, had decided

to introduce their own automobile in 1915.

Henry looked for other outside sources and found that Hercules had several engines available, one of which he chose for the new prototype unit-frame tractors. These first appeared in March 1915.

Hercules' four-cylinder engine featured a 4-inch bore and 4.5-inch stroke. According to historian Jack Heald, spark plugs on this engine were located on the right side—not on top—of the head, two at front, two near the rear. Heald believed the updraft carburetor probably was Hercules' own design, while the engine's exhaust collected in a single pipe at the rear aimed straight down. On the opposite side of the engine at the rear of the block, Hercules had its oil filler. Unitized construction of the first tractor consisted of the large automobile radiator followed by the engine block, the transmission housing, and the worm-gear rear-end casting.

The tractor's front axle was assembled from several steel pieces with left-hand steering, similar to automobiles. Heald learned of another engineer, Thomas L. Fawick, who produced a water pump for the Hercules engines, but Henry Ford soon overruled this for cost. He instead used the thermosyphon system of "circulation by percolation."

The first unit-frame prototype, which Farkas had plowing in the snow, appeared in early photos in March 1916. It had no hood or engine side panels. It was shot working at Fair Lane, pulling a single 14-inch plow. Second-generation prototypes appeared in May with hoods and louvered side panels. Farkas shifted steering to the right side to more easily watch the plow. His new manifold directed exhaust forward and down. The badge fitted on the radiator identified the tractor as Henry Ford and Son.

On June 11, Ford told *The Automobile* he had acquired more than 1,000 acres between Dearborn and Oakland where he would erect a plant to manufacture tractors and blast furnaces and other steel to produce Ford parts. The reason for the new construction was that material needed for production arrived in such small quantities that it interrupted manufacturing plans. Rouge construction continued, its contribution becoming more valuable as the impact of the European war became apparent.

During Sorensen's and Bricker's February 1917 visit to England, they came to understand that Europe would need a large number of tractors to feed itself. Henry envisioned making Model Ts and

tractors in Cork, Southern Ireland, his homeland. Work had begun on a plant there; however, if more tractors were needed to save a country, greater capacity was needed soon. Sorensen and Perry inspected several sites that could be purchased, including one at Dagenham, a London suburb east of Stratford. They looked at another, closer to the city itself. Sorensen and Bricker returned to Dearborn, leaving the two experimental tractors with Perry for the Royal Agricultural Society to test. These were nearly complete, only needing adjusting. Sorensen brought a two-bottom Oliver and a three-bottom Cockshutt plow as well. Ford's Trafford Park plant in Manchester prepared everything.

Matters accelerated rapidly at 1:18 P.M. April 6 when U.S. President Woodrow Wilson, no longer able to maintain neutrality in the face of German submarine warfare in the North Atlantic, declared war. Torpedoes took lives with increasing frequency on passenger ships and jeopardized trade since the previous October. Sensing coming commitments by U.S. manufacturing to America's own war effort, Percival Perry wasted no time.

On April 7, he cabled Edsel Ford who had taken

*T*est pilot Jimmy Smith, his cap raked over his eyes, posed on prototype 28 on April 4, 1917. (Smith was in charge of the experimental machine shop.) The new tractor plant was still under construction in Dearborn in the background. Four days later, Henry Ford agreed to send to England the machinery and tools to build these tractors for the British government. *Henry Ford Museum and Greenfield Village*

Charles Sorensen and several engineers visited England in April and May 1917, looking for tractor parts suppliers. The British government decided firms should produce airplane parts instead. Sorensen returned with a Ministry of Munitions (MoM) order for 5,000 tractors. Ford redesigned his tractor. These experimental tractors were labeled the X-series. This is possibly 6X. *Henry Ford Museum and Greenfield Village*

on increasing responsibilities in his father's tractor enterprise. Perry's now famous cable asked Edsel if he would "be willing to send Sorensen and others with drawings of everything necessary, loaning them to British government so that parts can be manufactured over here and assembled in [a] government factory under Sorensen's guidance . . . ? The matter is very urgent. . . . National necessity entirely dependent Mr. Ford's decision."

Henry Ford responded on April 8.

"Will comply with every request immediately . . . we will work day and night. Get full information possible on gear cutting, cast iron, malleable foundries and drop forge plants. We are sending full organization depending on your assistance at earliest possible moment."

The Royal Agricultural Society had not yet even tested the Ford tractor. That took place on April 24 and 25 in Cheshire on the estate of Sir Gilbert Greenall. The tractor impressed the five judges as reasonably suited to the needs of British farmers. Recognizing Ford's mass production capabilities, the Ministry of Munitions immediately abandoned its plans to produce its own tractors.

A dozen U.S. tractor makers and three or four English producers also participated in the trials at Cheshire. Representatives arrived with regular production machines. Only Ford provided prototypes. When the Ministry selected the Ford as its "official" tractor, there was considerable criticism.

While Perry's proximity to British power had impact, that alone could not support the selection. Ford's mass production technology pushed the decision along. No other maker had similar capabilities. When Ford spoke of producing 100,000 tractors a year, no one laughed. The Saunderson and the Marshall plants in England already worked at capacity. American-made tractors distributed in England through various local agents were stuck on docks in Liverpool, awaiting ground shipment. Ford's offer to build in Cork avoided that bottleneck.

There was one other factor. Prior to the eventful but unsuccessful Peace Ship voyage, Ford was merely an automobile manufacturing *company*. Its founder's wealth was acknowledged, but this was long before celebrities lived on business pages. With the Peace Ship and a subsequent 14-month effort in the Hague, all of which Henry paid for, Ford became as well known as his Model T. His commitment to peace and to production at low cost was widely understood and admired. No other tractor manufacturer brought to their dealings with the heads of state the force of Ford's personality and accomplishment.

The Automobile magazine reported in its April 19, 1917, issue that Ford waived patent rights on his tractor to permit government manufacture in large numbers. The request to produce Ford's machine followed British government observations of his tractors working 24 hours a day in English and French fields. Ford cabled specifications for each of the 1,000 parts in the tractor at his own expense to enable the British government to proceed rapidly in their manufacture. Description of a single screw, the magazine reported, required several hundred words.

A week later, an item in the magazine ran under the headline "England Needs Tractors—Machines Rented to Farmers." One brief paragraph stated, "The farm tractor situation in England is not in as clearly a defined and satisfactory condition as the food problem would warrant it being in. The Government after rigorously excluding tractors has announced that until May 31 anyone desiring may import unlimited quantities of them. . . . To this can

Jimmy Smith operated an X-series prototype, this one most likely was 9X, on a corner of the Fair Lane farm. The X-series tractors, of which there were probably 16 in all, were produced as Ford, Galamb, and Farkas innovated improvements over successive tractors. They were painted white for demonstration purposes as well as to make any mechanical problems fairly obvious. This hood was emblazoned with the words "Peace, Industry, Prosperity." *Henry Ford Museum and Greenfield Village*

be added the fact that the Government has commandeered a small number of tractors and is hiring them out at low rates to farmers requiring them."

Bredo H. Berghoff, an engineer hired into the Experimental Department in 1915, worked at that time designing tractor parts. He recalled times both thrilling and perilous in reminiscences recorded for Ford Motor Company in 1957.

"One day we were asked if we would like to take a trip to England. The English needed tractors to plow up their parks. It seemed more reasonable to take patterns across to England and have them make the parts and assemble it in England rather than take the risk of shipping whole tractors across. April 1917 was the worst month for sinking of ships. The ship that we went over on was sunk about a month after we left and the one I returned on was sunk two months after I left it.

"I don't know that each of us had a specific task to do when we got to England, but we were sent to find who could make the various parts of the tractors. We had all the patterns with us and a list of the manufacturers there who were in the business of machining parts similar to what we wanted."

The Automobile magazine followed the progress carefully, publishing a story June 7, datelined May 22 from London: "The British government has opened bids for the supply of parts to build 10,000 tractors of a standardized design. The machine will be known as the MoM (Ministry of Munitions), but it is to all intents a Ford tractor and doubtless represents the immediate result of Henry Ford's gift of his designs and data to Great Britain.

"It is stated that 3,000,000 acres of hitherto uncultivated land are to be tilled this year and that the Government itself will handle 1,000,000 leaving the other 2,000,000 to private enterprise. The 10,000 tractors to be built by the Government will be about half the total quantity required, which means that America will be relied upon to export as many as shipping room can be found for."

Sorensen explained that Ford production would begin slowly but increase rapidly, so Britain permitted importation during 1917 of 10,000 Mak-A-Tractor conversions kits from E. G. Staude of St. Paul, Minnesota. These kits (at $225 U.S. retail price) made tractors out of Model Ts that already were in England. Staude kits were renamed The Eros by the importer,

1917 Ford 9X Experimental
ℋistorians estimate that Ford
constructed 16 X-series
prototypes. The machines were
built in pairs, with each new pair
of tractors incorporating
improvements resulting from
thoroughly testing previous
tractors. This is number 9X.

possibly because the maker's name sounded German.

Britain's domestic tractor manufacturers' small
size and limited capabilities gave the country little
choice but to proceed with the Ford-built tractor. A
survey done in 1984 and quoted by Michael
Williams in his *Ford & Fordson Tractors,* (Diamond
Farms Books, 1985), revealed that in 1914 when the
war began, there were fewer than 500 tractors on
British farms. There was so little demand at home
that Britain's six manufacturers produced tractors

mostly for export. In 1917, when the Board of Agriculture ordered 400 Saunderson Universal tractors
with plows, it was more than the firm could handle;
it subcontracted some of the order. Yet this barely
doubled the tractor population in Britain.

Once the ambitious scope of the Ministry of
Munitions' needs were clear, selecting one mass-
producer providing thousands of identical
machines simplified spare parts inventories and
training procedures. British journals complained

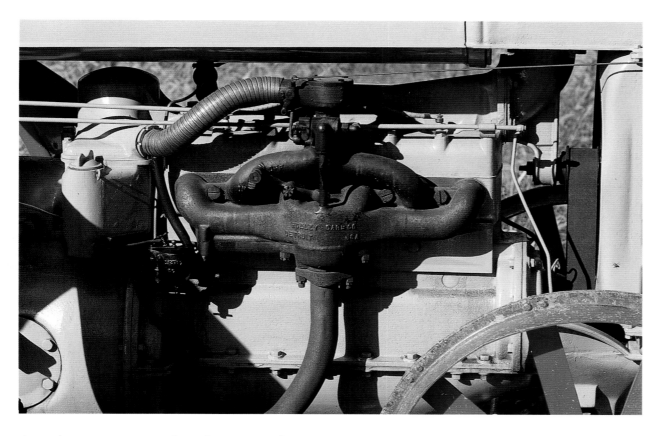

George Holley and his carburetors joined Ford's development team when Sorensen returned from England and Henry Ford decided to completely revise the prototypes the Ministry of Munitions (MoM) had seen. Eugene Farkas designed the engine, but Hercules manufactured it. Carburetion was provided by Holley Model 234 carburetors.

that selecting an imported machine was unfair to home industry, and U.S. manufacturers wailed over Ford's unfair advantage. Certainly shipping space allocated for farm machinery would be cleared first for the "government" tractors.

"When we were pretty well set," Bredo Berghoff continued, "and felt that we could go ahead, the heads of the Ministry of Munitions [decided] that if these manufacturers could make tractor parts, they probably also could make airplane parts. They needed airplanes worse than anything at the time."

German bombers had hit London. One site for MoM tractor manufacture was destroyed in raids on June 25. Three days later, the prime minister of England, David Lloyd George, wrote to Percival Perry from 10 Downing Street: "Owing to the changed conditions here, I very much regret that it has been found impossible to proceed with the manufacture of MoM Tractors in this Country. I understand that you are about to proceed to America in order to make arrangements for the production of these tractors in the United States, and I know that I may rely on you to do everything in your power to ensure the production of the greatest number of tractors for use in the United Kingdom.

"I regret very much that your plans in connection with the production of these machines have been altered, but I am certain that even under these circumstances, I am able to count on Mr. Ford and yourself to do your utmost to assist us in order that the Food Production program in the Country may not suffer."

Perry and the MoM directors reorganized priorities, asking Sorensen if the tractors could be manufactured in the United States and shipped over complete. As head of production, Sorensen knew Highland Park and Dearborn's capabilities better than

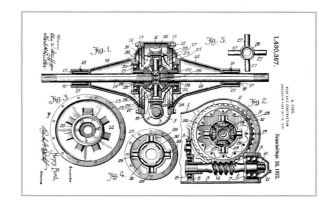

Eugene Farkas began developing underslung worm gear final drives in mid-1917, after Sorensen returned from England. This increased the ground clearance of the tractor, and it ran cooler because the bottom half of this final drive was immersed in oil. This prolonged worm gear life and no longer transmitted heat directly up the operator's seat.

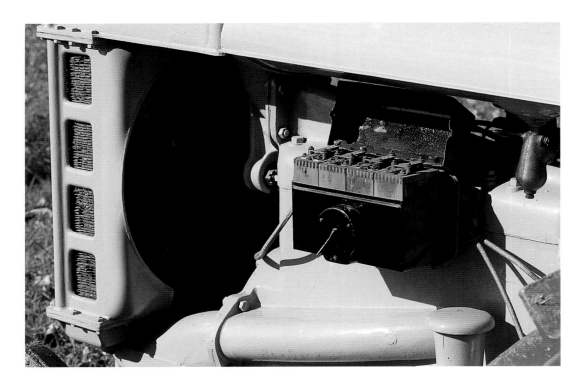

Early Hercules in-line four-cylinder engines had a distinctive oil-filler at the rear of the block. To ensure adequate cooling, Farkas perforated the radiator casting with ladder-like openings to allow additional airflow. The coil box bore no identification.

One unique feature of 9X is the "skirts" fitted to the sides of the fuel tank. These were added, probably, to deflect rain off the tank, from running onto the spark plugs on the top of the engine. Earlier prototypes had the worm gear on top of the rear end. Gene Farkas wondered about running the worm on the bottom. The tractor body would remain on the same level, but reversing the worm, and bringing the axle center line up higher, allowed increased ground clearance and a change to 42-inch rear wheels from 36.

anyone alive. He knew Henry Ford had acquired a new property in Dearborn, an old brick-making factory at Michigan Avenue and Brady Street, where he intended to manufacture these machines.

"We can build fifty in ninety days from now, with a rapid increase later. How many do you want?"

MoM's Lord Milner quickly said, "We'll take five thousand. But at what cost?"

Cost was an important question to Ford. As Sorensen polled the various independent suppliers throughout the United Kingdom, he derived a unit price of $1,500 per tractor if produced in England. This figure upset Sorensen who thought it far out of line but recognized it came from piecework assembled, not units mass produced. He knew they should cost less than $700 to make. To Milner's questions, however, Sorensen had to get to Henry Ford. The answer came back quickly: "$50 over cost. We'll make five thousand in Michigan at a unit cost of seven hundred dollars and start shipping in sixty days." Sorensen and the others packed up quickly and came home.

Gene Farkas, who was in Dearborn all that time, picked up the story: "Sorensen came back in July 1917. The tractor contract was based on the experimental models over in England. Mr. Ford just decided, 'Now, we'll design a new tractor.'

"These English demonstrators that Mr. Sorensen took over had the worm on the top. The size of the driving wheel was thirty-six inches. I came upon the idea that it would be better if we ran the worm on the bottom. The body of the tractor would be kept on the same level, but reversing the worm, and bringing the center line of the axle up a little higher, it took up the difference in the size of the wheel, which made the rear wheel forty-two inches instead of thirty-six.

"We also were designing the transmission housing and different parting lines [where casting molds separate]. Mr. Ford came up with the idea, 'Why divide it three ways? Why don't you make two castings, the engine block the first one, and the transmission clutch housing the second one?

"It was, of course, all hollow, a shell. . . . We made a plate and built the whole transmission on that plate as a unit. Then we would just slide it in and bolt it inside of that big housing. We got the word about four o'clock to change the design.

"The Foundry man and the pattern-maker were on my neck to get the information. The distance from the motor to the axle hadn't changed. All the internal mechanism hadn't changed. I just took a blueprint of the old housing and the new housing and pasted them together as one piece. Instead of waiting for a drawing, I just gave them a blueprint. Where the old joint was, I just filled that in free-hand and said, 'Well, this is the way it should be. Now go ahead and work to that." The pattern makers used old wooden forms they glued together, filling in where it had previously separated. They began creating new molds at 4 P.M. when Farkas returned to his drafting board to begin new drawings. At midnight, he and they were finished. The foundry staff took it from there, working through the night.

"Believe it or not," Farkas said, "by ten o'clock the following morning the casting was on the floor. It was still warm but it was done. There was this big casting.

"Joe Galamb was there, and he was as mad as a hatter because he wasn't consulted about the decision or the change in design. Right away he condemned it as being impractical. He said we would never get a casting like that into production. Sorensen advised Mr. Ford otherwise, and it never was changed for thirty years."

Four

AFTERMARKET MODEL T CONVERSIONS

Returning the *T* to *Tractor*

The barrage of publicity Henry Ford earned in 1911, 1912, and 1913 from experiments with Model T–based tractors hit unexpected targets. A number of backyard tinkerers and more than a few sharp business minds saw Ford's efforts for the good ideas they were. A trend, an entire industry in fact, may have been started by photographs and magazine articles published in 1915 that featured Ford's tractor experiments.

At first outside efforts to make tractors derived from the cars were unlike Ford's. Most of the kits based on the Model T and A cars and trucks didn't permanently change the vehicle into a tractor as Ford did. Instead, they gave the farmer the best of both worlds. Kits allowed owners to change the rear wheels and tires to larger steel-spoked wheels with grousers or studs for traction, enabling the farmer to pull a plow, harvester, or binder across the fields. The selling point of these conversions was that by unbolting the steel wheels and a minimum of necessary hardware, the "tractor" could be returned quickly to a car configuration to take the family to town for Saturday night's social or Sunday morning's church.

This is an extreme over-simplification of what these kits did. In many cases, there was nothing simple about the conversion itself. While some makers advertised that 20 minutes and $200 was all it took to convert the Model T to a tractor, that job

This 1926 Model T Roadster Pickup is fitted with a Fond Du Lac Tractor Company kit that was produced around 1921. Fond Du Lac was one of the several dozen makers who made solid, reliable, affordable conversion kits (still usable as road vehicles) but who failed during 1921–1922.

**1918 Model T
with Knickerbocker
Forma-Tractor Conversion**

This is a before-and-after-comparison starting with a 1918 Model T Roadster and ending with a 1918 Knickerbocker Forma-Tractor. The Knickerbocker was a conversion requiring less than an hour to change from Roadster to tractor or back.

more commonly took half a day. Even the simplest of these kits, made by E. G. Staude of St. Paul, Minnesota, or Pullford of Quincy, Illinois, were time-consuming for the initial setup. Once major pieces were permanently attached, the changeover still took an hour.

Which maker came first? Who sold most, who lasted longest, whose product was best? These are among questions that historian/collectors like Glenn Heim dig into relentlessly. After more than a decade of research, he has found quite a few answers. Heim has uncovered about 125 firms that claimed to pro-

duce kits. He has gathered fairly solid evidence for 65 of those claims, having found actual literature, order forms, instruction booklets, or parts lists. In an enormous facility in northern Illinois, he has about 50 kits representing nearly 40 makers.

"The first days of the tractor conversion kits were the result of early tinkerers," Heim explained. "One such maker was the Auto Tractor Company of Chicago and Niles, Michigan. This was sometime around 1915. These were not Fords, but they used the entire automobile attached to a large frame bolted to the back of the vehicle with very large aux-

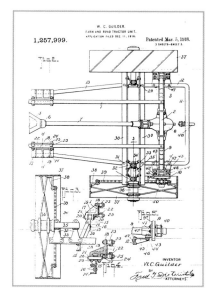

iliary rear wheels. They used reduction gears to effectively increase the pulling power for a plow. These people, and the few others already in business this early, got a lot of attention in publications like *Popular Mechanics*.

"People saw that this could be done and it started to click with them. Undoubtedly, some sharper guys looked at the Auto Tractor, with all its complicated fittings attached to an Oakland or something expensive, and recognized that it could be done simpler, and they could use Model T Fords since they were cheaper.

"Of course, there were so many pictures of Henry Ford's own experiments, with big wheels, two tanks above the radiator. Some of these people must have looked at the Model T and thought, 'Gee, if we put big wheels on it, it might work.'"

Ironically, about the time Henry Ford abandoned the Model T as a tractor, small industry embraced it. Starting in 1916, the marketplace

swelled. Perhaps as many as 75 of the 125 firms Heim has located came into business in 1916, 1917, and 1918. This market was surely encouraged by England's need for farm tractors. To any blacksmith with ambition, a photo of 10,000 Staude kits being unloaded at Liverpool must have been pure inspiration.

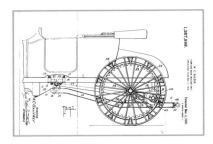

Walter C. Guilder of Springfield, Ohio, designed his "Farm and Road Tractor Unit." He licensed his patent to Knickerbocker Motors Ltd. of New York, which marketed it as the Forma-Tractor kit for Model T Fords.

Many tractor conversion kits were well-thought-out, well-made, and well-promoted. Knickerbocker Motors' $178 Forma-Tractor produced a lovely brochure with most of the image devoted to perfectly formed furrows. Eventually the price rose to $250.
Glenn Heim

Day's work done while still high sun

Car ready for road in fifteen minutes

KNICKERBOCKER FORMA-TRACTOR

Some of these kits sold for as little as $98. Others, in late 1917, reached $350. These high prices covered the costs of over-engineering and over-building. Manufacturers, such as Keystone Farm Machine Company of York, Pennsylvania, used 3-inch-diameter axles for their Multa-Power, where nearly all the others used 2-inch diameters. These kits also were intricate and difficult to assemble, requiring real skill, tools, and time.

Others like Staude's Mak-A-Tractor sold for much less. A Staude ad in a January 1917 issue of *Automobile Trade Journal* stated that "Twenty Minutes and $195 converts your Ford car into a guaranteed powerful tractor." It was one of the simplest and, according to Heim, one of the most common. Staude produced between 20,000 and 30,000 in its lifetime. Pullford, another of the easiest and most affordable, advertised that for $135 farmers could, "Make your Ford do the work of two or three horses."

That was the thrust of these conversion kits. At $150 to $200, these were not aimed at Bull or Lion or even Baer Ewing tractors (although the Multa-Power at $350 was in the same price league). Instead, Staude and others saw their market just as Henry

1914 Model T with Geneva Adapto-Tractor Conversion
E. G. Staude's Mak-A-Tractor, the Pullford, Geneva's kit, and the Knickerbocker were strong enough to survive the 1921 postwar depression. After 1922, however, even Knickerbocker disappeared.

Geneva Tractor produced a well-made "Adapto-Tractor" kit, a simple, easy kit selling for $168 in mid-1918. Geneva offered a front-mounted belt-pulley for $37. *Glenn Heim collection*

1922 Model T Pickup with 1918–1919 Pullford Conversion

*A*bout 125 manufacturers produced conversion kits from 1914 through the late 1930s. Like Henry Ford, they competed not with mainstream tractor makes but against the horse. By 1922, 75 of these manufacturers were out of business.

Ford saw his: smaller farms still using horses. Each kit produced a machine that was quite competent to pull a one- or two-bottom plow across a field.

"The heyday for these kits and their makers," Glenn Heim said, "was 1916 through the late 1930s. Many of the manufacturers came and went fast. Some didn't get started until as late as 1919, and by that time, they had really missed the market that was created by the need for food during World War I. Probably only Staude, Pullford, Geneva, and perhaps Knickerbocker were around in 1921. After 1922, Knickerbocker was gone.

"The postwar agricultural depression walloped most of the companies by 1922. The whole tractor conversion era began and ended neither abruptly

By 1930 and later, the price of Model Ts like this 1922 truck, dropped so much that the $175 1918–1919 Pullford kit was many times more valuable than the $15 Model Ts. Even so, the low cost of the Model T made it possible for a farmer to try out power farming for less than $200.

Pullford's brochure, quoting a price of $175, announced that its kit could be attached to any Ford in 30 minutes and removed in less time. "If you do not own a Ford, get one and attach a Pullford to it. Get a used car at a low price. Own a tractor and an automobile too." *Glenn Heim collection*

nor gradually. It came and went in waves. The first surge started in 1916 and ended in that recession of 1921–1922. When the economy turned back upwards in 1923, the next wave began.

"The ones that hung on," Heim continued, "that made it through the [nineteen] twenty-one–twenty-two depression and through the Great Depression, were those that adapted. Staude was the longest in business even though they changed name several times. They survived by moving into the turf industry and getting away from regular farming. Toro, Worthington, and Aarps were their competition; they didn't worry about International or Deere or the major manufacturers. Of the 125 that I know about, probably 50 came into being after 1923. Some of these, like Shaw, built in California, and Thieman, from Albert City, Iowa, stayed around until the beginning of World War II. These came after Model T engines. They used Model As and even Model Bs.

"Many of the kits became more valuable over time. After the Great Depression, farmers might have more tied up in the kit than it would cost them to buy a Model T for parts. A good Model T could be had for $5. This was Shaw's success. They came

along about 1923, after most others were gone. But they were ahead of their time for the Depression era to come. Their unique angle was to take old Model Ts and turn them into a little tractor. Shaw never had the kind of conversion kits where you could drive it weekends as a car. They were meant for permanent conversions after the car ceased its usefulness, or

1922 Model T with Shaw Manufacturing Conversion
Historian Glenn Heim observed that "Shaw's innovation was turning its gear teeth toward the outside of the wheel. This made it more difficult for dirt to pack into gear teeth."

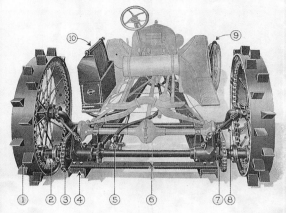

1. Bull Wheels—Strongly constructed of steel and iron. Size 48 inches in diameter, 8-inch face. With interchangeable internal driving gear, which insures long wear. Furnished with wedge-shaped lugs or angle irons. Either can be quickly removed.

2. Roller Driving Pinion—Made of hardened steel, practically wear proof. Driven from Jack Shaft and engaging internal gear on Bull Wheels.

3. Jack Shaft—Made of hardened steel and set in roller bearings, reducing friction to a minimum. Reduces high speed to mighty power. Multiplies the Ford's power 11 times. Has changeable sprockets which permits of variable speed with motor running at same speed.

4. Frame—Built of heavy trussed steel strongly reinforced. Extends entire length of car bracing it at every point. Note how car sets in frame relieving it of all strain.

5. Pump—Specially designed and built by well known and reli-

able pump maker. Driven with gear from Jack Shaft, circulates water in right proportion to speed at which Multa-Power is running.

6. Draw Bar—Built of steel with adjustable hitches.

7. Axle Sprocket—which replaces Ford wheels and drives roller chain to sprocket on Jack Shaft.

8. High Carbon Steel Axle—3 inches diameter, strongly braced. Carries weight of car and attachment.

9. Front Wheel Casings—of special tractor design. Thoroughly cover front tires and rims protecting them and making it unnecessary to remove tires. Makes steering easy.

10. Cooling System—Built of galvanized iron. Patent construction takes water hot from the motor, cools it instantly by aeration and holds it in reserve to be drawn as needed by the Pump on Jack Shaft.

Multa-Power, from the Keystone Farm Machine Company in York, Pennsylvania, made things unnecessarily complex. Its kit sold for $395 with gears, chains, auxiliary axles, and cooling systems. It must have taken an entire weekend just to mount. This was not a conversion but a permanent change. Glenn Heim *collection*

after the body had rotted, for example. In 1934 or 1935, a Model T engine and rear end could be had almost anywhere for a dollar and a half. A farmer could do a minor overhaul, grind the valves, and put in a new head gasket for maybe $10. The kit was worth much more, and so the farmer could keep working," Heim said.

"When Henry Ford took the Fordson out of the U.S. market in late 1927, this very suddenly gave new life to the kits. Some of the makers, like Pullford who had gone out in 1922, came back in 1928. Shaw influenced a lot of latecomers because they catered to the garden tractor industry, to the small truck farm. They had a big bearing on what followed.

"Shaw was very advanced mechanically for the time. They used an integral gear in the axle. Most used a big bull gear out near the wheel. A very few used chains, the most expensive, most complicated, most difficult, and now, the rarest. Shaw's innovation was turning its gear teeth toward the outside of the wheel. This made it more difficult for dirt to pack into the gear teeth from the furrow that was being turned. Also, Shaw mounted the rear axle upside down to keep the gears in the car's proper order, leaving them with two forward, one reverse.

"There is one common misconception that these conversions always ran in low gear. They never did this," Heim explained. "To operate a Model T in low

gear you had to always hold the pedal down. These ran in high gear. Shift the brake lever to high and just regulate the gas, just like driving the Model T. Regulating speed in high gear was done by a little hand lever. Made it simple and comfortable. The large reduction bull gears would have made speed over the ground too slow in low gear anyway. Most of the companies didn't bother inverting the rear axle because, with the car's reverse gear as the tractor's single forward gear, its speed was closer to Model T high gear anyway."

Shaw deleted the rear leaf spring. Instead, the kit included brackets to mount the frame rigidly. Shaw sought to get rid of that spring, which was harder on the rear drive bouncing and pounding over a field. The Fond du Lac Tractor Company sold two versions, one to use with the rear leaf spring, the other to remove it to make a more rigid machine.

These manufacturers policed themselves. In October 1917, makers of these kits formed the National Tractor Attachment Association in Chicago. Members included not only kit manufacturers such as Pullford and Geneva, the Unitractor Company of Chicago, and 3-P Auto Tractor Company of Davenport, Iowa, but also major suppliers such as Hyatt Roller Bearing. These groups created this organization to maintain standards and educate farmers to use the attachments economically and efficiently.

Historian Heim believes these conversions may have had more influence on freight and produce transportation than on farming. Pullford offered an adapter to tow farm wagons. Several makers offered "road lugs," grousers with flatter tops to do less damage to dirt roads than the taller versions. Some offered a higher pinion for road use.

"Farmers could not hook a trailer up to a Lion or a Bull for road use," he said. "This was a simple way for farmers to get trucks. The U.S. government took most of the regular production for use in the war. Some twenty or thirty percent may have been used strictly for hauling. It is certainly one of the origins of the term 'tractor trailer.' Gersix Manufacturing Company of Seattle made a tractor. The name came from Gerlinger, a truck maker and its six-cylinder engines that it used in the tractor kits. Gerlinger became Kenworth.

"There were regional variations, too. Yuba Manufacturing, in California, already made partial crawler tractors. They made a Model T conversion

called the Bearcat. It was a full-crawler. You just dropped their body and tracks onto the Model T chassis and bolted it down. A couple of other California makers produced half-track adaptations for the sandy soil out there.

"Because Henry Ford abandoned the Model T tractor idea, there has been a misconception for many years that these kits were all junk," Heim continued, "that they all overheated, that the Model T wasn't right for a tractor. That's not the case.

"The Model T was good for these *kits*, even though it was not good as a real tractor to compete against other tractors. They could not pull a three-bottom plow. There were tractors out there that could, but they were very expensive. These machines were perfect for a single-bottom plow, definitely for small farms, truck farms, farms formerly run with three or four horses. When these kits were available, good draft horses cost three, four, five hundred dollars. Plus the cost of horseshoes and the land set aside to feed them. If you already had the car, these things were an unbelievably cheap way to get into tractor farming."

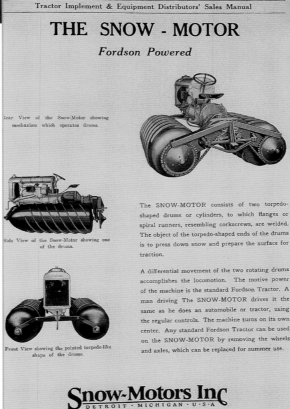

Tractor Implement & Equipment Distributors' Sales Manual

THE SNOW - MOTOR
Fordson Powered

Rear View of the Snow-Motor showing mechanism which operates drums.

Side View of the Snow-Motor showing one of the drums.

Front View showing the pointed torpedo-like shape of the drums.

The SNOW-MOTOR consists of two torpedo-shaped drums or cylinders, to which flanges or spiral runners, resembling corkscrews, are welded. The object of the torpedo-shaped ends of the drums is to press down snow and prepare the surface for traction.

A differential movement of the two rotating drums accomplishes the locomotion. The motive power of the machine is the standard Fordson Tractor. A man driving The SNOW-MOTOR drives it the same as he does an automobile or tractor, using the regular controls. The machine turns on its own center. Any standard Fordson Tractor can be used on the SNOW-MOTOR by removing the wheels and axles, which can be replaced for summer use.

Snow-Motors Inc
DETROIT · MICHIGAN · U·S·A

[B-123]

Fordson Snow-Motors Conversion

One of the most unusual conversion kits was this one produced by Snow-Motors Inc. of Detroit, Michigan, replacing front wheels and the entire back end of the Fordson with twin spirals operated by chains. The steering wheel operated a differential-steering system. James McIvor and this machine delivered U.S. mail during the winters in the 1920s and 1930s from Truckee, California, to North Lake Tahoe, Nevada.

Detroit's Snow-Motors Inc. listed its product in the annual Tractor Implement and Equipment Distributor's sales manual. *Higgins Collection, University of California, Davis, Library*

Five

BIRTH OF THE FORDSON

Cable Fordson, Dearborn

Ford and his son, Edsel, who was nearly 24, guaranteed that tractor activities remained independent from Ford Motor Company by founding Henry Ford and Son on July 27, 1917. When letterhead was produced, a cable address was established in the style of the day by abbreviating the company name to Fordson.

To keep finances separated, Henry Ford opened a new bank account in early 1916 to reimburse Ford Motor Company for development expenses incurred by the new firm. Joe Galamb prepared accounts for Frank Klingensmith of work done on Model T tractors out of the Highland Park plant before tractor operations moved to Dearborn. Galamb reported that by December 1, 1914, five tractors were built, four used at Highland Park (the industrials) and one sent to Fair Lane.

He had files: materials purchased outside for the tractors came to $1,966.92; those from existing stock totaled $1,805.84. Design time, from hourly pay logs and drafting materials were valued at $7,300. Experimental Department labor came to $11,744.86 (calculated as two-thirds of all experimental's work); labor from other departments was $2,500. They marked up labor charges 1.3 times for overhead. The grand total was $46,810.76, paid from the new account. Subsequently, Ford spent another $550,000 on Model T tractor development before he felt it had gone as far as it could. Gene Farkas remained in charge.

This 1918 Fordson F, serial number 8118, was one of the first Fordsons delivered to the United States. Some accounts say that while North American deliveries began with serial number 7,260, the next 1,073 went to Canada. Others claim distribution was shared between Canada, Michigan, and other states as well as Ministry of Munitions (MoM) tractors through the next several thousand machines.

Fordson Model F domestic manufacture began around April 23, 1918. For reasons no one yet knows, serial numbers skipped exactly 3,000, quitting at 3,900 and resuming at 6,901. The first Fordson, using Holley Model 234 carburetors like the MoM tractors, is generally accepted as the 4,260th one built, serial number 7,260.

On October 6, 1917, Henry Ford, standing far right, posed with the very first MoM tractor and the men who created it. Standing next to Ford is Charles Sorensen, Ford's chief of production. Opposite them at the extreme left is engineer Bredo Berghoff. From the bottom left, seated on the planks, are engineer Richard Kroll (with his head down), Mead Bricker (Sorensen's assistant), Louis Scott (mechanic), engineer Herman Reinholt, Frank McCormick (tractor operator and tester, in dark shirt), Ernest Kanzler (Ford's personal secretary), and chief tractor engineer Eugene Farkas (dark suit). Sitting beside Berghoff up on the loading dock is George Brubaker, left, and William Moore, former national president of the National Good Roads Association, both of whom were involved with national distribution. Above Moore, tractor engineer John Crawford rests his hand on the radiator; Jim Daly and Roy Bryant are at the rear above Ford. *Henry Ford Museum and Greenfield Village*

"We didn't sit down seriously to design the new tractor until we went into the war, although we kept on working on new designs," Farkas was quoted in the company archives. "I laid out rear axle housings three or four different ways and built them all, tried them all, and discarded them." Farkas modified the design of the wheel spokes, putting a bend into the previously flat pieces. This caused slight compression, fitting them tightly, eliminating a troubling rattle. He also designed the four-cylinder engines that Hercules would manufacture, similar to Model T engines but using a 2-inch-diameter crankshaft instead of 1.25-inch."

George Holley, who traveled to England with Sorensen, was part of the Ministry of Munitions (MoM) development team from the start. He convinced Ford that air entering the carburetor could be drawn through water to eliminate the dust. He made the original air washers that first appeared on the later experimental tractors.

In September 1917, Lord Alfred C. W. H. Northcliffe, head of the Permanent British Mission in the United States, visited Dearborn. He was concerned

1918 Fordson F

With deliveries to state war boards just beginning, Henry Ford and Son opened a floodgate of interest and demand for Ford's affordable farm tractor. This 1918 model, serial number 7770, was one of those distributed either in Canada through the Food Board as the *Greater Power Fleet* or the United States from War Preparedness Board county offices.

The first 1,000 or so Fordson tractors (including 16 X-series tractors, about 50 preproduction models, and two originally sent to England) used Hercules-built engines with the oil fill at the rear of the block. After that, the oil fill was located at the front.

over production delays with a tractor approved and ordered months before. Northcliffe learned that Henry Ford, still a perfectionist, thought the tractor needed improvement, and he would not produce it until it was ready.

Quoted in Allan Nevins' *Ford: Expansion and Challenge: 1915–1932* (McMillan, 1976), Northcliffe, ever the diplomat, was direct: "We understand your objection. We ourselves have many new military devices in blueprint, but we have to use the weapons and machines we have, and try to beat the Germans with what we've got. We need a tractor. Yours is the best we can get. We can't wait for the perfect tractor; we need what's available and we want you to produce it."

Ford accepted that and production began. Then President Woodrow Wilson severed diplomatic ties with Germany on February 3, 1917. While Ford believed war would not involve the United States, he promised to put his factories at Wilson's disposal.

TRACTORS ON THE LINE

"*At* the Rouge," Theodore Gehle said, "tractor production started February 23, 1921. Actually it was probably ready to go before that but . . . we did exercise an extremely tight line on inventory." Gehle had handled raw materials purchasing at the Highland Park plant, and he moved over to the Rouge, continuing to work for Sorensen.

"Tractor operations were on the first floor, and they had two railroad tracks inside the building for freight cars to unload and load their materials." These arrivals were timed so precisely that workers often unloaded subassemblies from freight cars, which they reloaded with completed tractors. By year end, Rouge workers manufactured nearly 36,800 Fordsons (more than half the 69,123 produced in 1920 but at a comparable pace, considering the nearly five-month shutdown).

Ford introduced the "progressive" line at the Highland Park plant in 1910, more a sequential conveyor line that jerked along in fits and starts. By spring 1913, Clarence W.

Avery, a manual training instructor from Detroit, divided up 29 steps necessary to assemble a magneto, giving one function to each of 29 men. The conveyor cut assembly time from 20 minutes to 13. A year later, at Avery's direction, they raised the belt to a more comfortable working height, and assembly time dipped to 7 minutes.

Once this technology reached the Rouge, its effects were conspicuous. Milling machines placed alongside moving conveyor lines milled both ends of six Fordson engine blocks at once. Another hole-tapping machine drilled in three directions at the same time from any of its 59 drill shafts, completing 25 engines an hour. Overhead chain conveyors carried transmission subassemblies from various work stations to the engine housing for insertion and assembly. These were inspired by what Avery and William Klann, a master machinist of exceptional skill and speed, saw in Chicago's meat-packing houses.

1918 Fordson F with Moline Implement Cultivator

*M*oline Implement Company was among the first to expand Fordson farming capabilities. This two-row cultivator probably was manufactured as early as 1920 or 1921. The owners got a bit carried away finishing their Fordson.

Ford's contract with the British government was for 5,000 tractors delivered as rapidly as possible. For the next several months, his entire output was committed. Two days before the first tractor was shipped, however, Herbert Hoover, director of the U.S. Food Administration in Washington, wrote Ford. Hoover saw American farmers feeding the world and rewarding themselves for their work by buying cars. Hoover wondered if enthusiasm for motor vehicles could be directed back to the need to raise crops.

"As we will be short of labor," Hoover wrote on October 6, 1917, "and as there will be a drain on work animals through war, would it not be possible for your agents throughout the country to devote themselves to persuading farmers to buy tractors instead of pleasure cars? My impression is that the farm tractor is becoming more and more important and that it might be possible to make use of the national emergency to give it a wider extension in use."

Hoover was preaching to the leader of the converted. Henry already had increased production to accommodate Britain's needs. The limit to greater output was not desire for tractors, but it was Ford's facilities themselves.

"They had to set up another building for the tractors," Gene Farkas recalled. "Building [Number] Thirteen

Moline's cultivator added 400 pounds to the Fordson. Farmers could adjust its beams to accommodate rows of 34-to-46-inch width. Moline claimed the installation, and setup took an hour. The single front wheel improved maneuverability.

Gene Farkas completed a half-scale drawing of the Fordson on February 26, 1919, showing transmission changes, including a belt pulley bevel gear behind the clutch. It also showed the "rainbow" coil box featuring a bold Fordson logo beneath a broad arch. *Henry Ford Museum and Greenfield Village*

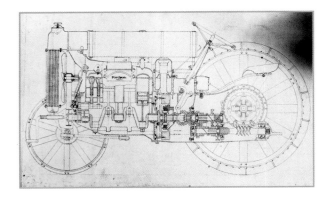

*H*alf of the Fordsons produced on January 30, 1919, sat under covers awaiting shipping. The covers, delivered with the tractor, identified the machines as made by Henry Ford and Son, Dearborn, Michigan. Workers in the background assembled rear wheels. *Henry Ford Museum and Greenfield Village*

was laid out to build them, and even a regular chain driven assembly line was provided to pick up the parts and pull them along. The men would stand in one position to tighten up the bolts and nuts as the tractor went along."

This enlarged facility on Brady Street turned out 259 tractors in 1917. Jack Heald reasoned it took the entire first week of October to manufacture the first tractor that came off the line October 8, "trying out each conveyor, learning how to handle the castings, and figuring out the best way to lay out parts to put them together." When workers knew their jobs, parts were in appropriate bins and the conveyor line moved evenly, the pace reached one per hour, working six days a week.

A cable, dated December 5, 1917, addressed to Sorensen, came from Perry: "First tractors arrived." It had taken more than seven months. In late 1917, Henry Ford and Son had hired Eber Sherman as "Traffic Expediter." Sherman soon was successful getting tractors onto ships to England; however, submarine warfare in the North Atlantic again slowed freight movement to a crawl.

Perry raised the stakes on February 18, 1918, relaying England's desire for 5,000 more MoM tractors. Ford promptly cabled back his commitment to another 1,000, promising to let Perry know about the rest by March 15.

By the end of February, 1,731 Ministry of Munitions Farm Tractors were completed. The assembly rate in March reached 56 per day, 7 every hour. The first thousand, including prototypes sent to England, plus the perhaps 16 X-designated development tractors, and the 50 or so preproduction models, used Hercules engines produced at Canton, Ohio. These first ones had the distinctive rear oil fill. Later MoM tractors ran engines with front oil fillers.

Knowing that by March 3 they would have completed more than 1,800 MoM tractors, Ford somewhat prematurely cabled Lord Northcliffe in London on February 28: "We have shipped to date 1,800 assembled tractors and parts for another 1,800 knocked down [crated with wheels unmounted but included]. Only 10 percent of this has been loaded aboard ship. We have made good time in getting goods to seacoast. . . . Your officials do not get them aboard ship. Three thousand tractors lying on the dock do not help food problems anywhere. . . . Canada and this country are begging for these machines. Each tractor in England can produce fifty times its weight and bulk this season and in shipping [they] should have preference over food. We . . . suggest that if they cannot be moved in time you release them to us and we will put them to work in Canada and this country."

On March 15 when Ford was to notify Perry about 4,000 more tractors for the MoM, he instead agreed to produce 1,000 tractors for Canada. The Food Board at Ottawa had created a *Greater Power Fleet*. Then Ottawa wanted another thousand as well. Ford promised delivery to begin around April 1. Shipping was still slow; Ford diverted tractors destined for MoM to Canada while factory output remained seven or eight an hour.

The U.S. government established County War Boards. Major agricultural states were allowed 1,000 tractors each. Farmers applied to their county agents for permits to buy one, promising to keep the tractor in constant operation on their farms or make it available to neighbors. Eber Sherman still had trouble getting tractors on ships, so Ford moved them elsewhere, completing orders as he could.

The U.S. government had worked with Ford before this, although that involvement came at Henry Ford's request. He wondered about developing the equipment that might be used with his tractor. He approached International Harvester Corporation (IHC), which he did not consider to be a competitor, seeking advice.

What came from IHC was a loan of engineer Bert R. Benjamin to Ford. Head of the IHC Experimental Department from 1916 to 1921, Benjamin developed the Motor Cultivator and was the driving force behind the first successful cultivating tractor, the Farmall.

In 1917, under agreement with the War Production Board (on which his boss, Alexander Legge, was a board member), Benjamin joined Ford and Son in Dearborn to develop implements for the Ford tractor. He also proposed modifications to make it compatible with McCormick-Deering equipment.

Before year end, Benjamin returned to Chicago and set out to design an IHC-produced package to convert the Fordson into a cultivating tractor. (Loaning Benjamin to Ford may seem an altruistic effort, but it provided IHC numerous benefits. IHC had not yet developed assembly line technology, and it was not at all certain its ideas for a high-speed automotive-type engine for farm tractors would work. Benjamin brought new experiences back to Chicago.)

Through 1917 and early 1918, Ford's tractors were shipped without identifying marks on them. Fulfilling a patriotic and humanitarian mission, Ford kept his name off the MoM Farm Tractors. Everyone knew who made them; he made a good profit ($50 each on 6,000 tractors), and he was satisfied. On tractors shipped to Canada and around the United States, however, he stenciled "Henry Ford & Son" on the radiator.

Around April 23, he replaced the stencil logo with a more durable insert. Foundrymen slipped this into the radiator patterns when they poured the shells.

Henry knew of the Ford Tractor Company in Minneapolis and wanted no association with them. "Henry Ford & Son" was a cumbersome logo; fitting that on radiators required small letters. It was difficult to read across a field.

Highland Park Fordson manufacture didn't use assembly line production when this photo was taken. The system shown was called a "progressive line," which was operated by a conveyor belt and chain introduced in 1910. Overhead, a monorail system, similar to Chicago's beef-packing plants, carried gearbox subassemblies to the line. Henry Ford Museum and Greenfield Village

Final engine check at Highland Park was done when tractors rolled forward and were plugged into the electric motor-driven crank. For this mid-April 1919 photo, Sorensen had a white-painted tractor inserted in the lineup. The electric motors spun the engine fast enough to start it within 10 seconds, sometimes less. Henry Ford Museum and Greenfield Village

The Gleaner Combine Harvester Corporation of Independence, Missouri, offered both a promotional brochure and instruction manual. The Fordson-powered machine boasted a 30-bushel grain bin and carried an 8-foot, 3-inch header. *Duane and Carol Helman collection*

1921 Fordson F with 1925 Gleaner Universal Harvester Thresher
*G*leaner production reached 200 in 1925, assembled by Butler Manufacturing in Kansas City, Missouri. Fordson was the only tractor on which this Gleaner could be mounted.

1920 Fordson F with 1928 Belle City Corn Picker
*D*uring 1919 production, production parts switched the ladder-side radiator shell to a solid casting. Belle City Manufacturing produced corn pickers and other mounted harvesting equipment from its factory in Racine, Wisconsin.

The company name, abbreviated for use on cables, had a nice ring. Jack Heald reported that Ford produced some 3,200 unnamed Ministry of Munitions farm tractors before Ford felt product identification was acceptable. Thereafter, tractors shipped worldwide were known as the Fordson.

Within three months, Canada received 1,073 Fordson tractors and more U.S. states became interested. Wisconsin ordered 500, Iowa 1,000, Kentucky 100, Nebraska 400, Ohio 1,000 (with one delivered to Harvey S. Firestone of Firestone Tire and Rubber, in early May). Virginia ordered 200 and Tennessee 100, and Massachusetts, Vermont, New Hampshire, Connecticut, and Maine combined wanted 1,000, all through the county boards. Allocations were made based, in Michigan for example, on one Fordson for every 12 square miles of working farm lands. Organized by county agricultural agents, this "community cooperation idea" asked each farmer to agree "to lend his tractor at a reasonable price for the benefit of his neighbors whenever he can spare it from his own needs."

This satisfied Henry Ford's every motivation. Providing the greatest number of farmers with an affordable tractor removed the greatest amount of "drudgery from the backs of man." Every Fordson delivered exposed other families to the benefits of tractor farming and the suitability of the Fordson. Of course, in most regions, the times when tractors were needed were the same from farm to farm. This would induce those farmers who had delayed an expenditure to buy their own Fordson.

Ford Takes Control of the Motor Company
Back in June 1915, Henry Ford initiated his plan for his Rouge River site. He knew that Highland Park was a limited facility with little available land surrounding what he already owned. His plans to produce a half-million or more tractors and cars annually never could be realized on those 56 acres. This was possible at the Rouge. Horace and John Dodge worried about this facility; however, they mistakenly presumed it existed solely for tractors.

Brookville Locomotive Company of Brookville, Pennsylvania, produced yard engines based on Fordson tractors, but records indicate that Charles Sorensen's staff assembled this one (and perhaps one other like it) to use as materials tugs during the summer of 1919. *Henry Ford Museum and Greenfield Village*

The farm tractor wars that Henry Ford declared with his February 1921 price cut accelerated introduction of motorized cultivators. In mid-1922, Gene Farkas devised this stubby attempt. Its front wheels took power and steered using the differential. Rear wheels were simply castors to support the engine and radiator. Farkas narrowed a Fordson front axle to use as the rear axle of this prototype one-row cultivating tractor. It had one speed each forward and reverse. Drive wheels were half-width Fordson rear wheels. *Henry Ford Museum and Greenfield Village*

Until August 1916, an uneasy peace lingered between Ford and his shareholders. Planning continued for the Rouge, and Farkas and others forged ahead with tractor testing. In August, however, Ford cut car prices 10 to 20 percent and announced he would use $50 million in accumulated profits to finance Rouge expansion, not to pay generous dividends.

The Dodges filed a lawsuit on November 2, 1916, arguing that backers expect full portions of the profit from their investment. They won. In early December 1917, Henry Ford was ordered to disburse $19 million. He appealed. Most of the decision was overturned in February 1919. Ford still had to distribute the dividend, and future "excess" profits of the company had to be distributed to shareholders.

Henry's response was quick. His stockholders, blind to the benefits of long-term expansion and implementation of his ideas, were "parasites." He resigned as president of Ford Motor Company on December 30, 1918, "to devote time to building up other organizations with which I am connected," namely Henry Ford and Son. The board of directors elected Edsel Ford as president on December 31. Henry escaped with Clara, Edsel and his new bride, Eleanor Lowthian Clay (they married the day before the Dodges filed suit), and Charles Sorensen, to the Los Angeles area.

On March 5, 1919, the world learned what Henry Ford did on his vacation. A Los Angeles *Examiner* reporter, Otheman Stevens, got an unanticipated scoop interviewing Ford. Henry told Stevens he planned "to make a better car than he now turns out and to market it at a lower price, somewhere between $250 and $350 . . . through another company. . . ." Henry Ford and Son would produce not only tractors but now a Fordson car and a truck also. None of the Model Ts would be carried over.

This news sent panic through the streets of Dodge. The brothers understood it. Ford had walked away from his car and his company. The world knew him as a manufacturer who built reliable vehicles millions could afford. The Dodges knew a Fordson would devastate them: Their car might compete but not their Ford stock. By mid-July 1919, Henry Ford had reacquired every share of Ford Motor Company stock, borrowing much of the $106 million to do it.

Ford bought out his minority stockholders and began in the fall of 1919 to consolidate the two companies. Ford Motor Company took over tractor sales and the service department. Henry Ford no longer needed to answer to—or tolerate—anyone but his own ethics, morals, ideals, vision, or conscience.

The Fordson Comes to the United States

Henry Ford and Son began domestic Fordson tractor production around April 23, 1918. The first three weeks of the month were occupied with changeover from United Kingdom and Canadian export models. Production slipped to about 300 tractors a week as workers struggled to get proper parts onto each tractor. Ford Motor Company had not yet completed the MoM tractor orders. The newly designated Model F tractor, the first one actually called Fordson, appeared with a freshly cast radiator housing sometime in 1919. Earlier radiator shells were easily identifiable because of a noticeable seam around the logo and sometimes not-quite-true alignment. Now the logo was squarely positioned and cleanly blended into the casting. A small toolbox also bore the new name.

Gene Farkas recalled its history: "We made a toolbox mounted right on the dash. McCormick had charge of the assembly. Long before we went in the tractor business or designed the tractor, he was with Mr. Ford on the farm as a farm mechanic. He was a friend of Mr. Ford's."

George McCormick lived on the farm next to Henry Ford's parents, a neighbor in whose company Ford grew up. McCormick was a frequent evening guest, discussing politics with Ford's father, William, and machines with Henry.

"He picked out all the tools that should go with the tractor," Farkas continued, speaking of the older man, "a Westcott wrench, an open-end wrench with a socket wrench on the other end, and a good screwdriver. They even copper-plated them so they wouldn't rust. They were excellent, too." Through 1918, the box bore the Fordson logo embossed in small print onto the cover. Beginning in 1919, the box swelled slightly and the logo grew greatly.

Henry sent his first 10 Fordsons to friends and longtime supporters, including Thomas Edison and botanist Luther Burbank. Curiously the serial number sequence of the tractors, stamped on engines between the front two exhaust ports by Hercules, skipped 3,000 numbers, jumping from 3,900 to 6,901. Perhaps, knowing Ford had about 3,000 more tractors to build to complete the Ministry of Munitions order, Hercules pulled numbers out when domestic shipments began. (Hercules publicized in the February 15, 1918, issue of *Agrimotor* that it had "received an order from the Ford Motor Company of Detroit for 65,000 motors for foreign tractors . . . to be delivered at the rate of 100 a day and are designed for shipment to Cork, Ireland. . . .") Sadly, no one knows the real reason for this serial number sequence break. Fordson F production is generally regarded as beginning with the 4,260th tractor pro-

duced, which has serial number 7,260.

These were glory years in American agriculture. The United States had won the war and America now fed the war-ravaged world. Farmers were first-class citizens enjoying generous incomes and public respect for their contribution to success overseas. They had money to spend. Many became convinced during the war of the value of tractors. In 1910, banks began to finance purchases of automobiles and trucks. In 1913 farmers found bankers willing to extend credit for tractors. Two-thirds of Ford vehicles were sold on time payment plans, usually with 25 to 35 percent down. Edsel favored it; Henry disagreed. It was a matter that father and son seldom discussed. Families worked hard in fields and factories during the war and saved their money because there were so few consumer goods available. The pent-up demand for tractors, automobiles, and trucks increased employment. What's more, war-weary Europe needed everything. It was an illusion, a bubble that had to burst. Through 1919, though, this house of cards rose higher.

Ford Experimental Farms

"About this time, in 1919," Fred W. Loskowske explained, "the Ford farms were pretty big." Loskowske would have known; he worked for Ford at Fair Lane Farm beginning in 1914 and was general

French and Hecht were among the first to offer solid rubber wheels for Fordson F tractors for industrial applications. The small wagon fitted around the operator appears to have a bracket to hold a road license plate. *Duane and Carolyn Helman collection*

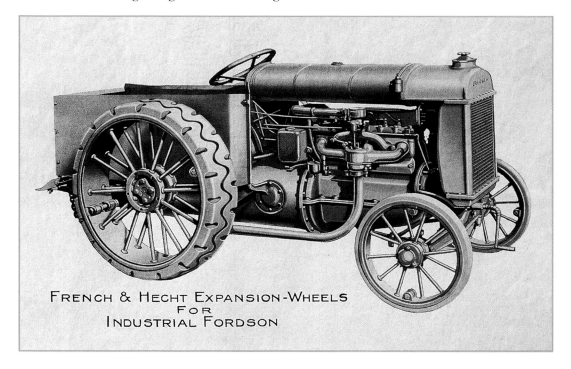

FRENCH & HECHT EXPANSION-WHEELS
FOR
INDUSTRIAL FORDSON

manager until 1950. "He had . . . I'd say around four thousand acres of wheat. He must have had pretty close to five or six thousand acres all around there.

"At that time, Mr. Ford ran a lot of experimental work. There'd be a lot of different guys here with plows. . . . We take these plows in the field and work them, give them a good try. . . . Mr. Ford was very interested in it all. When they'd get a machine like that, I'd get it a-going, and [he'd] usually come out . . . along about two or two-thirty in the afternoon and watch it work.

"What [we] were anxious about was to get a plow that would stand up to the tractor. That was the big item with the boss, and the boss was great on tools.

"When they decided on the Oliver plow, the boss must have bought, I daresay, seventy-five, maybe a hundred Oliver plows. We had some double-bottoms and single-bottoms. The boss didn't like the double-bottom because it wasn't turning the furrows over. So he got hold of Oliver, [who] made an

1922 Fordson F with Trackson Model F Full Crawler

*T*rackson Company, based in Milwaukee, Wisconsin, produced two types of the "Full Crawler" on the Fordson tractor. This version, the Model F Two Ton, added 2,150 pounds to the tractor, yet boasted only 4-psi ground pressure.

*A*n extremely compact unit, the Trackson F measured only 99 inches long, 56 inches wide, 54 inches tall, and operated on a 46.5-inch track gauge. Standard tracks were 9.625 inches steel alloy, although customers could order 12-inch manganese steel for gritty or abrasive soil conditions. Steering was accomplished by track brakes operated by the maple steering wheel. Trackson provided an "emergency hand brake" for locking the tracks on hills or when otherwise needed.

eighteen-inch, single-bottom that could pretty near do as much as a double-bottom. They got it to do a wonderful job, 'cause the boss was bound to plow *deep*. . . . He figured bringing up that dirt and mixing it up would grow better crops."

Finally Oliver settled on a two-bottom, 14-inch model, the No. 7, from a heat-treated steel alloy that weighed 25 percent less than comparable plows. Oliver developed a lifting mechanism and depth regulation device with its control levers located within reach of the seated operator.

"Henry Ford & Son will not directly market any of the power farm equipment used with the company's tractor," reported the May 16, 1918, issue of *Automotive Industries*. "Mr. Ford long ago requested cer-

tain manufacturers of farm equipment to design and build implements used exclusively with his tractor. This was the reason behind the development of the No. 7 Oliver engine gang plow. . . and the engine double disk harrow, designed and built by the Roderick Lean Mfg. Co., Mansfield, Ohio."

The Tractor Wars

Labor unrest in the United States first hit manufacturers such as Ford in 1919. The healthy economy had raised the cost of living. Organized labor sought higher wages. Strikes disrupted production at several Ford suppliers, reinforcing in Henry the determination to produce everything, from car bodies to tractor engines, at the Rouge. He spent $60 million

1922 and 1925 Fordson F with Hadfield-Penfield Rigid Rail Model X Tracks

The Hadfield-Penfield Steel Company of Bucyrus, Ohio, got into the Fordson accessories business in late 1922, introducing its Rigid Rail Track system. In the foreground, a 1925 Fordson with a clutch brake sits near a 1922 Fordson. In weight and performance, H-P's Rigid Rail crawler system came slightly behind Trackson's Model F Two-Ton and ahead of its Model D Three-Ton crawlers.

1923 Fordson F with Ricardo Head and Hamilton Transmission

When was a Fordson not a Ford? When it has parts from half a dozen other makers who created products to improve performance of Henry Ford's Fordson. Most apparent here, besides pneumatic rubber tires, is Waukesha's Dynamic Thermostat combination intake/exhaust manifold with Zenith's carburetor. Behind the Waukesha manifold was a Wehr number 1404 Super-Power Unit intake manifold. Wehr claimed its manifold increased power by one-third. It fed a high-efficiency cylinder head designed by England's Sir Harry Ricardo, a master of combustion engineering. The green housing lower left was a New Idea power take-off housing from New Idea Spreader Company, Coldwater, Ohio.

bringing the plant to its potential from 1916 through 1918. He invested another $15 million in ore mines and forests to guarantee steel and wood supplies, ensuring independence from outside suppliers. To Ford, these were basic survival tactics.

"In my contacts as buyer both here and in Europe," Theodore Gehle explained, "it was not our policy, written or by instruction from our superiors, to buy at ruinous prices. Our instructions were to buy from the right sources who had the right equipment and the right organization who knew how to produce economically."

One such source was Hercules, run by engineer Charles Balough, who had designed the Model T engine. Hercules, however, failed soon after Fordson production exceeded 100 per day. Gehle explained, "This man, Charlie Balough, [didn't] have enough foresight to see that as Ford makes his own engines, his cost will go down, and Hercules' costs must go down or Ford would be paying him a premium. Some people might call that unscrupulous buying. I don't. It's just good business."

These practices paid off. By the end of 1918, the first year of sales in the United States, Ford overtook IHC as the world's leading tractor producer, turning

The Hamilton Transmission, number 1279, manufactured by Standard Gas Engine Company of Oakland, California, replaced Ford's worm gear with a spur gear, allowing greater speed reduction, ground clearance, and cooler operation. A Perfection Type F Air Washer from the Handy Cleaner Corporation of Detroit cleaned engine air. (The connecting hose to the Zenith carburetor is missing.)

1923 Fordson F with Lawn Wheels

This 1923 Fordson F rode on lawn wheels, made from rolled steel 15 inches wide at rear and 9-inch wide fronts, produced by Whitehead and Kales Company of Detroit. Ford introduced the transmission disc brake operated by the clutch pedal. Intake was the Kingston Regenerator.

out 34,167 Fordsons. Despite Henry's desire to centralize every element in the manufacture of his tractors, he spread production beyond Cork, which was in full operation by July 1919. (By year end Cork completed 300 new Fordsons, and 3,626 were assembled in 1920.) At Kearney, New Jersey, Ford produced 75 tractors a day, delivered up and down the East Coast, to the Caribbean and South America. In July 1920, monthly Fordson production reached 4,188 at Dearborn, 2,341 at Des Moines, 2,101 at St. Louis, 810 at Kearney, and 326 at Cork. The daily average was 375, although on June 29, Ford's five factories completed a one-day record of 545 Fordsons.

For dealers things were tough. When Henry regained control of Ford Motor Company, he shifted tractor production to the bigger company. Fordson dealers with retail sales agreements with Henry Ford and Son got plenty of notice but had no tractors to sell after July 31, 1920. Ford had to provide his company branch houses, authorized dealers, and distributors with tractors. Fordson dealers retained only exclusive distribution of approved equipment. The

1924 Fordson F with Trackson Model D Full Crawler
*T*rackson's largest Full Crawler was the Model D Three Ton, which weighed 4,500 pounds without the Fordson, 6,300 complete. It offered greater flotation with overall length of 119 inches on 12-inch tracks with a track gauge of 57.5 inches. These were used often in logging and snowy conditions more than in agriculture.

1924 Fordson Industrial
*V*isually, Fordsons changed subtly in 1924. The gray color was slightly lighter. Ford replaced the maple steering wheels with hard rubber after farmers complained the wood dried out in the elements and some broke. W&K produced wheels for several tractor makers, some of whom offered turning brakes on the axles, hence the drums inside these wheels.

effects were widespread; Henry Ford's car and truck dealers in cities had no wish to carry or service Fordsons while hundreds of Ford and Son dealers now needed a tractor to sell to support sales and service operations. Yet, within a year of canceling agreements, Ford formed new ones with new independents (and some old ones) to sell Fordson tractors and implements without cars or trucks.

Ford's cross-town competitor, GM-founder Billy Durant, acquired Samson Iron Works in Stockton, California, makers of a heavy orchard tractor called

the Sieve Grip. Durant missed the opportunity to buy Ford for $8 million in 1908. His bankers questioned the investment. Since then, Durant often guided his actions by Ford's activities, but Durant's interest was not in a tractor's capability to help the farmer.

"The idea of selling tractors spurred Durant's imagination," Lawrence Gustin wrote in his book, *Billy Durant—Creator of General Motors* (Eerdmans, 1973). "He had ideas of revolutionizing the business of selling farm implements." Durant invested millions to move Samson tooling and supplies to

1926 Fordson F with Nichols & Shepard Corn Picker-Husker
This unrestored artifact operated off a power take-off supplied with the picker, off the drive pulley shaft. Nichols & Shepard, in business since 1848, produced this machine solely for Fordson tractors.

Nichols & Shepard Company of Battle Creek, Michigan, were famous for Red River Line harvesters. The company took pride in continuous operation through the Civil War and World War I, until Oliver Farm Equipment Company acquired it in 1929. *Higgins Collection, University of California, Davis, Library*

Janesville, Wisconsin, and to develop a Fordson look-alike, the Model M.

On September 21, 1920, Ford reduced prices of his cars to keep sales up and his plants and workers busy. Claiming a backlog of 146,000 car and tractor orders, he hoped to energize the economy. Instead, it continued to tighten; he used the slowdown to shut Highland Park tractor operations on October 1 and move them to the Rouge.

As Europe got back on its feet, American farmers found fewer markets and smaller prices for their produce. Cash flow slowed universally. On Christmas eve, Ford closed all his plants, saying it was to inventory completed vehicles and supplies on hand. In January, the commodity market hit bottom. Ford, paying only managers' salaries by now, still faced a financial crunch; with taxes and loan installments due, he owed nearly $30 million.

A competitor proposed solutions. Dr. Edward A. Rumely, grandson of Meinrad Rumely who

founded the threshing machine and steam traction engine company, produced OilPull tractors in 1910. During 1914, Rumely sold hundreds of large prairie sod busters across Canada. The company held loans on them. When crops failed, the banks called due loans Rumely made to acquire several implement makers. M. Rumely Company went into receivership in January 1915. Edward Rumely recovered his financial footing; however, the family lost the tractor firm, something he did not wish on Ford, whom Rumely admired. Rumely suggested Ford create a nationwide farmers' credit company to finance purchases of tractors, equipment, and automobiles. There would be far less risk because only disasters of biblical proportions ruined crops everywhere. Rumely also proposed Ford offer $200 million in stock to the public. Ford opposed buying on credit, and issuing stock would return him to the situation he'd just borrowed millions to eliminate. Ford had another solution.

"The Fordson tractor price was cut $165, from $790 to $625 in January [19]21," Theodore Gehle recalled. "I remember when Mr. Sorensen wanted

cost figures on the tractor before that price cut. . . . The price was not based on cost figures. The actual cost was higher than the price."

Ford reopened Highland Park on February 1, 1921, even though shipments of tractors (and cars) never stopped. Ford, who refused to borrow from bankers, required his dealers to pay on receipt of merchandise, which he shipped according to his supplies not their demand. Dealers might complain, but none wanted to lose a franchise; they went to the banks. In January, Ford shipped 1,138 Fordsons, 1,932 in February, and another 4,708 in March. This broke the economic logjam, creating an upward spiral. As Ford shipped more tractors, farmers felt encouraged by his confidence in the economy. Fordson demand increased. Ford hired back more workers; production, shipments, and demand increased further. Ford produced 69,123 Fordsons during 1920. U.S. tractor production that year totaled 203,000; despite the tight economy, Henry Ford led the business.

Competition Heats Up

Through 1921 and 1922, Ford maintained its dominance of the tractor market while the competition sought ways to unseat the Motor Company.

Wehr Company of Milwaukee produced its "One Man Power Grader" beginning in 1925, frequently configured to use Trackson's Model F Full-Crawler tracks. Kammerdiener Photo Studios of Minneapolis shot this one working on May 30, 1932. Henry Ford Museum and Greenfield Village

On July 27, 1926, the Division of Agricultural Engineering at the College of Agriculture, University of California at Davis, balanced its 1919 Fordson F (fitted with later rear wheels) on its fenders to certify stability and protection offered by Fordson fenders. The chained front axle maintained balance. The standing technician provided scale and assurance of its safety. Higgins Collection, University of California, Davis, Library

FORD BOATS, BUSES, AND PLANES

Henry Ford liked to use his company as a resource pool from which to draw parts and materials for experiments. As an imaginative and intuitive mechanic, he frequently knew what to expect from his experiments. During the decade that began with Fordson production in 1918, Dearborn, Highland Park, and the Rouge factories began to get special machinery and equipment and to work more progressively and imaginatively. This period was the early renaissance of creative applications for Ford engineering.

World War I Ford Production

Once Henry Ford agreed to provide factory and labor resources to U.S. war efforts, several projects came to his facilities for manufacture and assembly. The most well known was the Liberty aircraft engine. Ford also produced light tanks, the "Whippets." When not solving these manufacturing challenges, Ford pressed his engineers to experiment with other applications for his peacetime products.

"During the First World War," Jimmy Smith told Ford Motor Company interviewer Owen Bombard, "we took the tractor engine and built tanks. They were big things, more like conveyors to carry equipment. Of course, they had guns in them and . . . we only built two of them. The Army came to look at them." Charles Sorensen proposed using two tractor engines, one operating each track. Operators turned it by speeding one engine up and slowing the other down. These went no further than prototypes, completed and tested just as the war ended. The day the Armistice in Europe was announced, Ford halted war materiel production immediately and ordered the machine tools for that work removed from the factories or reconverted without delay to peacetime products. At peak production, Ford turned out 250 Whippets daily. Within three weeks, the company produced 1,000 cars, trucks, and tractors a day.

The Ford Boat

Mechanical engineer Harold Hicks joined Ford in 1919 as an engine designer. In late 1924, Edsel, who enjoyed racing powerful boats, looked into mass-producing a small boat powered by the tractor engine. Farkas asked Hicks to make it work. Hicks drew a reverse gear, using the bevel gear cluster of the Model T rear axle. Shipwright Jimmy Lynch from John Hacker Boat Works came in January 1925 to build the hull.

"This boat was tested in about June 1925," Hicks said, "but it was not too much of a success. It was made rather square-ended in the aft part in order to suit production purposes." That created problems for a speedboat; broad, flat sterns had too much wetted surface. The boat would not plane sufficiently. Several marine tractor engines were built and installed in tenders on the *Henry Ford II* and the *Benson Ford*, Ford's Great Lakes ore carriers. In those hulls, meant for harbor plodding, they succeeded.

"From a design standpoint," Hicks continued, "they seemed to work well. The difficulty there was that about that time, Ford went out of the tractor business. That ruined the supply source for the engines."

Fordson-Powered Trucks

The mid-1920s were good times for Ford's experimental engineers. Henry Ford had still other ideas for Fordson engines and his young, enthusiastic engineers.

Laurence Sheldrick joined Ford April 27, 1922. "One of the first jobs I had . . .," he explained in his oral reminiscences recorded in late 1958, "was the Fordson truck. Mr. Ford decided to produce a truck using components of the Fordson tractor, the engine, radiator, worm, and worm gear out of the tractor rear axle for the truck rear axle." This came out of the Fordson threat Henry Ford announced in an interview that appeared in the March 5, 1919, Los Angeles *Examiner*. Once Sheldrick completed the first prototype on the floor in the old tractor building at Dearborn, engineering built six more. Gene Farkas also was involved.

"This truck actually came about after Mr. Ford purchased the Lincoln plant [in February, 1922]," Farkas explained. "He thought with our tractor motor and the Lincoln rear axle we could make a truck chassis good enough to carry a school bus. His idea on the truck was unique at the time. He wanted to put the driver alongside the engine . . . put the cab right over the engine. The radiator projected out maybe four inches in front of the dash and the windshield. Joe Galamb made the drawings for the body, and we had the Budd Wheel Company in Detroit make up several sample bodies."

Sheldrick got a commuter-type and an intercity-type bus body. He stretched two additional truck frames to fit them. Assembled at Dearborn, they later shuttled employees around the factories. Ford used the seven trucks around the Dearborn and Rouge plants until they wore out and were scrapped.

"We brought the driver right next to the engine," Farkas explained, "and the transmission was away at the back. I had a remote beam to pivot in between the distance to shift gears. They didn't have much power, although we did increase the compression. We had about thirty horsepower in those engines. That could have been one thing that prevented going into production on them. . . . Our smallest two-ton truck had more power. The tractor engine at that time . . . didn't have the refinements a truck engine should have," Gene Farkas concluded.

The Ten-Propeller Airplane

That didn't deter Henry Ford from trying even wilder applications. The nation's obsession with flying meant that for Fordson development, not even the sky was the limit.

Henry and Edsel got involved with William Bushnell Stout in late 1922. Stout advocated all-metal airplanes over spruce or plywood, which most aircraft makers used at the time. Spruce was lightweight and strong, but, like all wood, it was subject to rot. In July 1925, Stout Metal Airplane Company became a division of Ford Motor Company, constructing Ford's Trimotor airplanes.

Stout and Ford engineers experimented with engine placement below, in, and above the wings. While most Trimotors used Wright air-cooled radial aircraft engines, one clever variation was built and patented.

"We laid out an aircraft job," Laurence Sheldrick recalled in 1958. "In 1928 the airplane activity was hot and Mr. Ford had some rather novel ideas about aircraft. . . . His idea was that one set of propellers would do the lifting and take the

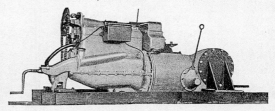
7n late 1924, Edsel Ford proposed that Ford manufacture small speed boats powered by Fordson engines. Gene Farkas worked with engineer Harold Hicks to produce several prototypes with Model T rear axles. The resulting hull shape was better suited to slow speeds; these became tenders on Ford's ore ships, remaining in use into the 1950s. In Fernandina, Florida, Lasserre Moto Company started making marine conversion kits earlier that year, offering 24 horsepower on kerosene. Higgins Collection, University of California, Davis, Library

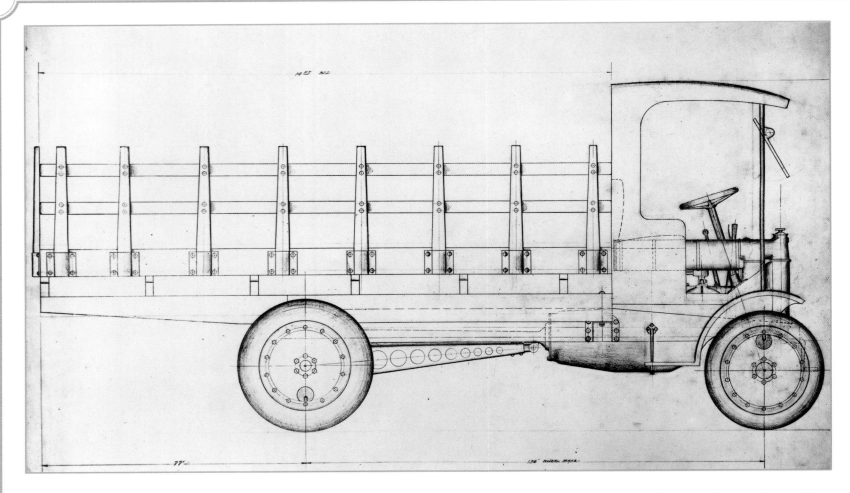

While Henry and Edsel Ford visited Los Angeles in 1919, Henry planned to regain control of his company. He announced that Henry Ford and Son would make not only Fordson tractors, but also cars and Fordson trucks. Gene Farkas drew plans in September 1920; chief engineer Laurence Sheldrick supervised prototype assembly beginning mid-1922. *Henry Ford Museum and Greenfield Village*

plane off the ground while the horizontal set of propellers gave the forward effort.

"This engine of 1928 was made using a lot of the tractor engine parts—pistons, connecting rods, axle housing parts to support the propeller shafts. . . . It had absolutely not a chance of ever getting off the ground." (The application described Fordson engines recast in cylinder pairs. Ford's vertical and horizontal propeller aircraft design was awarded patent number 1,749,578.)

"It was really . . .," Sheldrick continued, "just a bunch of heavy junk. Mr. Ford had [Karl] Schultz working on it principally. I can still see that very plainly. It was right in the northeast corner of the Engineering laboratory building [the former tractor plant in Dearborn]. I don't know if that is the one he asked [Charles] Lindbergh's advice on or not. He probably could have shown it to him because Lindbergh was around there in late 1927 and 1928. I can imagine what Lindbergh said though."

The Kiddie Tractor

Producing Trimotors greatly reduced engineering at the Rouge plant. Tractors, with no changes anticipated, had just Gene Farkas and Howard Simpson. Ford gave them a new assignment.

"I think the new Engineering Laboratory was in the process of being built, which might date it around 1925 . . . when I designed a little tractor with a planetary transmission in it," Simpson said. It was "for this miniature farm that Mr. Ford was interested in, over at his estate . . . part of the threshing outfit [including a miniature steam engine] that he made for the Hy-Ben-Jo-Bill."

Hy-Ben-Jo-Bill was the acronym Ford created for Edsel's four children, his and Clara's grandchildren. The oldest, Henry II, born September 4, 1917, was nicknamed "Hy." Benson, "Ben," was born in 1919; Josephine, "Jo," was born in 1923; and William Clay, "Bill," arrived in 1925. Ford was wild about his grandchildren. At Fair Lane he played games with them and taught them farming, showing them how to plant and harvest by hand.

"Mr. Ford . . . wanted a tractor that would be just the right size for an eight-to-ten-year old boy," Simpson explained, "and he wanted the planetary transmission and the Model T radiator. . . ."

Simpson ordered a unique radiator housing cast to fit around the Model T core. He created a "Fordsons" logo, in honor of its several designated operators. Once the single casting cooled and Sorensen's foundry men checked it for soundness, they destroyed the pattern.

"We took a Model T engine and radiator and built a planetary transmission, which I designed," Simpson continued. "I believe we used a Ford car axle and built a subframe and put a hitch on it so we could pull a little plow. It was just a toy."

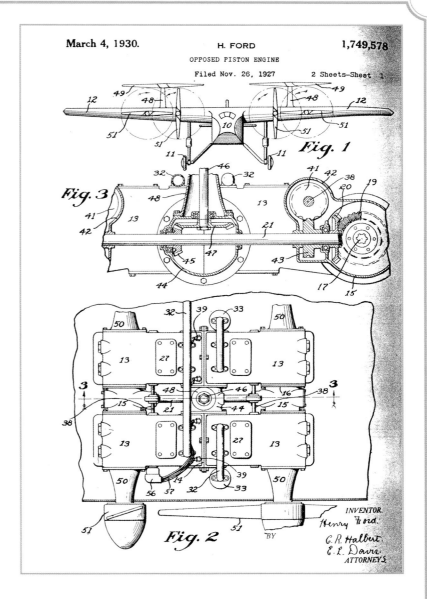

Under Henry Ford's direction, young engineer Karl Schultz created an aircraft adaptation for Fordson engine parts utilizing not only vertical propellers but also horizontal (lifting) rotors as well. A prototype was built which, as chief engineer Laurence Sheldrick characterized it, "had absolutely not a chance of ever getting off the ground."

*H*ammer Blow Tool Company produced a variety of farm tractor farming tools and machines from their plants in Wausau, Wisconsin. These Horseshoe Lugs are sometimes known as potato masher lugs. *Higgins Collection, University of California, Davis, Library*

1926 Fordson F with Horseshoe Lugs

*C*alled the "Lugs that make Good," these Horseshoe lugs were nicknamed "potato mashers" because they resembled potato whisks. Manufactured by Hammer Blow Tool Company of Wausau, Wisconsin, these bolted onto existing Fordson rims and cleats. Hammer Blow Tool promoted Horseshoe Lugs as essential to steep hill or side hill plowing or for sand or gravel soils.

Former industry leader IHC was not content to follow the upstart Ford and developed an entirely new line of McCormick-Deering tractors. General Motors (GM) also plotted to take a piece of the tractor pie and introduced Durant's Samson Model M in May 1919, priced at only $650 and designed by GM engineer Arthur Mason. Mason's design looked like a Fordson, but it dissatisfied Durant. He ordered his struggling tractor division to acquire an odd contraption called the Jim Dandy motor cultivator, a gasoline-powered machine operated with reins, just as a horse would be. Durant figured it would have great appeal to farmers who missed working behind a horse. Called the Samson Model D Iron Horse, it marked the beginning of the end of GMC's chairman. Durant envisioned Samson as supplier for the farmer's every need, offering cars and trucks, as Ford had done with Henry Ford and Son. Ford, of course, threatened this as a strategy to win back his own company. GM's board of directors overruled Durant after learning the tractor "investment" exceeded $33 million. They shuttered Samson early in 1923.

"A common delusion in what is called salesmanship has to do with selling against a rival instead of to

the public . . . ," Henry Ford wrote in 1931 in *Moving Forward*, produced in collaboration with Samuel Crowther. "A business which takes its ideas from other businesses either through fear or emulation and merely copies them has nothing which can really be called a foundation. . . . We have never, in settling our own designs or prices, given the slightest attention to what anyone else was doing in the same field."

In February 1922, with an eye to keeping his plants working at capacity, his labor force employed, and his products affordable to as many customers as possible, Henry Ford decided to cut the price again. On February 5—the day before the seventh national tractor show opened in Minneapolis—he brought the price down $230, to $395. The ripple effect of this made clear how large a fish Ford was in the pond he inhabited.

Alexander Legge, IHC's general manager, got word of Ford's new price while visiting his truck plant in Springfield, Illinois. Stunned, he matched the cut and threw in a plow to attract the buyers' attention.

Agrimotor published specifications of tractors sold in America in each edition. Its February 1922 issue gave additional news: "Just previous to the opening of the seventh national tractor show on Feb. 6, several manufacturers announced rather drastic slashes in the prices of their tractor models. . . .

"The price of the Titan 10-20 tractor has been reduced from $900 to $700. This price cut, together with the cut made by International Harvester Co. on the International 8-16 . . . includes also either a tractor plow or a disk harrow at the option of the buyer if the tractor is purchased before May 1, 1922. In making these reductions, President Harold F. McCormick . . . makes the following statement: 'This reduction is not justified on any present or prospective reduction in manufacturing costs. It is made chiefly to meet competition and enable our dealers to retain their position in the tractor trade.' " In addition, GMC cut its Model M from $665 to $445, Waterloo Boy dropped its 12-25 horsepower tractor from $1,075 to $675, and Wallis reduced the 15-25 from $1,600 to $995.

Henry's belief in price reductions spurring demand, increasing sales and production, absorbed losses from 35 percent cuts. IHC's situation was different. Legge had, lighter, more efficient tractors coming: International's new McCormick-Deering 15-30 was headed toward full production. The model's smaller sibling, the McCormick-Deering 10-20, was timed for launch later in 1922. Left with too many obsolete 8-16s and 10-20 Titans, Legge became an industrial hero, rising to Ford's challenge and cutting prices to "stay in the tractor business." He couldn't lose: selling 8-16s and Titans at 80 cents on the dollar was a shrewd means to turn potential losses into a windfall.

Re-engineering the Fordson

As International Harvester and other makers introduced new tractors to contest Ford's market supremacy, the Fordson's shortcomings became noticeable. The tractor had developed a reputation from its behavior when its plows stuck. A young University of Michigan graduate, mechanical engineer Howard Woodworth Simpson, took on that challenge. He was 26 when he joined Ford and Son in 1918. As a college graduate, he was in a minority at Dearborn, and just days after he started, he was sent to Fair Lane Farm to operate a tractor.

"That was supposedly experimental work, but actually it was just farming," Simpson recalled. He did that experimental work for a few weeks. "While I

was on the farm I heard of the tractor tipping over and injuring somebody in the yard of the plant where they were trying to pull a tractor out of a mud hole.

"I decided that was something that needed correction and I became interested. I had been driving a tractor several days. . . . It never occurred to me that such a thing could happen."

In late 1918, Simpson transferred through a range of assignments common to young talented engineers rising through the company. Gene Farkas had his own chief draftsman, Walter Gage. When Gage left in 1919, Simpson got his job. But Simpson worked upstairs at the tractor plant, rarely seeing Ford when he came to work with Farkas downstairs. When the economy shuddered to a halt and Henry shut down the tractor plant in October 1920, Simpson worked only a short while longer.

"I was laid off about the first of the year, and about the first of April, Gene Farkas and Joe Galamb appeared at my home and asked me to come back to

1927 Fordson F with Wehr One-Man Power Grader
The Model D Wehr One-Man Scarifying and Grading Machine was another complex accessory designed for the Fordson. Built in Milwaukee, Wisconsin, the grader used Illinois Steel 8-inch I-beams, and the Fordson was fitted with the Trackson Model F Full-Crawler tracks steered by the front wheels. Without knowing how Wehr determined its serial numbers, it's impossible to guess how few of these were built. This unrestored but recently worked grader was serial number 3885. Its primary use for the past 20 years was clearing fire roads through mountains during the summer and opening winter access once the snows fell.

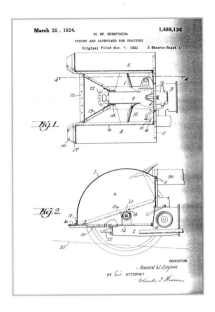

Howard Simpson worked on the problem of Fordson's rising front wheels during January and February 1921. He concluded that full fenders with long lips at the rear would eliminate any risk. After designing and testing a set, he applied for a patent he assigned to Ford Motor Company for only the costs of filing the application.

design a new worm drive for the Fordson," Simpson said. "I remember during that three months I devoted my entire time to developing a cure for this overturning problem. By that time my ideas had crystallized on what should be done because I had analyzed remedies proposed by different people."

The Fordson "problem" was analyzed in trade journals and newspapers. A writer named Grant Wright, with *The Eastern Dealer*, a farming machinery trade journal in New England, attacked the tractor by name in his article headlined, "Fordson Killings." In it, Wright named every victim of an accident, singling out Ford and ignoring other companies whose machines overturned. Such moral high ground was perhaps understandable. Fordsons constituted nearly one-quarter of the tractors in use on American and British farms. They were the best-selling tractors in the world. Ford was a large target and Wright took his pot shots.

The Fordson distributor in Kansas City, Missouri, G. T. ("Go To") O'Maley Tractor Company, published a lampoon-style magazine at the fifth annual national tractor show in Kansas City, February 1920. It was reproduced a month later in the March 15 issue of *Agrimotor*. An item under the heading "Fordson Turns Over Three Times" characterized the tone: "Much has been said about Fordson tractors turning over and we have tried on numerous occasions to get first hand information, but have never succeeded until this day. But now we have it and quote herewith from a letter just received from R. U. Worthy of Confidence, Ga., Feb. 16, 1920. 'Dear Sir: I want you-all to know that I have turned over three times as much with my Fordson as I did with one mule last year.' "

Outside manufacturers introduced safety systems against stuck plows in 1920. The "Calumet Automatic Hitch," the Meili-Blumberg "TractorStop" hitch, and Farm Specialty Company's "Quick Stop" tractor hitch were three among dozens selling simple linkages that sensed rapid changes in hitch tension and disengaged the clutch. Others, such as Rutledge's "Stabilizer" produced mercury-switch-activated magneto cut-outs to kill the ignition if the tractor passed an angle of 25 degrees.

"The best thing to do," Howard Simpson continued, "was to put some fenders on the tractor with some pads or tail pieces out behind, which would engage the ground and prevent overturning."

He went to a Ford dealer with fenders he'd

made. He put them on the tractor and photographed them. Afterwards he took them to the country, put them on a Fordson, tipped it every conceivable way, and took more pictures. He applied for a patent, and when he returned to work, he offered the patent to the company, asking only to recover the $80 patent attorney's fee. When the patent was issued, he assigned it to Ford.

"About 1923 they were adopted as optional equipment on the Fordson tractor. Joe Galamb's assistant, Walter Fishleigh, meanwhile, also had gotten a patent for a design subsequent to [mine]. Ideas of both Fishleigh's and my design were incorporated in the production of the fenders."

Fishleigh was one of Simpson's professors at Michigan. His fender had pads on the bottom end. Fishleigh, Simpson, Galamb, and Gene Farkas talked about Fishleigh's design; they planned the toolbox to cover the pad, giving the fenders a second function.

Simpson continued: "Among the remedies that would prevent overturning and yet not require making the tractor longer was putting added weight on the front end. That incidentally was later adopted when the wheels were changed from steel to cast iron and the weight increased from about sixty pounds apiece up to about two-hundred-thirty pounds apiece.

"There was a lot of misconception in the industry and in the minds of dealers and farmers who thought the tipping was a matter of the way the load was hitched. My observations and tests proved that this had little to do with it. In fact, if there was any load hitched to the drawbar of the tractor, it tended to keep the front end down. Most accidents occurred after they had unhitched the tractor and then had locked the wheels by placing rails or beams under them in order to give them traction for the wheel to climb out of a hole. When the wheel could not climb out, the whole tractor would turn backwards."

The problems that the Fordsons endured publicly troubled other manufacturers too. These caused the entire industry to look at performance characteristics that designers knew were essential. Because of this, they devised independent rear turning brakes to aid in tight maneuvering, they increased tractor wheelbases, and they added weights to the nose. Many tractors in the early 20th century were liable to this risk. Ford provided a tractor for small farms. The prevalence of Fordsons throughout America made his machine more noticeable.

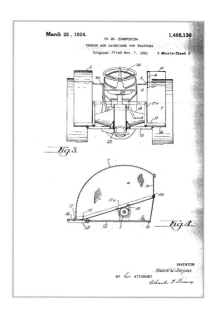

Simpson returned to work in March where he encountered his former University of Michigan engineering professor Walter Fishleigh. Fishleigh had designed a similar fender. Farkas combined elements from both (including Fishleigh's idea of a toolbox in the space created by the rear lip) in a fender available in 1924.

The End of the Fordson in America

Competition in America eroded Fordson sales after 1922. New tractors not only from IHC but also John Deere, Allis-Chalmers, Hart-Parr, and J. I. Case Threshing Machine showed that the once-innovative Ford tractor had aged.

Ford had diverted engineering and development resources from his tractor toward a replacement for the Model T, which ended production in May 1927. These factors, combined with strong domestic challenges, forced him to think about Fordson production in America. From England to Russia, however, European demand remained high and production continued overseas.

In January 1928, Henry Ford, Edsel Ford, and Charles Sorensen agreed to end U.S. manufacture of the Fordson. It may have happened because Ford needed the facilities for his new Model A. Just as likely, Ford stopped because he felt defeated by the tractor price wars and technology skirmishes that he initiated in 1922. Dealer complaints over his warranty reimbursement policies and rigid delivery methods put them at odds. Ford warned them he would as soon not produce tractors as accede to their demands. With sales slipping against IHC's popular 10-20, Ford withdrew.

"I believe," Howard Beebe said, "Mr. Ford stopped tractor production at the Rouge and moved it to Ireland because the majority of our sales were with Russia . . . manufacture would be closer to market. It was just a question of not having sufficient demand in this country to absorb production." A tractor production engineer as early as 1917, Beebe helped start up operations in Cork in 1926.

1925 Five-Eighth-Scale Fordson

Howard Simpson was Gene Farkas' assistant during the late 1920s. In the summer of 1925 Henry Ford asked Simpson to design a little tractor for a miniature farm Ford established at Fair Lane for his grandchildren, whom he referred to as "Hy-Ben-Jo-Bill" (Henry II, Benson, Josephine, and William Clay). Ford told Simpson to make the tractor "the right size for an eight-to-ten-year old boy." Simpson and Farkas used a Model T axle, cut down and remolded, and implement wheels up front with specially cast six-spoke rears. They used a Model T steering wheel and cast a smaller tractor seat.

Six

FORDSONS IN EUROPE

Seeking a Superior Fordson

Although Henry Ford eventually ended Fordson production in the United States, European interest and United Kingdom manufacturing remained strong long afterward. It was not an easy task, however. Updating and operating factories abroad proved more challenging than Ford first imagined.

Cork, Ireland, was never the perfect answer to Ford's question of where in the United Kingdom to produce his tractor. While the first Fordson drove off the line July 3, 1919, one day ahead of schedule and with a shamrock boasting its origin painted on the radiator, the entire operation still was troubled. First, costs to improve and develop the factory were greater than Ford expected. He doubted his mass-production assembly lines could support the effort. The factory was located on the River Lee beside an Irish railway line. While Northern Irishmen were considered more work-oriented, Henry Ford believed he should provide industry where it might make workers more industrious. Cork's second problem was that Ford's hope for industriousness never materialized. Another difficulty was that Percival Perry resigned in October 1919, disagreeing over sales philosophies between the United States and the United Kingdom. (He would return within 10 years, his views intact.)

There was more. Southern Ireland mined no coal or ore. These came up river by ship or over land by rail. A seaman's strike crippled Cork in October

Dagenham Fordson Ns introduced pneumatic rubber tires as an option by the 1936 model year. They were not a popular choice at first because farmers felt many conditions demanded the traction of steel wheels and tall lugs.

Throughout the world, Fordson Industrials were popular tractors. An Industrial with a crane rigged to a trailer strung telephone poles in this photo shot somewhere in the southwest United States just before Christmas 1927. *Henry Ford Museum and Greenfield Village*

Herbert Hoover's Relief Administration authorized shipping nearly 25,000 Fordsons to Russia between 1920 and 1927. The Allied American Corporation staged trials and demonstrations throughout the country. Russian workers prepared tractors for exhibitions in Novorossisk in February 1923. In 1926 Ford briefly considered opening a factory there. *Henry Ford Museum and Greenfield Village*

1920. Nothing moved on the rivers. Once that labor problem was resolved, coal miners in England and Ireland struck, giving shippers and railway operators no way to move and little to carry if they could.

Then hearts stopped in Dearborn. The *Chicago Tribune* reported, "Cork Burned December 12, 1920. Following a 'military ambush' involving the British army and citizens of Cork, members of the Royal Irish Constabulary went on a rampage burning nearly the entire central city of Cork. Damage estimates finally reached 10 million pounds sterling as all but one commercial business were destroyed."

Sorensen cabled for a report on December 13. Edward Grace reported back. The Fordson plant at the river front escaped attack. The Works were in no danger; military martial law was invoked and the Black and Tans were routed.

No matter. Henry Ford's homeland wasn't behaving as he hoped; he had too much at risk. He suspended operations immediately after New Year's Day 1922. Sorensen received a cable back from Grace on January 7: He had 150 tractors in stock but very few new orders.

Politics overtook whatever stabilizing value the plant offered in the work community. The Irish Free State was created in early 1922 with similar independence to Canada, setting its own customs and tariffs. Automobile parts and entire tractors from Cork could be taxed. Henry, Edsel, and Sorensen agreed with ending tractor manufacture there and cutting production back strictly to Model T parts. Just 1,443 Fordsons came out of Cork in 1922 for distribution throughout Europe. Peter MacGregor and Edward Grace, Ford employees in charge of production at Cork, packed up everything and returned to Michigan in 1923.

Fordsons to Russia

During that period and after, from 1920 to 1927, Ford Motor Company shipped, at the request of Herbert Hoover's Relief Administration, about 25,000 Fordsons (and nearly as many Model T trucks) to Russia. Their need came from a nationwide crop failure and famine in 1920. Changes in politics and hardships from their own civil war made their requirement greater. By 1926, with 20,000 Fordsons already delivered, Ford con-

Kutsukian and Hyde, Ford distributors in Brussels, Belgium, used a winter parade in late 1926 to demonstrate the urban pulling power of industrial Fordsons, dressed to look like Belgian draft horses. *Henry Ford Museum and Greenfield Village*

Six years before Ford Motor Company Ltd. introduced its Fordson All-Around, it was developed in Dearborn's Experimental Department. This prototype, photographed December 14, 1931, showed some features that were carried over into production as well as some tool mountings on the front axle that were not. *Henry Ford Museum and Greenfield Village*

Ford's Imperial Cultivator provided a three-row, spring-loaded spade attachment. This was mounted to the rear axle, bolted onto the X-webbing-reinforced rear axle extensions and the rear wheel outside hubs. Ford's Experimental Department devised the prototypes using Cork-produced Fordsons. *Henry Ford Museum and Greenfield Village*

sidered opening a factory there. He sent Bredo Berghoff and four others to examine sites and conditions. Amtorg, the American Trading Organization, a Russian ministry in Moscow, organized a four-month visit.

Berghoff found thousands of operators well satisfied with the tractor, at least until it came to service. Parts produced in Cork or at the Rouge and imported into Russia were fine, worked well, and cost a fortune. Russian-made parts, of inferior metallurgy and ineffective heat-treatment, were cheap and worthless. Lack of machinery knowledge often did more damage than using inferior replacement parts. In one case, Berghoff discovered, the operator had run out of gasoline and refilled the fuel tank with thin crude oil, destroying the engine.

"Sometimes we found they weren't using Fordson parts, but parts made in Leningrad where they started making them in preparation for making a tractor later on. This was pirated manufacture, especially the pistons.

The major difference was the Russian parts were roughly machined and the thickness varied in the castings and no doubt the weight of the pistons would be quite a bit more than Ford pistons. They were mixing in various pistons indiscriminately so the motor was off balance all the time," Berghoff is quoted in the Ford Motor Company archives. Berghoff guessed that a third of the Fordsons his group saw during its 7,000-mile journey no longer ran.

"They lacked repair equipment," he said. "Some places had quite good equipment but not enough of it. There were so many tractors that they just couldn't service all of them in a reasonable time." This was not universal, however. In other areas, operators understood machinery. On some farms, machines plowed more than a thousand hours in a season. In the Volga Region, farmers operated Fordsons around the clock, headlights blazing 24 hours a day. Fordsons outnumbered IHC tractors and other European makes by more than 10 to 1.

Tiflis Equipment Fair

Ford and competitors from the United States and Europe put on an equipment fair in Tiflis, the capital of the Republic of Georgia. While trying to set up, it rained every day for three weeks straight, turning their demonstration plots to deep mud. When the rain stopped, exhibitors still had to build their displays, allowing the ground to dry into a surface tougher than concrete.

"There was a great big Allis-Chalmers tractor," Berghoff said, "that came in with four plows to start with. They cut off one after another. . . . They couldn't do much plowing with two plows because [they] were out of balance then; they couldn't run straight.

"They had their troubles, we had our troubles because the tractor had a tendency to stand on its rear wheels once in a while. Herman Luedtke [a Dearborn tractor engineer] suggested that we needed a weight on the front axle. . . . [S]omeone said, 'You'd make a good weight. You weigh more than any two of us.' He thought he ought to make himself useful so we tied him on the front axle. He held onto the hot radiator with some rags and stood on that front axle for hours." Amtorg requested each participant to plow seven inches deep through the concrete-like surface.

"Then after the plowing contest they wanted the various tractors to haul cannon over the mountains. They had no roads but just an opening in the rock. It was a slippery surface. We knew that Mr. Ford wouldn't be too happy to have his tractors haul cannon. . . . Someone had to haul a wagon across the mountain for supplies or something. [We] suggested the Fordson tractor be used for that supply wagon. That worked out all right. Most of them didn't make much of a showing climbing those mountain roads. The steel cleats on their wheels would spin on the slippery rock. The Fordson had rubber tired wheels on it and, therefore, could travel faster than the rest."

Berghoff even found Russian-built Fordsons, called *Krasny Putilowitz*, identical in every way but materials quality and reliability. He shipped two of them home for inspection.

Back in Dearborn, Berghoff advised Ford against investing in Russia, or more correctly, the Union of Soviet Socialist Republics. Sites he saw in Taganrog were English-built structures that were left to rust. Lenin was dead, Trotsky would be exiled, and Stalin was sure to become dictator. Everything was set to be

state controlled, influenced, or obstructed. Factory hierarchy involved not only a plant manager who understood manufacturing operations and products but also a political appointee with more influence. Ford decided he would not invest in the Soviet Union.

Instead, in May 1929, the Soviet Union invested in Ford. In an agreement with the Supreme Economic Council of the USSR, under Joseph Stalin's first Five-Year Plan to increase industrial output, Ford provided plans, information, training, and equipment necessary to establish a factory capable of producing 100,000 cars and trucks a year. In exchange, the Soviet government would purchase 72,000 Ford vehicles over four years. Only Ford-made parts would be allowed for repairs. Soviet engineers already had pirated the Fordson, so Berghoff and others helped them clean up mistakes in manufacturing. Real Fordson tractors would continue to be available to them, sold from regular production built in England. Former Cork boss Peter MacGregor eventually toured the Krasny Putilowitz tractor factory, which boasted it completed two machines each day. It was in near-hopeless disarray, its 800 workers lazy and disorganized. Tractor output never exceeded 20 in any month. In 1928 MacGregor learned the Soviet Union would build a new Putilowitz plant in Stalingrad, and it was updating

*H*oward Simpson and Gene Farkas developed at least three prototype row-crop Fordsons. Two of these carried Imperial cultivators. They bolted rear axle extensions onto existing hubs and attached wheel extensions to the narrow 54-inch French and Hecht "Skeleton" wheels on this prototype photographed New Year's Eve 1931. *Henry Ford Museum and Greenfield Village*

1936 Fordson N Standard Agricultural

Fordson production, interrupted by the move from Cork in 1933, resumed in Dagenham later that year, though total English output was small. In 1935, Ford Ltd. added orange trim to the previously solid blue tractors, painting logos and wheels in bright contrast.

Dagenham Fordsons carried more than 4.125x5.00-inch four-cylinder in-line engines with new manifolds aiming the exhaust straight up. The University of Nebraska tested a Cork-built, gas-engined N in April 1930; University testers rated it at 26 belt pulley and 14 drawbar horsepower.

others in Leningrad (opened in 1923 but not operational until 1924) and in Kharkov. Berghoff visited Stalingrad near the end of his stay.

"We didn't see industrial plants in Stalingrad at that time but we did see the cornerstone which had been laid for the new tractor plant. It seems the farther away you were from Stalingrad, the bigger the plant was going to be; the more tractors they were going to produce," Berghoff said. "At one place they might say it would be thirty thousand, at another place twenty thousand, ten thousand. Everybody read figures in the papers so they knew. That was 1926 and in 1930, they built the plant. The cornerstone was laid because . . . they liked to get together, celebrate, and report progress.

"They had a beautiful picture of the plant which was to be built. . . . I asked them why they had enormous coal piles in the middle of the oil district.

"'Well, this is an artist's idea of what a plant ought to look like.' As a matter of fact, they had no idea what the plant was going to look like when they showed up here in the States in 1929 when I became their consulting engineer. They suggested twenty buildings for their tractor plant and I said, 'Why not just have one building instead of twenty?'

"'Oh no, that isn't the Russian way.'

"Later I found out it was a Russian custom to have many buildings like they have at the [Putilowitz] Works in Leningrad where I think they had 300 buildings. The idea was that if anyone started trouble in one of the buildings, they could segregate the trouble right in that building."

Figures released from the three plants, always notorious, announced they produced more than 50,000 Soviet-built Krasny Fordson tractors in 1932. They published no reports of trouble.

U.S. Production Ends;
the United Kingdom Gears Up

Soon after Ford stopped U.S. production of the Fordson in January 1928, Amtorg in Moscow ordered more Fordsons to supplement so-far-unsuccessful Soviet efforts. Ford's factory closing left him unable to fill the Russian order, so Amtorg bought tractors from International Harvester which, after a fairly good showing at Tiflis, wanted to invade Soviet soil.

When Percival Perry, who earned the title Lord Perry for assisting British agriculture during the war, appeared at Dearborn to patch up old disagreements, he and Ford recognized opportunity. Perry knew Ford's Dagenham facility in Essex was expanding, though it couldn't be operational until 1932. Demand for the tractors was high, both from domestic dealers willing and able to sell the slightly dated Fordsons and from foreign markets where Fordsons were quite competitive.

Because Ford Motor Company Ltd. was independent, Perry proposed it take over production in the United Kingdom when Ford offered him Fordson tooling for a small investment. In five years since formation of the Irish Free State, political and tariff climates were calmer in Cork. The river city now made sense as a temporary home for the Fordson. The plant, always conceived with tractor production in mind, had capacity unused since it ended there in 1922.

Henry Ford, who cared first for tractors and second for all other vehicles, was very pleased. He was back in business in his native land, offering employment where none had been.

Debugging Cork

"I didn't have anything to do with getting the Cork Plant started," Howard Simpson stated, "but I did have a lot to do with getting them out of trouble afterwards. I went over there in the spring of 1930. Their major difficulty was heat treatment of steel and the quality of steel. The heat treatment would turn out batches of gears with very brittle teeth, and they would break under load. There was a lot of trouble with the Cork tractors because of gear breakage . . . a problem of British supply and metallurgy.

"I was only there a few weeks. . . . They were adopting standard American design with certain changes and improvements that we had recommended. . . . I spent most of my time on tractor design," Simpson continued. "We worked out a new air cleaner . . . governors and new carburetors and manifolds. We played with cylinder heads and tried to increase compression and power. We worked out gear designs to do away with that worm drive that was so inefficient. . . . After the tractor moved to Ireland . . . I started to work on a planetary transmission for the tractor. I did a lot of different designs, four speeds and so on. These tractor projects never got beyond the blueprint stage. Mr. Ford would say, 'Keep working on it.'

Dagenham engineers trimmed Howard Simpson's and Walter Fishleigh's Fordson F fenders when they adapted them to the English N models. This permitted tighter turning with the tractor and towed implements, allowing greater maneuverability.

One significant element of the Fordson All-Around was Dagenham's introduction with this model of individual rear brakes to improve turning and maneuverability characteristics. The wider rear track, necessary for row-crop farming, allowed Howard Simpson to fit the drums onto the rear axles.

Kerosene-fueled Fordsons were less energetic performers than their gasoline-engined twins. At 1,100 rpm, the in-line four produced a maximum 13.6 drawbar horsepower and 23.2 horsepower on the belt pulley. All Fordson Ns through 1945 had three-speed transmissions.

"I had a big board . . . covered with blueprints of different designs. He would come in, often bringing Edsel, and discuss them and I would keep working along. He just never seemed [at] the point to do anything serious about it, but he wanted me to keep working.

"I was also working on a steering brake to make a sharp turn. . . . Other tractors [had them] and a self-energizing multiple steering brake seemed to be the way to get a brake into the present construction of the Fordson without hanging a big drum on the outside and requiring an extra means for holding the drums and mechanisms. . . .

"We designed one power take-off, coming off ahead of the main clutch, for the Fordson and it was built over in England. . . . There was some demand there to make the Fordson available for row crops so the wheels could be spread out to straddle two rows of corn. We built them up experimental on the Ford-

1936 Fordson Row Crop All-Around

Dagenham introduced its Row Crop, or All-Around, near the end of 1936, as this tractor, serial number 802230, indicates. Developed by Howard Simpson in late 1931, manufacturing tools and dies were developed during 1932 as Cork production was closing down.

Ford Motor Company Ltd. introduced the All-Around primarily for U.S. tractor customers. Early models featured brake pedals operated from the rear of the axle. The left-side pedal of this machine was inverted for easier operation.

son . . . ," Simpson said. "Mr. Ford didn't show any interest in the Fordson tractor after it went over to England. He was only interested in new and experimental design."

Evolution of the English Fordson

Despite Henry Ford's lack of interest in the Fordson, developmental work continued on the tractors. Most of this took place at the enlarged Dagenham, England, plant, which replaced the Cork facility. Production ceased at Cork after four years with just 31,461 tractors built.

The engine cylinder bore was enlarged from 4.00 to 4.125 inches, providing nearly a 20 percent drawbar horsepower gain, from 12.3 to 15.5 horsepower. Simpson also replaced the old thermosyphon cooling system with a pressurized water pump.

The Model N English Fordsons were, ironically, the first foreign-built tractors tested at the University of Nebraska in 1930. These tests—numbers 173 and 174—included a clerical error. Records read that Nebraska tested Model Fs. The fact they were equipped with the larger 4.125-inch bore engines and

1938 Fordson Row Crop All-Around

*D*uring regular production in 1938, Ford Motor Company Ltd. spruced up appearances of the 20-year-old design by painting the entire tractor orange. This was done as much as anything to appeal to farmers captivated by other makers' tractor styling—redesigned sheet metal and re-engineered operator platforms.

*H*igh-compression heads and gasoline carburetors enabled Fordson Model N engines to produce nearly 30 horsepower through the late 1930s. Reinforcing rods tied the extended front axle housing to the engine oil pan on all row-crop English Fordsons. Dagenham manufactured these Row Crops until October 1944.

the serial numbers—757447 and 758223—clearly indicate they were Model Ns produced in Cork.

Heavier cast front wheels with five stout spokes and the Simpson/Fishleigh toolbox fenders were standard on the Irish Fordsons. Production at Cork peaked at 15,196 tractors in 1930 but plummeted to just 3,501 in 1931 and to 3,088 through 1932's partial year. In its final year at Cork, Fordson introduced ribbed radiator shells. It changed from American Bosch magnetos to German Bosch units. As stocks of toolbox fenders expired, narrower versions (shorter, with no toolbox) appeared. Simpson continued testing and learned that the rear overhang was unnecessary. The additional weight wrapping over the wheels kept tractors from rising up. He devised a smaller fender that still protected operators yet allowed greater implement maneuverability.

The last 1932 Ns were painted blue with red wheels, a startling contrast to long-standing gray. Ford reduced the price of "Standard" Fordsons to 156 pounds ($624; they peaked at 280 pounds, $1,120, in 1919 after introduction at 250 pounds, $1,000, as MoM versions). Neither price cuts nor appearance changes had any effect on sales. When Dagenham was ready, Perry relocated production nearer supplies of raw materials and talented workers.

Manufacture began in Dagenham on February 19, 1933. Only 2,778 tractors were produced that year (in deep blue with orange trim and wheels), and just 3,582 more were produced in 1934. Ford Motor Company Ltd. introduced pneumatic rubber tires as a factory option in 1934, mounting Dunlops on home market Ns while exports to the United States appeared on Firestones.

Because Ford Ltd. was a separate entity from operations in Dearborn, N tractors came into the United States through Sherman and Shepherd in Brooklyn, New York, which also distributed Ferguson's "Irish" plows.

Henry Ford never revealed his feelings about exiling domestic tractor production to Cork. A large group of his domestic dealers, on the other hand, acted on their frustration with the short supply of tractors from Ford. In March 1929, many of the Fordson dealers formed the United Tractor and Equipment Corporation. They created a tractor, the United, produced under license by Allis-Chalmers.

The venture was relatively short-lived, as the dealers were quick to jump back to Fordsons when English production became available. The United foundered and disappeared by 1933, and Allis-Chalmers continued producing the tractor as its Model U.

When the world finally shook off the Depression, Dagenham output tripled to 9,141 in 1935 and jumped again in 1936 to 12,675. Introduction of the All-Around, the "tricycle" tractor known as the Fordson Row Crop in America, helped boost sales.

Until 1935, all Fordson Ns were "Agricultural" models. Then, Ford offered "Land Utility" tractors, modified "Industrials" featuring pneumatic tires, a toolbox to carry what was needed to change tires, a muffler mounted below the tractor, optional extra brakes, and even bulb horns.

Aftermarket manufacturers bought "Skid Units," as historian Allan Condie referred to them in his *Fordson Model N 1929–1945*. These chassis, delivered on skids, went to independents who attached crawler tracks and even locomotive wheels.

Condie explained that modest profits from Fordson tractors (both Ns and earlier Fs) meant that spec-

ification, engineering changes, or developments had to be recoverable in cost. It's likely that Case's Model CC Row Crop, with its front wheels supported by a pedestal cantilevered below and out from the radiator, inspired Fordson's All-Around. A "pigeon roost"–type steering linkage connected the steering box to the front pedestal on both tractors. Splined extensions bolted onto existing half-shafts to widen rear track. Howard Simpson designed the All-Around in Dearborn years earlier. Yet he completed final details in Dagenham on the eve of production in 1937.

"That was a so-called three-wheel tractor with very high wheels [for] added clearance. The front wheels were close together to go between a row of corn . . . [made of] heavy cast iron, and the increased length made it necessary to have so much weight in the wheels because of the increased leverage of the wheelbase," Simpson explained. Simpson raised top speed to 4.3 miles per hour, and dealing with rear tire and front suspension considerations, chose French and Hecht wheels for the All-Around/Row-Crop model. According to Condie, these were popular in eastern England and on potato farms in Scotland. For 1937, Dagenham's steering-gear redesign incorporated a worm-and-pinion system lubricated by high-pressure oil; a Handy Governor Company oil-bath air cleaner replaced the water bath-type that let dust pass through in air bubbles. Rear axle brakes

*Dagenham changed from the "Chicken-Roost" steering linkage used through 1937 to a smoother-operating worm steering gear for 1938. In addition, U.S. Row Crops were available with a single front tire.

1940 Fordson Model N Standard Agricultural

In response to worries that bright orange tractors stood out too clearly against green English fields, Dagenham began painting its Model Ns green starting in late 1940. This color scheme continued until Fordsons went out of production in early June 1945.

greatly improved maneuverability. In 1937 brake levers rose up the backside of the axle, but in 1938 Dagenham revised the operating linkages so brake levers worked off the front, providing more comfortable, convenient access and better control. English farmers first saw oil bath systems on demonstrator Fordsons at the Royal Agricultural Society show in June 1937. They recognized it most easily by the additional tall stack above the fuel tank, opposite the exhaust. They heard about new, high-compression cylinder heads and domed pistons. With an optional vertical-shade fitted in front of the radiator, farmers controlled engine temperature to ensure proper

function of the fuel vaporizing system.

Still, to some observers, Fordsons appeared in 1937 as yet another too-long-lived Ford product, like Model Ts with 20 years on the clock. Dagenham exported less than 5 percent of its output to the United States, the least forgiving of any market for Ford's steady tractor. Even though Ford relocated the power take-off (PTO) in 1936 and it offered the row-crop tricycle in 1937, none of this improved sales.

In November 1937, Dagenham changed from dark blue paint to orange, or "harvest gold," with black trim. (Some prototypes appeared in orange

with blue wheels. In regular production, wheels were orange, a decision made on cost of labor and materials.) This more vivid color choice likely confronted an industry-wide trend for brighter colors and styled bodywork. Manufacturers hoped to make their tractors not only more reliable and better performing, but more attractive, banking on strong influence from farmers' families on purchases. Dagenham fitted 9-inch-wide rear wheels to increase traction without compaction.

Some of the problems with the English Fordson persisted. Simpson slightly increased the compression ratio, which provided more power with no problems for U.S. operators where gasoline was the fuel of choice. In Britain, where lower octane fuels were used in farming, the high-compression engines suffered under hard work. Connecting rods and crankshafts broke. Simpson and his colleagues made fast improvements. They replaced steering gears on Row Crops in 1938, provided better brakes, and switched to Ford's own oil-bath air cleaner system.

This progress, however, was in marked contrast to what Simpson felt he'd accomplished back in Dearborn during this period.

Fuel tanks denoted the country of origin, as they had starting with Model Fs in 1918. Dagenham engineers scribed ignition quadrants with a break to prevent operators from advancing it too far when gasoline was no longer widely available as a tractor fuel.

To save metal during World War II, Dagenham cut back the size of rear fenders starting in 1940. This also reduced production time because workers could mount the fenders after fuel tanks and instrument panels were installed.

Early in 1940, Dagenham emptied its stockpile of German Bosch magnetos. Ford Ltd. adopted American Bosch units or those made by Wico before Lucas models appeared. Most wartime Model Ns ran on kerosene or tractor vaporizing oil (TVO).

Seven

THE V-8 EXPERIMENTS

Wild Ideas

and

Sleight of Hand

"**O**ne day in the middle of July 1931, the Old Man rushed into the Experimental Department looking for me," Gene Farkas said in the Ford Motor Company archives. "He was excited. 'It's time we begin a new tractor,' he said."

The "Old Man," Henry Ford, was days shy of his 68th birthday. He had waited patiently through fourteen years of federal investigations and legal maneuvering. With the dismissal of all charges against the Ford Tractor Company of South Dakota and Maryland, with the death or disappearance of all the participants, and with no further claims on the name, Henry Ford had his own name back. For almost four years he had done without a tractor. It was time to begin a new one, one that would bear his own name.

Ford thrust his best young talent into the work. He dusted off John Fritz's principle and applied it liberally: "Let's start it up and see why it doesn't work."

He pushed his engineers, stretching their minds and their patience. Where each change to the Fordson had improved the tractor, some of Howard Simpson's experiments for Ford on a domestic tractor seemed senseless, if not wrongheaded.

"The factory keeps no records of experiments," Ford said in his book, *My Life and Work*, (Garden City, 1926). "Foremen and superintendents remember what has been done. If a certain method has formerly been tried and failed, somebody will remember it—but I am not particularly

*K*arl Schultz developed this simple V-8 prototype built on ordinary 1935 Ford truck steel frame rails, using the 85-horsepower V-8 engine and a great number of production truck parts, including a 1935 truck grille.

In late fall 1936, after Howard Simpson had produced numerous tractor designs, Henry Ford told him to go ahead, but to develop one-wheel drive using his new V-8 engine. By January 1938, Simpson had his oddly configured machine running, shown here in a field that is now the parking lot for the Henry Ford Museum. Henry Ford Museum and Greenfield Village

In April 1938, Ford sent Simpson and his tractor to test at Ford's Georgia farm south of Savannah. As he recalled years later, "We could plow with it, but the thing would sort of roll like a rowboat in a heavy sea." Henry Ford Museum and Greenfield Village

anxious for the men to remember what someone else has tried to do in the past, for then we might quickly accumulate far too many things that could not be done." Ford felt this was the trouble with records.

"If you keep on recording all of your failures you will shortly have a list showing there is nothing left for you to try—whereas it by no means follows because one man has failed in a certain method that another will not succeed. . . ." He learned that lesson at Michigan Car 40 years earlier. It made clear to him the value of putting fresh minds to a problem after others of comparable skill and ability were exhausted.

Ford's commitment to trying every idea led to strange products at times. One such effort was the one-wheel-drive tractor Ford asked Howard Simpson to design.

The trail to this unorthodox machine began with Ford's quest for a V-8 engine. Earlier Ford had challenged his engineers to make a V-8 engine in a single cast-cylinder block. He had many applications for it in mind. Chevrolet introduced an in-line six in late 1929, and Ford felt technology slipping away from him. By May 1930, design engineer Karl Schultz

completed a one-piece V-8 prototype. Two dozen more were cast, assembled, and tested during the next 18 months, each reducing manufacturing cost and improving performance. Ford took over the project himself, ordering expensive new tooling in the height of the Depression to produce these engines economically. He spent millions. Then on March 31, 1932, he unveiled his 65-horsepower V-8.

The success with the V-8 engine invigorated Ford, who declared to any reporter or observer who would listen, "I've got back my old determination." With his new engine in his pocket and rising competitor Chevrolet held at bay, he pushed Simpson and Schultz harder on tractors. He gave them the V-8 months before the world would see it.

"On December 4, 1931," Simpson recalled, "Mr. Ford told me to design a tractor with large wheels and with an engine speed of fifteen to sixteen hundred rpm." Simpson's memory was clear because he started a diary that day of assignments he received from Ford. His diary, blueprints, and reminiscences are now in the collection at the Research Center at Henry Ford Museum. He had investigated tractor design and especially ground clearance for row crops and wheel track adjustment to accommodate different crop row widths.

"Mr. Ford would stop at my desk every day," Simpson explained. "He always had ideas and wanted to discuss different things. He didn't want to go ahead and build anything. He just wanted to investigate all different possibilities. . . ."

Ford wanted planetary gears, eliminating bevels totally. He proposed double-reduction planetaries. He resurrected the cylindrical fuel tank ahead of the radiator from his Model T prototypes 15 years earlier,

MODEL 39 EXPERIMENTAL

This two-to-four-plow machine was labeled a "General Purpose Tractor-58-inch tread-shown for plowing or cultivating narrow row crops 28–30-inch rows." It is one of the series of tractors designed as Model 39. Howard Simpson introduced many features updating the Fordson. He fixed a pivoting front axle to the transmission tube, with front wheel brackets providing clearance for narrow row crops such as beans and potatoes. He also connected his steering gear to steering brakes using enclosed rods. He specified a Ford Model B V-8 engine cut in half and four-speed transmission, and he allowed a top road speed of 12 miles per hour (with rubber tires). He designed rear axles as hollow tubes to reduce weight, with reversible rear wheels to increase tread to 78 inches. Simpson angled the belt pulley (driven through a bevel gear off the engine-speed driveshaft) 22 degrees off the axis of the tractor to clear the front wheels. His note in the side elevation behind the engine referred to a "latch to limit swing of the front end to 30 degrees either way and to lock when front wheels are moved together." With few adjustments, Simpson's configuration converted a standard tractor to a narrow front. After it was patented, Ford decided not to produce it; Avery Farm Machinery introduced the idea in the late 1930s as its Ro-Trak. The photo was dated September 23, 1932. *Henry Ford Museum and Greenfield Village*

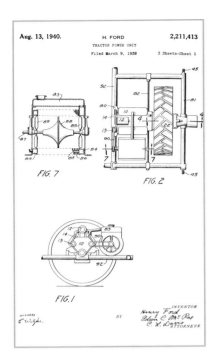

to reduce fire hazard and get weight further forward to shorten the tractor. A compact machine, Ford maintained, was more maneuverable. He suggested using 60-inch wheels with 4-inch lugs. On December 21, Ford and Simpson discussed the general-purpose tractor concept. He wanted his tractor as light as possible, yet capable of extremely deep plowing.

"On January 10, 1932, he asked the weight of the tractor I was designing," Simpson said. "I said about twenty-eight hundred pounds. 'It shouldn't weigh more than two thousand pounds,' he said, 'You don't need weight to give traction. A cat doesn't need weight to get traction, and neither does a tractor.'

"On June 7, 1932, Mr. Ford stopped at my desk about nine-thirty in the morning. He had proposed locating the transmission on the axle shaft, that is, transversely mounted. That morning, he asked about relocating it to the more conventional engine shaft configuration." Simpson had done this already in a three-speed planetary gear design with gears surrounding gears. "By telescoping the gears this way, it made a very short and compact job. Then he said I could put all the men in the place on a new tractor."

After a few words about power take-off configurations, Ford walked away. Later that afternoon they talked more about gear reductions. Simpson put that

day in perspective 24 years later.

"When Mr. Ford said I could have the whole factory to build a new tractor, that was sort of a burst of enthusiasm. If I had taken the whole department, Sheldrick's men and everybody else working around there, why, there wouldn't have been anybody else left to work on trucks and cars. . . ." Simpson was unsure if that was a test or a tease. He chose not to take over the department.

The next day, Ford said he needed differential brakes on any tractor they built to get shorter turn-

While Howard Simpson was embarrassed by his transversely mounted one-wheel-drive, V-8-powered tractor prototypes, Henry Ford thought enough of the system to apply for patents in March 1938.

Simpson built two versions of this midengine, one-wheel-drive tractor, the first using Ford's 60-horsepower V-8. The second, with the enclosed rear wheel, ran with the larger 85-horsepower engine. Simpson understood Ford's desire to try every idea, to see why it might not work. *Henry Ford Museum and Greenfield Village*

Through the winter and spring of 1938, Karl Schultz developed a unit-frame tractor, using Ford's new in-line six-cylinder. By April, Shultz had his prototype working in the fields at Fair Lane. He had used the lightest-weight materials possible. Its first day in the field, the rear axle housing broke. *Henry Ford Museum and Greenfield Village*

ing, a system that IHC's Farmall had pioneered. Ford appeared with Ray Dahlinger, another design engineer like Simpson. They discussed parameters for a new tractor: light, powerful, "and above all comfortable so the driver would want to drive it." Simpson did so many designs and studies, he started numbering them to tell one from the next, should Ford walk back in one day and tell him to build a prototype. The designs quickly mounted up.

Two months later, frustrated by so much work but so little progress, Simpson told Ford he felt he'd accomplished nothing. Ford said he was satisfied, reminding Simpson, "We fussed around two years on the Fordson and then when the right time came, we designed it in a single week."

In September 1932 Simpson told Ford he'd heard farmers were returning to horses because they could not afford gasoline. "He immediately said, 'Alcohol, that's the answer. They'll have to make their own.' " Within weeks, however, Simpson had another innovative gasoline tractor for Ford.

"I have a quarter-size sketch of a row crop tractor showing an extensible front and rear axle [using] a Model B passenger car engine," Simpson said. "It also shows wire wheels which Mr. Ford was very partial towards at that time. This could be changed from the plowing-type of tractor to the row-type of tractor by detaching two front wheel brackets and moving them around and bolting them onto a central pad. In doing so the radius rods were removed. Other layouts had it in position for row crops. The front wheels are brought close together so they could run down the middle of the row. One of the other companies adopted this idea and put it into production." When Avery Machinery Company introduced it in 1938, the company called it the Ro-Trak.

"A Model B engine was used in [several] instances. Mr. Ford was constantly playing with the idea of a light engine. He wanted to use passenger car units wherever possible. [Many] of these layouts are designated for Model 39. This was a mythical model as we had to have some tractor model number to be working toward. All this experimental work was charged to Model 39."

Ford noticed a Simpson blueprint showing the belt pulley set on a twenty-degree angle, allowing the belt to clear the front wheels instead of dragging over them. He had Simpson produce a sample and they found that it worked.

"I mentioned rubber tired wheels for plowing," Simpson said, "and he said, 'Never mind that. Work on the mechanism of the transmission and the wheels will take care of themselves. We are going to build a real tractor. Make this room all tractor in here. Get in samples of different kinds of construction.' "

Ford stopped back three days later. "Maybe rubber-tired wheels *will* be okay to plow with," he told Simpson.

"It was quite a strain working with Mr. Ford," Simpson said. "I would try to do all these things to satisfy him, and yet I was not able to go ahead and just design a tractor with my own ideas.

"I put a power lift on the implements, the cultivator in particular," he said. "This was a vacuum power lift [with] a large ten-inch cylinder mounted on the rear of the tractor with leverage arranged to lift the cultivator when the operator opened a valve." He made another system using exhaust gas pressure. Of course, all this experimental work was sporadic and without any definite aim at going into production.

Ford was approaching 70. Through his lifetime he'd worked with machines and, mostly, with forceful decision makers. Men who were gentle, sensitive, and acquiescent, such as Howard Simpson and Ford's own son, Edsel, were a challenge to Ford, who challenged them back, pushing them, pressuring them, working them, thinking it would toughen them. It didn't work.

Simpson was pulled from tractor work to design a new planetary transmission for Ford's Model B. This, Ford told him, was so they could adapt his design to tractors as well. "The tractor is your meat," Ford told him. Just before this, they had discussed

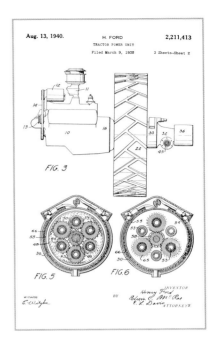

In its side view, it is easy to understand Ford's claim for the novelty of Howard Simpson's one-wheel-drive tractor. With a planetary gear system within the driving wheel, it is an efficient package. Unfortunately, it did not provide performance to match its originality.

While the 1938 truck grille still had the V-8 logo at the top, Karl Schultz chose Ford's straight six to power his unit-frame prototype. He cast an oversized oil sump out of aluminum to use as a stressed member. Ford staff photographer Ann Hood made these pictures on August 29. In early October the entire prototype broke in half, the aluminum sump failing under load. *Henry Ford Museum and Greenfield Village*

These French and Hecht rear wheels were common to Allis-Chalmers tractors, while Schultz took pressed steel wheels from the 1936 passenger carline for the front. Overall, the tractor stood 11 feet long on a 7-foot, 7-inch wheelbase. It was 6 feet, 5 inches to the top of the exhaust pipe and 6 feet, 6 inches wide. It provided 1 foot, 11 inches ground clearance to the engine oil drain plug, but 4 inches less below its battery box.

the upcoming presidential election, Herbert Hoover against Franklin Roosevelt in November 1932. Ford believed Hoover would win. Simpson heard farmers were for Roosevelt.

"Well, I don't see any relief for the farmers for a long time," Ford told him. "What they need is a cheap tractor and that is what we are trying to do here, let the farmer find a greater number of uses for his product." (Ford practiced what he preached, later raising thousands of acres of soybeans to use their oil in machining processes and developing synthetic materials from their extracts to produce automobile body parts and even tractor seats.)

Simpson toiled on transmission and drivetrain configurations for automobiles, not returning to tractors until late 1936.

"Then, after endless hints and conflicting orders, I finally got orders to build up a tractor. In 1936, Mr. Ford told me to build one up, but before I could lay it out, he stopped me. He wanted a one-wheel-drive tractor. I told Mr. Ford a one-wheel tractor couldn't take all the

power that our V-8 engine had. But he said he wanted 'to try out all the lousy ideas,' regardless, so he could be sure in his mind what the best thing would be.

"The three-wheel tractor that was built in 1938 was a different model number. . . . Layout 46 is a design for a Model B engine mounted crosswise directly in front of the rear axle. . . . That put all the weight on the back of the tractor, which gives ideal traction. Of course, the idea was to mount the implements on the front end of the tractor and thus provide weight to hold it down."

Ford wanted everything designed around the Model B V-8. Through the next year-and-a-half, Simpson drew and assembled an oddly configured prototype. Its engine was mounted transversely in the middle of the tractor frame, driving one wheel only. Ford knew that driving the tractor through the middle would lessen the risk of rearing up as it crossed uneven fields or furrows. Laurence Sheldrick had done a light car prototype with the small V-8 transversely mounted on the rear axle, known as design 44B7001. Ford began hinting to the world that his interest in tractors had returned, that he was developing prototypes.

"What the world needs right now," he said publicly several times through the fall of 1937, "is a good tractor that will sell for around two hundred and fifty dollars." In January 1938, using a Model 52 136-cubic-inch engine, Howard Simpson got one running. The price was right, but the technology was not.

"It worked fine on the varnished floor of the laboratory, but it wouldn't pull a pickup truck with the brakes on. We demonstrated it to numerous people in the building in February and March, and I was quite ashamed of this design inasmuch as Mr. Ford was bringing different people in to see the thing."

The drive wheel was set back 30 inches behind the driver on a 58-inch tread width. The wheelbase was 76 inches. Simpson's planetary gears were compact. Ford saw no problems in the unorthodox configuration. At least, he had no problem showing the world this ungainly machine.

"He had the president of the Oliver Farm Equipment Company, Mr. Cal Sivright, and Mr. McAllister, president of International Harvester, and Mr. Johnston, chief engineer of Harvester, to look at it with very many other notables, including Paul Gallico [the author and screenwriter], and Eber Sherman, Tom Micklejohn, and Elmer Schatz, who were all Ford tractor dealers. They all looked at it and tried to think of something nice to say about it, but they couldn't.

"I took it out and maneuvered it around outdoors, and it tipped over sideways as I had predicted."

Whether Ford showed off this machine to the world because he believed in it or due to a crafty desire to keep the competition off-balance is unsure. Whatever his intentions, this odd tractor struggling across the field would have made a lasting impression on the industry observers invited to see it work.

Ford sent it with Simpson in April 1938 to the Georgia farm he'd acquired in 1925, to undergo field tests through the winter. Ford's plantation farm at Ways Station was 20 miles south of Savannah. This sea-island region previously raised rice, and Ford felt America should produce more. He converted some of his acreage back to rice. By 1935, he'd enlarged his holdings from his original 100 acres to encompass about 100 square miles of the area, renaming it, and the small community surrounding it, Richmond Hill, for a region near his ancestral home in Kilkenny, Ireland.

"We couldn't pull as much with this V-8 engine as the little Model B Allis-Chalmers engine could pull. I would hitch it up and it would get stuck pulling the plow. We'd have to pull it out with the Model B. We took this one down to Georgia and also another one with an eighty-five horsepower, standard, large V-8 engine. The Allis B could pull more than either one.

"This first tractor tended to tip up in front because it was so light. Mr. Ford had us pile sandbags and bricks on the front end. . . . We could plow with it but the thing would sort of roll like a rowboat in a heavy sea.

"On the second tractor we made it a little heavier and put two front wheels on it. Mr. Ford didn't like that because it looked 'like a bedstead.' That is the way he wanted it and the way he got it because he was in every day when I was designing it and building it. He looked it all over, and I kept changing it just the way he wanted." Ford became obsessed with eliminating any chassis configuration that might lift the front off the ground.

"Mr. Ford had a reporter out from Savannah and took a picture of us." Karl Schultz ran the tractor extensively over four weeks in Georgia. Ford sent Simpson back to Dearborn, telling him to leave his drawings behind for Schultz. Ford wanted detailed information about the entire range of implements a working tractor should operate. Simpson completed that in late April. Ford set Schultz to work on another tractor idea, "apparently because these three-wheel screwball designs hadn't worked out," Simpson recalled.

Ford asked Wisconsin Ford distributor Tom Micklejohn to buy a second Model B Allis-Chalmers and send it to Richmond Hill. Schultz would tear it down, measure it up, and make "a copy of the A-C, more or less, except that [Schultz's row crop tractor] had a little larger engine, a one-fifty-six-cubic-inch six-cylinder, and it has some kind of crazy planetary gears in the wheels. It's just another nightmare.

"That three-wheel idea he had me do was his own. The basic idea was simplification," Simpson continued. "If he got a simple powerplant with the gears all planetary and the axle reduction all in one compact little unit, it would be cheap to manufacture and all you would have to do is bolt this unit right on

The engine was standard Model 51 221-cubic-inch, 80-horsepower V-8 with its Stromberg number 97 carburetor. Ford's truck V-8s produced about 138 foot-pounds of torque over a 1,700- to 2,200-rpm engine range, but they were not especially fuel efficient. Engine compartment covers were vertical louver panels from the 1935 truckline.

the back end of a standard passenger car V-8 engine with a drive wheel and everything on it, and you would have a tractor. You would have a power package that was ideal for manufacturing purposes.

"Then the question was, what to do with the thing to get it to plow. With only that one wheel [with power], you just couldn't steer that tractor. If you got the pull of the plow just one-quarter of an inch off of the center of [the] pull of the wheel, the tractor would wander all over the field and you couldn't steer it back into the furrow. Mr. Ford insisted upon that single wheel because that was part of the package deal. That was what he had in mind, and it was a brilliant idea, except that it didn't work. It was like taking a horse and cutting off three of his legs and putting little wheels on him and expecting him to pull with one leg. You can see how clumsy a horse would be, and that is just about how clumsy the tractor was."

In April 1938, Henry Ford sent Karl Schultz up to the Fair Lane workshops to develop a new tractor there. By September, he had it out in the field plowing. "The tractor was impractical," Simpson recalled, "and the rear axle housing broke on the first day because it was so light and weak." This used Ford's newest in-line six-cylinder engine coupled to the lightest materials Schultz could create. Schultz persevered.

"He must have worked quite a long time on it," Simpson theorized, "to develop these tractor designs. One was a two-cylinder job and one was a four-cylinder. I think he even designed the engines, which was a major project in itself. Imagine one man not only designing it but every little detail, every washer, rod, casting, transmission, and gear. The reversible lugs on the wheels was a major project. It was just impossible for one man to do a decent job, let alone in secret without conference with anybody."

That was another of Ford's engineering characteristics. Along with avoiding experimental records, Ford believed engineers worked best in isolation, without influence from their peers. The secrecy between projects was legendary. Yet it reinforced his belief that one man's reported failures might taint another's attempts. Isolated efforts insulated imaginations.

Then, in early September 1938, Henry Ford learned that Adolf Hitler had a car with "an air-cooled pancake floor engine," the Porsche-designed Volkswagen engine. Ford set Schultz to design one. In October, Karl Schultz's lightweight six-cylinder

prototype broke in two in a field at Fair Lane. The chassis failed right through the middle.

Eber Sherman, still U.S. distributor for Dagenham Fordsons, was a frequent lunchtime visitor of Henry and Edsel at the Dearborn Inn. He saw Simpson regularly as well, stopping by his drawing board for a chat. For some time, Sherman encouraged Henry Ford to produce a new, more modern tractor. A week before it split in half, Ford and Sorensen assured him that Schultz's prototype was ready for production. Sherman approached Simpson to orchestrate a meeting with Ford about another tractor, one built in England.

"I couldn't arrange a conference," Simpson remembered, "so Eber and I just happened to be out there when he was coming along. . . ." Simpson saw the Ferguson tractor when he was in England. He brought back information. Sherman had built plows for Harry Ferguson in the early 1920s, and he was anxious to recoup his $100,000 investment.

"He wanted to bring one of these Ferguson tractors over to show to Mr. Ford. . . . He started in to tell Mr. Ford of what a wonderful tractor this Ferguson was and right away Mr. Ford said, 'Well, get one over here and let us see it.' Then he walked away."

Schultz selected the 1 1/2-ton truck four-speed transmission and rear end. He equipped this prototype with regular foot brakes, left- and right-hand brakes, and an emergency brake. Its PTO and belt pulley were unique to this tractor, as were the final drive hubs.

Ford Experimental

This tractor is an odd mix of mystery and certainty. There are no records of this machine among the reminiscences of tractor engineers working at the time, yet the origination of the pieces of this tractor is obvious, either coming from regular production parts bins or else specially cast or formed for this prototype.

According to the owner, there were three of these machines built, two of them assembled with Ford's in-line six. This, the only survivor, did so because it was used on Ford's Fair Lane Farm for farming purposes during the lengthy Ferguson lawsuit. The entire front end is fabricated, not cast.

THE FORD-FERGUSON SAGA

Mr. Black, Meet Mr. Ferguson

While Henry Ford charged along building every-thing from Fordsons to one-wheel-drive V-8 tractors, Henry George Ferguson sold, tinkered with, and improved on early automobiles and thought about tractors at his May Street Motor Company.

Harry, the name Ferguson preferred, was born in Growell, Northern Ireland, on November 4, 1884, the fourth of 11 children born onto the 100-acre farm of Jim and Mary Ferguson. A slight lad, he was pulled from school at 14 to work the farm; he hated the tasks, the chores, and the horses.

Harry's oldest brother, Joe, left for big-city Belfast chasing his fascination with machines. Harry endured six more years of farming before he could follow his brother. After joining him, Harry studied engineering at Belfast Technical College.

The two brothers raced motorbikes and cars to publicize their business. Harry and friend John Williams convinced Joe that building airplanes would be another great promotion. After a series of crashes, Harry kept his plane aloft long enough to join history as Ireland's first aviator. Fame for Harry followed, but Joe wanted none of it, and they parted company. Harry opened May Street Motors in 1911 and soon hired Willie Sands, a 20-year-old with inborn talents for design, engineering, and mechanics.

In 1914, Harry changed his business name when he began selling imported tractors. Harry Ferguson

Harry Ferguson used wooden models in hundreds of demonstrations to explain how his unit-plow system worked. The model illustrated the superior efficiency and safety of the Ferguson System. *Henry Ford Museum and Greenfield Village*

Harry Ferguson (center, with hat) was forced into farming at home with his parents, a lesson that taught him he must make any tractor he might produce to be operable by a young boy. His partnership with English gear maker David Brown to produce his Ferguson tractor yielded just such a machine. *Henry Ford Museum and Greenfield Village*

Ltd. distributed Overtimes, the Waterloo Boy export model. He knew the best way to sell anything was by demonstration. Aware from his own experiences of the need to mechanize agriculture, and at government request, he and Sands began to teach Ireland about tractors. Operating Overtimes, Sieve-Grips, IHC Moguls, and Hart-Parr Little Devils, they learned as much about tractors and plows as they taught about mechanical farming.

Plows were still horse-drawn implements. Tractor hitches, sitting higher than horse rigging, pulled up the plows where horses pulled them down. For tractors, plow makers enlarged shares to make use of the tractor's additional power. But no one altered hitches or their geometry.

What worked for horses made tractor plowing a challenge and occasionally life-threatening. Horse-drawn plows stopped immediately when they struck a rock or tree root below the soil surface. Tractors, with more power and rotating flywheels maintaining the momentum, also reacted automatically: They reared up. Ferguson and Sands encountered this situation on every tractor they operated.

Frustrated by the plows and concluding tractors were far too heavy (his Overtime was more than 4,000 pounds; Sieve-Grips and Little Devils were 6,000 pounds each and Moguls were nearly 9,000 pounds) when their demonstration season ended, Ferguson and Sands planned a new plow system.

In December 1917, the E. G. Staude/Eros Model T conversions were available in England. Ferguson was intrigued by its lightness. Sands took Ferguson's plow concept and made it into a two-bottom prototype with cast-iron beams and shares. Designed for the Eros, they eliminated the usual seat and wheels. It weighed just 220 pounds, a third of anything else available. Ferguson knew lighter alloy steels could reduce its weight further.

Sands attached the plow frame to the Eros below the rear axle and ahead of it. Levers and compensating springs adjusted draft depth and allowed the plows to ride over sunken rocks or tree roots. If plows caught, a sheer pin gave way, separating it; if a plow stuck, it tugged the nose of the Eros to the ground instead of allowing it to rise.

Ferguson and Ford (Motor Company) Meet

As Ferguson introduced his Eros plow, he learned that Ford planned to produce tractors in England for the Ministry of Munitions. While this was not the perfect tractor for Britain, its price, at 250 pounds, was so far below a Model T with Eros conversion that it eclipsed the competition.

Harry Ferguson and Willie Sands saw the MoM tractors and concluded the hitch problems still existed. Ferguson felt it was a chance to sell plows, however. He learned that Sorensen was in London to review manufacturing sites; he and Sands gathered their drawings and quickly left.

Ferguson biographer Colin Fraser quoted Ferguson's opening remarks in his book, *Harry Ferguson, Inventor and Pioneer* (John Murray, 1972). "Your tractor's all right as far as it goes," Ferguson reportedly challenged Charles Sorensen, "but it doesn't really solve any of the fundamental problems." Ferguson praised the size and weight of the machine; however, he declared that efficient farm mechanization came when implements were not appendages towed behind the tractor but were rigidly mounted *onto* it while still being quickly removable to accomplish other tasks. Sorensen agreed but saw no way to accomplish this. With a flourish, Ferguson and Sands

Ferguson developed a more sophisticated model demonstrating his unit-plow system. This used an electric motor to apply even pressure to two models. Ferguson's unit plow, represented as "The Safer Way," hugged the platform while towed plows and engine torque lifted up "the old way." *Henry Ford Museum and Greenfield Village*

unrolled drawings of the Eros and its plow.

It was a curious meeting. Sorensen knew metal and production and could communicate with Sands. He was intelligent and perceptive, so he understood Ferguson. He knew his boss, so he recognized the potential in Ferguson's idea. But he was not prescient, so he did not trust his first impression. Years later, he wrote in his autobiography, *My Forty Years with Ford* W.W. Norton, 1956), "Had I foreseen the consequences of that meeting, I would have avoided it."

Ferguson anticipated a healthy plow market from the 10,000 Eros kits in Britain. He was too far into Eros plow production to abandon it for the MoM tractors. Sands adapted the Eros model to Ford's machine. They sold out their Eros plows because of the large supply of the kits. Then they both dove into the MoM.

The problem of rearing up that existed with all tractors seemed particularly to affect the MoM machines. Ferguson and Sands revised the Eros plow and hitch for the government tractors, resulting in their Duplex hitch using upper and lower sets of par-

allel links. On top of the plow Sands formed a pyramid frame and attached the two top links from the peak of the pyramid to the normal hitch location on Ford's tractor. The pyramid and top links forced the tractor nose down when a plow stuck. In tough going, the Duplex drove the front down further, creating the effect of a tractor weighing much more.

Ferguson and his employee Archie Greer traveled to Cork in 1921 to test their plow behind Fordson tractors. The plant provided assistants to operate tractors, while Ferguson and Greer watched and worked. One of those tractor operators was Patrick Hennessey, who had been a German prisoner of war and came home shell-shocked. According to Colin Fraser, Hennessey was adept at tractor work. Production line and field work were deemed "therapeutic." Hennessey, Fraser reported, "remembered in particular that there were some blazing rows. Ferguson had fixed ideas about plow design, and if anyone tried to shift him from these, or was openly in opposition to them, the scene was set for a rousing argument."

After thorough testing and field use, and after its patent was granted, Harry Ferguson felt emboldened. The war was over for a couple of years. Recalling the encouragement Sorensen had offered, Ferguson wrote asking for an opportunity to show the new plow to Henry Ford. Sorensen invited him to Dearborn.

Ferguson wanted steel beams cast for his plow at the Rouge (no one cast steel in Belfast at the time). Sorensen's hospitality was huge. Sand's bronze beams were molded, recast as steel, and Sorensen set a date to demonstrate the plow to Henry Ford.

Ferguson explained operations and the geometry to Ford, who was impressed. Following a few rounds of plowing in a field near the Rouge, Ford was intrigued. His interest, though, was greater in Ferguson than the plow. Ford told Sorensen to hire him.

Ferguson declined. Sorensen raised the wage three times; each time Ferguson declined. Ferguson wanted Ford to manufacture his plow, selling it with the Fordson, as partners. His rebuff annoyed Ford. He asked Ferguson to sell him patent rights. Again, Ferguson smiled and declined. Ford saw Ferguson and Sands off, suggesting they visit Oliver Chilled Plow in South Bend before they left America. Because the people at Oliver felt protective of its position with Ford as primary plow supplier, engineers greeted the Irishmen and their plow with little enthusiasm, judging it not a practical development.

Despite Oliver's chilly reception to Ferguson's plow, Harry Ferguson remained active and undaunted. During the decade between his first visit with Ford and the new invitation via Eber Sherman, he and Willie Sands continued developing their plow.

The biggest obstacle they had to overcome was stabilizing plow draft. They accomplished this in 1921 using a small wheel at the rear of the plow. This bothered Ferguson, who felt it compromised his "unit principle." Without a wheel, the tractor carried the plow weight, enhancing traction on the rear tires. The depth wheel, as it was called, bore some of that weight.

Ferguson had hoped to produce his plow in Ireland. Failing that, he looked back to America. One Ohio manufacturer agreed but quickly reneged. Ferguson called next on disc-harrow maker Roderick Lean in Mansfield, Ohio. They agreed, and Ferguson returned home to find Willie Sands improving the draft control. Sands replaced the depth wheel with a small skid riding the bottom of the furrow. Linked to

the Duplex Hitch, the skid responded to tractor motions over soil irregularities. Ferguson was pleased; Sand's skid returned plow weight to the tractor. Roderick Lean, through their licensee, Vulcan Plow Company, was producing Ferguson's depth-wheel plow; Sands devised an adapter to replace the wheel and its links with the skid. Ferguson and Sands patented the skid version in December 1923.

The next year Roderick Lean went bankrupt. Ferguson returned to America where he encountered Eber and George Sherman, who exported Fordson Model Fs to Europe and Model Ns back to the United States and distributed them in New York state. They watched the plow and thought it was a well-turned-out moneymaker. They established Ferguson-Sherman Inc. in December 1925, with manufacturing in Evansville, Indiana.

In Ireland Sands continued to invent tractor-operated implements for the Duplex Hitch. His skid was not foolproof, however. Plow draft was influenced by more than the tractor's angle on the soil; Sands observed that soil density had an effect. Heavier soil created more friction, which the draft-control engine-governor interpreted as increased depth. It raised the plow. They devised an "Apparatus for Coupling Agricultural Implements to Tractors and Automatically Regulating the Depth of Work," patented in June 1926. This was fundamental to Ferguson's system. Ferguson, Sands, and Archie Greer created a mechanism that worked either manually, by a system of two motors, by hydraulics, or even taken off tractor final drive that sensed engine speed variations from changes in plow draft. While the mechanical configuration *appeared* to be the easiest to adapt, the hydraulic system worked best.

Sands connected a horizontally mounted hydraulic pump, basically a cylinder and piston, through a linkage to the top of the plow pyramid, carried over from their earlier efforts. When hydraulic oil filled the cylinder, it raised the plow. Lowering the implement required opening the cylinder valve. Gravity did the rest, pumping oil out of the cylinder. This was all simple. Complications arose when the tractor moved over uneven soil. Sands prepared a sensor that responded to changes in implement draft nearly instantaneously. Ferguson, Sands, and Greer experimented with pumps and cylinders, never quite achieving what they hoped. Using a Fordson tractor, they continued to work, even after learning that Ford planned to end Fordson production in America.

This news stunned the Shermans with their inventory of 2,000 Ferguson plows in Evansville. (They sold out their supply after becoming importers for Ford's Cork-built tractors. Demand eventually exceeded plow supplies.) There remained little work at Harry Ferguson Ltd., however, and Willie Sands left to establish a bus company.

Ferguson and Greer persisted. They received another patent after sorting out linkages to force trailing implements to follow tractors exactly. This involved the same converging geometry that stabilized vertical movement. In early 1928, Ferguson perfected a three-point hitch, using fittings on the rear axle housing to connect the implement by twin linkages. Satisfied, Ferguson and his wife, Maureen, returned to the United States in the fall of 1928 to find a new manufacturer. Allis-Chalmers was intrigued and bought a 90-day option. The Fergusons returned home to find Willie Sands, retired and wealthy from a larger company's purchase of his successful bus line, again offering his services.

Allis let its option expire while Willie and Archie struggled to eliminate problems that overheated the hydraulic oil. Under some circumstances, this started the plow cycling up and down, a behavior they called "bobbing." While there was still no maker in America, Ruston-Hornsby in England reworked its new tractor design so Ferguson's draft control plow would fit. Rover Car Company, and Ransome-Rapier Motors, planning to produce tractors, met with Ferguson. Morris Motor Company, still another auto maker, expressed interest in tractor production, but then withdrew. Morris' board felt uncomfortable investing in a new vehicle.

The Black Tractor

Ferguson recognized that even though Fordson production surged in 1930, the world was in a Depression in 1932. No major company seemed ready to invest millions to produce a new tractor. Fordsons remained the lightest tractors available, though IHC's Farmalls were more versatile and highly maneuverable. Ferguson concluded that he might provoke interest only if he spent his own funds to build a sample tractor to demonstrate his ideas on unit implements.

Ferguson, Sands, and Greer began working out this tractor's characteristics and construction. Fergu-

son hired John Chambers as second draftsman to work with Greer on necessary drawings while he sought suppliers. The David Brown Company was recognized throughout England as a quality gear maker. Transmission and steering pieces would come from them. The Fordson's early Hercules engine, as used in the Ministry of Munitions tractors, made sense to Ferguson; he ordered an 18-horsepower version of the newest model. They mounted their latest three-point hitch, which placed the single link on top and two links below. They built the hydraulic pump into the tractor instead of bolting it on.

What developed in their workshop was a tidy, small machine, lower and less substantial *looking* than a Fordson, but actually slightly larger. Ferguson painted it black, and to this day no one knows if this was homage to Ford's choice for the Model T or simply Ferguson's own method of understating the evidence of competent engineering. The "Black Tractor" was born in 1933 and Ferguson sent it out immediately to get dirty. Ferguson, Sands, Greer, and Chambers had done the tractor, a new plow, and

*D*avid Brown built and sold few of the Ferguson tractors. Some farmers felt it had too little power to pull their own plows; others objected to buying a new plow to use on the new tractor. Here a small crowd watched a southern Irish farmer turn over large ribbons of earth. *Henry Ford Museum and Greenfield Village*

1938 Ferguson Type A

The first of these Ferguson Type A tractors was completed in May 1936 by David Brown Tractors Ltd. of Huddersfield, England. Production models followed very closely—but not exactly—the details of the prototype known as the Black Tractor, which Harry Ferguson and Willie Sands assembled in Belfast in 1933.

several cultivating tools, one for potatoes, another for row crops, and the third for normal purposes.

The tractor got muddy and their humor blackened. Problems existing in previous versions reappeared, even after modifying the "leaking valve" mechanism that reacted quickly to soil contour changes. The system still overheated hydraulic oil, and the tractor and plow bobbed across the field.

Then Sands had an idea. Draft control had been tied to the two lower links. The hydraulic pump constantly adjusted these links under tension. This overheated the oil and caused the pump to leak or fail. Sands wondered if, instead of using the oil under pressure pulling on the bottom two links, it might be less labor for it if it were on top to pull the plow up by compressing the cylinder. Gravity and the point of the plow slicing through the soil would bring it down and keep it there. Tests and more tests showed that Sands had nearly solved the problem; it diminished the bobbing as well. It was time to find a manufacturer.

Ferguson and Trevor Know, his young tractor demonstrator, showed the tractor and plow to groups from Craven Wagon and Carriage Works, owned by one of Sheffield's larger steel companies, using land adjoining David Brown's private air field. Brown was

impressed, but so was Craven who signed on. Ferguson and company moved to Sheffield to help production start up. He demanded complete control of the engineering and specifications of raw materials. He and Sands were loathe to allow any modifications to either hitch or hydraulics. Ferguson asked his partners to use American steel specifications, believing the tractor would be more marketable in the United States if it met those standards; however, Craven's parent companies were steel mills with, they believed, some knowledge of the materials.

It is easy to imagine Harry Ferguson smiling at the principals and remarking, "Your steel is fine, as far as it goes. . . ." It didn't go far. Their agreement unraveled before one piece was cast or pattern formed. Ferguson had spoken with David Brown, who wanted the project no matter where it was with Craven. Brown visited their solicitor in London, who confirmed difficulties dealing with Ferguson. Brown asked if Craven would be willing to turn over the agreement to him; the lawyer, quoted in Colin Fraser's *Harry Ferguson: Inventor and Pioneer*, replied that Craven, "would be delighted but you would be a bloody fool."

Despite fair warning, Brown and Ferguson became partners. It was a merger with odd side-effects. Ferguson, nearly 50 by this time, had become an insomniac. With worries of tractor production off his mind, he found himself thinking very creatively during the late silent nights. He reconsidered Sand's hydraulic depth control system. He knew that relocating the hydraulic control valve to the suction side of the pump would stop oil flow in or out of the pump. This blocked oil in the pump cylinder and held lower links rigidly in place. An increase in draft pressure, when, for example, the implement dug deeper, exerted additional compression on the top link, allowing the pump to suck in oil, but no more than necessary to return the implement to its preset depth. A decrease in draft allowed oil to escape the cylinder, lowering the implement. A manual override lever alongside the operator's seat could adjust depth and raise or lower the implement at the row ends.

This provided an unexpected effect when an implement struck some submerged object. The enormous compression of the upper link forced the valve not only to the point where it filled the cylinder, keeping the implement depth constant. It also forced it to the drain holes beyond. This temporarily jammed the implement deeper into the ground, hauling down the front wheels and barely lifting the rears up to spin harmlessly. They could not dig in and flip the tractor. When the operator reversed the tractor away from the obstruction, the implement momentarily unloaded and lifted up to full raised position. Once past the obstruction, the operator reset the implement and went on. Ferguson's System was complete.

Preproduction test tractors appeared in early 1936. Bowing to nationalism, they switched from Hercules to English Coventry Climax engines. They priced the tractor, called simply the Ferguson, at £244, $976, some $336 more than Fordsons. They chose battleship gray paint. Demonstrations in May impressed farmers. In June they sold their first Ferguson, the 12th one built. Harry Ferguson set up

Rear wheels, 37 inches in diameter but 0.50 inch thick, were apparently Ferguson options. While they are uncommon, they resemble the "telephone dial" wheels Ferguson used on several sets of scale models for demonstrations. Caulkett grousers rimmed the steel disk.

Ferguson provided individual rear turning brakes mounted far out on the axle rather than inboard as other makers had done. Outboard brakes required less mechanical effort. These tractors used the final version of Ferguson-Sands hydraulics and the three-point hitch before Ford's engineers worked on it.

training programs for dealers and customers. His sessions dealt with care and maintenance as well as implement techniques and equipment adjustments for various conditions.

Some problems recurred initially with the hydraulics. Seals, bushings, and sleeves twisted, slipped, or failed. The biggest setback they suffered was "the System" itself. Farmers with Fordsons, Internationals, or other makes already owned implements they pulled behind their tractors. This new machine used dedicated implements. Although these each cost just $112, this was an additional expense to fully utilize the Ferguson System. By 1937 production slowed to fewer than 20 a week; sales were slower than that. Ferguson's advice to Brown sounded like Henry Ford: Cut prices to increase sales, production, income, and

profits. Brown felt the tractor needed improving, a near-heresy to Ferguson. Others told Brown they wished it had more power to tow their existing implements. Ferguson would not listen. Brown hired other engineers and designers, and he prepared a more powerful machine he'd manufacture with or without Ferguson's blessing. Ferguson shrugged it off, long since resigned to whatever Brown might do. He had other friends who were helping.

Ferguson and "Layout 46"

In January 1938, one of Ferguson's friends, George Sherman, saw Howard Simpson's odd one-wheel-drive tractor. He wrote Ferguson on January 24 with a brief description and rough sketches.

"It is a 3-wheel tractor of unconventional design.

. . . I understand [it runs] three to thirteen miles an hour in high and about two in low. The driver's seat is ahead of the motor so that the driver is really sitting up in front. The gas tank is part of the driver's seat. . . . The frame is made out of two inch pipe and the combined job . . . weighs [around] 1900 pounds, including an operator. The tractor is quite awkward to steer and requires about eighteen feet to turn around in. . . . [A]ccording to published reports it is going to sell for $375 or less. . . . Personally, I cannot conceive of this type of tractor working. . . ."

Ferguson's ongoing correspondence with George and Eber developed undertones and codes. Their letters are almost school-boy-like in unbowed optimism for the success of great projects. And while Ford is clearly the object of many theories, schemes, and discussions, he is never mentioned by name. He was referred to only as "Black," as in "any color so long as it's. . . ." Ferguson's response on January 21, 1938, to Sherman was typical:

"We have never been so confident of our great future as we have been since reading details of the various new light tractors, including Black's, which

Production Ferguson tractors used Coventry Climax–based in-line four-cylinder L-head side-valve engines of 3.125-inch bore and 4.00-inch stroke. At 2,000 rpm, these engines provided 20 horsepower. Like the Fordson that Ferguson hoped to replace, his tractor engine had neither electric start nor a water pump. After the first 500 Ferguson Coventry Climax engines were assembled, Coventry introduced a new engine. David Brown bought the tools and dies and produced the next 800 engines in his own name. This Ferguson tractor is powered by the Brown-built engine, which used a Fairbanks Type J magneto, Donaldson air cleaner, and a model FBK349 carburetor.

Ferguson adopted the unit-frame idea of the Fordson to accompany his unit plow. His version comprised four components: the Coventry Climax engine, the clutch housing, the David Brown three-speed transmission, and the rear axle. The tractor measured just 9 feet, 6 inches from the tip of the crank to the tail of the lower hitch arms.

Greenwich Village High School boys looked over the Ferguson tractor before trials began on November 8, 1938. Harry Ferguson had demonstrated the capabilities of his tractor and its plowing system to Henry Ford for five days, mostly in private. *Henry Ford Museum and Greenfield Village*

After a long run through hard clay, Henry Ford, seated right, told Harry Ferguson it was time to talk. The weather was beautiful on that late fall day; they borrowed a table and chairs from Ford's neighbor W. R. Brewer. Under the watchful eyes of Ferguson's daughter, Betty, and his partner, Eber Sherman, a Ford photographer recorded the meeting for history. *Henry Ford Museum and Greenfield Village*

you and others have sent to us. . . ."

Referring to Black's tractor, he went on, "Our feeling is that perhaps all this is a bluff . . . intended to drive us into his arms. Anyway, we feel all the happier that we are postponing our demonstrations to him. There isn't one word about an implement in the whole of the report we received, and from that standpoint, the report is sheer nonsense, because what on earth is any kind of a tractor going to do even if it be given away for nothing, if there are no unit implements?

"If that marvelous negotiator, Eber, can get Black to build a tractor for us on terms of mutual confidence, I am sure that we are open to do business. I feel that if he will leave the implements to us and build the tractor, we will be prepared to leave the tractor field to him and build the implements. It would be a question of mutual confidence, and if anyone acted unfairly towards the other, then that other would be free to do as he wished. . . ."

The Handshake Felt Around the World

On February 4, 1938, Ferguson wrote back to George Sherman, commenting on Ford's Simpson-designed tractor.

"We can see no hope for this machine. Even with our wonderful principle we require under some

Through the fall of 1938, even as Harry Ferguson showed off his tractor and plow at Fair Lane Farm, Howard Simpson and Gene Farkas continued to innovate. One creation was a system to raise and lower a tractor through internal gearing. A rack and pinion worked the front axle of what appears to be a standard-tread Fordson All-Around.

Howard Simpson accomplished rear axle height adjustment through a set of rotatable, telescoping, rotating planetary gears in the final drive hubs. Ford's patent application explained that this system made the same tractor useful for cultivating relatively tall corn or, at its lowest position, for heavy plowing.

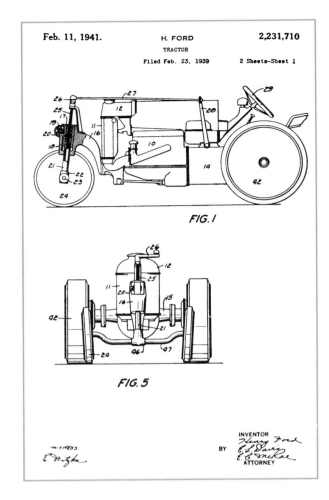

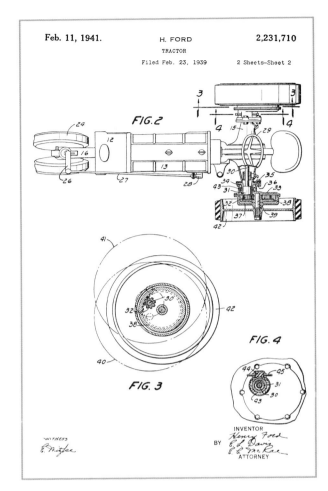

severe conditions all the drive we can get from two wheels . . . as would taking advantage of all the weight available. . . . The new Black design throws away a lot of that. . . . Indeed we [have] the feeling that this thing is a bluff to cover a simple little tractor like our own which he may be developing." Ferguson offered other options for them.

"It is quite possible that Chrysler or General Motors or some big parts maker would build a tractor for us. . . . This really is a big opportunity for somebody like Chrysler." Ferguson stressed that Chrysler need only acquire the Ferguson tractor machine tools and it could go into business. His organization would handle implements and train Chrysler dealers to sell a Ferguson-Chrysler Tractor. But his true objective remained constant.

"Surely the big chance now is to let Black find out [his] tractor is not a success. . . . Backed up with his intense desire and ambition to do something for agriculture, surely he would be open-minded about

building our own tractor, modified to suit, on the right terms.

"If we can demonstrate to him at the right time, he will go ahead in cooperation with us and on terms we can accept." In Ireland and in New York, several spiders began putting finishing touches on the web.

In Dearborn, immediately after his "chance" encounter with Henry Ford, Eber Sherman, who had no further desire to invest in Harry Ferguson, asked Howard Simpson about getting the tractor to Dearborn.

"Sherman turned to me," Simpson recalled, "and said, 'Who's going to pay for this? I don't want to pay for it. Who is going to get it over here?'" Eber Sherman got Ford to pay for it, bringing several Ferguson tractors over, not just one. Simpson had first encountered Ferguson back in 1921, working with him when Ferguson wanted Ford to adopt his Duplex Hitch plow as standard equipment for the Fordson. "Sherman built some up and sold them, and Mr. Ford gave me the job of redesigning the plow. Ford didn't like to take a product in and accept it as it was. The minute he looked at a thing he wanted to improve it."

In late October 1938, Ferguson sailed for New York with fellow aviator John Williams. At sea, they encountered Leon R. Clausen, president of J. I. Case. Clausen once was a visionary: He was the Deere and Company board member in 1922 who authorized Deere's first 1,000-tractor production run of Model Ds. According to a Case "legend" reported by Robert Pripps in *Case GP Tractors* (Motorbooks International, 1996), Ferguson, who seized opportunity whenever he thought it knocked, "offered [his] three-point system to Clausen, but Clausen was not interested, saying that real tractors had enough weight and did not need such a system."

The Ferguson Demonstration

They landed in New York on November 1, 1938. Eber Sherman and Sorensen arranged for the demonstration at Fair Lane, giving Ferguson two days to get set up. When Ferguson got to the farm, he first encountered a landscaper named W. R. Brewer. Brewer and his wife owned land at the entrance to Fair Lane. They promised to sell to Ford, who encouraged them to remain until they were ready to move. As neighbor farmers, they knew the Fords like no one else did.

"Harry Ferguson brought his little tractor over here from England while we were at the estate," Brewer said, his reminiscences also in the collection at Henry Ford Museum. "He brought his own petrol. He wouldn't use American gasoline. Mr. Ferguson said to me, 'Can we get things ready for when [Ford] comes back?' "

Brewer directed him into Fair Lane's fields, near the entrance of the estate by his cottage. He staked out half an acre as Ferguson, Chambers, and Eber Sherman prepared the Ferguson for Ford's return on November 3.

According to Colin Fraser, Ford brought Ed Malvitz, Karl Schultz's assistant and tractor evaluation driver. Ferguson had asked Ford for an experienced operator so he might walk alongside Ford to answer questions that came up.

"We started the plowing," Brewer said. "We dug furrows. We dug a ditch about three feet wide and eighteen inches deep. We'd skip five or six feet and dig another one.

"That little Ferguson would run along there, dig down in, climb out again, run into another, climb out again. After it finished, they went along and measured it and there wasn't half an inch difference. That plow stayed right there. That suited Henry. . . . For the first few days nobody came over. Henry wanted to see what he could for himself. . . . Then he began to bring all the others in to see it." Tests ran for six days, from the third through the eighth. Ferguson saw Ford and Brewer talking often.

"He was very worried about it," Brewer explained. "He said, 'I will lose everything if Mr. Ford doesn't buy that tractor, not only all my own money but all my friends' money as well.'" Ford brought out engineering prototypes for comparison. He hauled out a Fordson and the Allis-Chalmers Model B, on which Simpson and Schultz based some of their work. Nothing matched the Ferguson. Ford told Brewer he admired the power the small tractor produced, and he marveled at the improvements Ferguson had made in his plow system.

"They kept thinking up tests trying to stall the little engine," Brewer recalled. "Every night Mr. Ferguson would say to me, 'Has Mr. Ford said anything? Does he like it?

On November 9, Eber Sherman delivered the assembled spare Ferguson tractor to the Ford Airport terminal where Experimental Engineering operated. Later that morning, Henry Ford and Sherman asked Howard Simpson to begin immediately to redesign it to prepare it for production. Henry Ford Museum and Greenfield Village

Ferguson and friend John Williams brought along to Michigan cases of implements and other equipment transported from David Brown's Park Works at Huddersfield. In them, Simpson found fresh Dunlop rubber tires. This example was a very late-production tractor with the David Brown–built Coventry Climax–based engine. *Henry Ford Museum and Greenfield Village*

" 'No, he hasn't said anything to me.'

" 'If he doesn't like it, I'm a ruined man. I've borrowed every dollar I could get and spent every cent on it.'

" 'Well,' I said, 'Give him time.'

"It was pretty nearly the finish of the tests. There is a big cornfield of about 300 acres on the other side. It was all heavy clay . . . so dry we couldn't plow it anymore, and we'd just let it sit there, waiting for rain. That thing had dried until it was just like a cement field."

The eighth of November was, as Colin Fraser described it, a classical North American fall day, "fresh and slightly misty in the morning with a bright warm sun in the afternoon." It was nearly cloudless and almost 70 degrees when the guests arrived. That morning, Ford asked about that particular clay plot.

" 'Brewer, how did you leave that field down there?'

" 'Well,' I said, 'we took our equipment in. We couldn't do anymore to it.'

" 'Let's go down there and look at that,' he said.

"So we went down and Mr. Ferguson looked at it. 'Mr. Ford,' he said, `you don't think a little tractor like this would turn that over? That would take a five-ton tractor!' "

Ford had invited some executives and the entire Greenfield Village High School out to the demonstration. Sorensen stood by with Eber and George Sherman. Only a few tractor engineers were present, among them young Harold Brock. Strangely, Sheldrick, Schultz, Simpson, and the others were not included.

" 'Go ahead,' Mr. Ford said. 'It won't hurt to try.'

"So Ferguson started it," Brewer recalled. "Henry, walking with his hands behind his back like he did when he was thinking, got in the furrow right behind the plow, and I got behind him.

"That little tractor kept going and going. There would be strips fifteen feet long that the tractor would turn over, and the strip wouldn't even break, it was so darned hard. It was like you had turned a cement curb over and it laid there.

"We got all the way down to the other end. Ferguson was so tense, so nervous, that when he got off that tractor he could hardly stand.

" 'Well,' Henry said, 'I think we can talk business now.'

"They went into our house and got our kitchen table and the two chairs." The two came back out, sat down, and began to discuss what each wanted and hoped. Ferguson knew Ford by reputation; Ford knew Ferguson from regular reports from Sir Percival Perry. Now, Ford had observed the man and his machine in his own fields. Ferguson's tractor performed faultlessly.

The conversation at Brewer's table got to business. According to Colin Fraser, Ford offered to buy outright Ferguson's patents on the hitch and plow. Fraser reconstructed their conversation.

"You haven't got enough money," Ferguson reportedly said to Ford, "because they are not for sale at any price, to you or anybody else." In light of Brewer's comments about Ferguson's concerns and insecurity, this boldness seems perhaps to be Ferguson's historical revision years later and not the honest recollection of the limited bargaining power of someone in debt and on edge for six days.

"Ford countered, 'I'm determined to go into the business. You need me and I need you. So what do you suggest?'

" 'A gentlemen's agreement,' Ferguson said. 'I've spent my whole career thinking out [this] idea, and I've put everything I and my family have into it. . . . I'll trust you, if you'll trust me, and I'll put my services at your disposal for future designing, education, and distribution. . . . For your part, you'll put all your resources, energy, fame, and reputation behind the equipment and manufacture it in volume, at low cost. I'll sell it.'"

They agreed. Ferguson would have full authority on design and engineering. He would distribute the tractors, taking delivery where Ford chose. Ford would manufacture the tractor and assume all the risks of manufacture. Either one could end the agreement at any time, without obligation to the other, for any reason whatever. Ferguson stipulated that Ford's plant in Dagenham eventually would build the tractors with his system as well.

"I was there for that," Harold Brock recalled nearly 60 years later. "I saw them stand up and shake hands. The whole thing was a very formal situation, despite the fact that they were outside sitting at a small kitchen table. They were outside because it was just a beautiful day."

W. R. Brewer was close by as the two men, hunched together over his table, looked earnestly into each other's faces and came to terms.

"They got around our kitchen table and [made] up these suggestions and ideas for the tractor. . . . I heard a lot of things said that I wasn't supposed to hear, so I didn't hear them. Henry trusted me not to know anything, and I didn't know anything. I've worked around private talks long enough to know how to forget them."

Ford and Ferguson posed for photographs and spoke with the people gathered there, then they left. Ferguson, John Williams, and Eber Sherman talked together as they loaded up the tractor and the crowd dispersed.

"We missed the furniture," Brewer recalled. "Henry drove by that evening and said, 'Mr. Brewer, how much do I owe you for that table and those two chairs?'

" 'Why, aren't you going to bring them back?'

" 'No,' he said, 'we sold them to the museum.' "

On November 9, 1938, the morning after the historic handshake agreement, Simpson had visitors.

"Mr. Ford and Eber Sherman came past my desk

and asked me to go down to the airport terminal," Simpson said. "They had one of the Ferguson tractors and various implements there. Some of them were still in the crates. Mr. Ford said he wanted me to redesign the Ferguson tractor and reduce the weight. Mr. Sherman then turned over a lot of drawings to me. It looked like Ferguson and Ford had already arrived at some understanding of how they were going to carry on their business."

Two days after that, late on November 11, Ford came past the Ford Airport terminal where a small engineering staff still worked after the TriMotor airplane project was completed. He stopped in and asked Simpson to ride with him. Ford drove a meandering route, ending up at the small house still standing on Fair Lane Farm that he and Clara had when they first married. He spoke quietly to Simpson, telling his young engineer about a heating system he designed and installed, an early kind of forced-air heating. He went into great detail.

Simpson, who had been in Ford's presence when he spoke of personal things, but who knew he was not a confidant, was unsure what really was happening. Minutes later, Ford fell silent. Then he turned to Simpson and told him he "felt he had gotten something wonderful in this Ferguson tractor principle."

*H*enry Ford learned the value of dated photographs in his legal victory over George B. Selden's patent infringement case in November 1910. Ford, long a photography enthusiast, used pictures to establish the evolution of ideas, a practice he continued. His photo department shot all angles of the Ferguson tractor before Howard Simpson dismantled it. *Henry Ford Museum and Greenfield Village*

Nine

CREATING THE N

A Ground-Breaking Machine

After agreeing to go into business with Henry Ford, Harry Ferguson and John Williams hurried home. Ferguson had to separate from David Brown to avoid a conflict of interest. (In another term of the "Handshake Agreement" Ford personally loaned $60,000 to Ferguson. This, recorded by Ford's secretary Frank Campsall, set up Ferguson in distribution with the Shermans.) Ferguson invited Willie Sands and John Chambers to work in America. Archie Greer would maintain operations in Belfast.

Separating from Brown was easy. His dissatisfaction with Ferguson's personality and his tractor made the split a painless resolution to a painful situation. From July 1936 through December 1938 they sold only 1,200 tractors. Brown believed in his larger, heavier machine, and he launched the VAK1, with Sands' hydraulics in July 1939.

Ferguson and his group landed in New York on January 25, 1939, continuing to Dearborn where Henry Ford surprised them with Ford's engineering accomplishments during their absence. After Howard Simpson dismantled the Ferguson to examine and measure its parts, Ford asked Karl Schultz to design two prototypes with full Ferguson hydraulics on lighter tractors. Schultz built one unitized lightweight with Ford's English truck four-cylinder engine and an ultralight two-speed transmission. The second used an air-cooled two-cylinder with a duplicate gearbox. (Ford

Starting in the 1950s, aftermarket manufacturers created kits to increase ground clearance of Ford tractors and other makes by using larger rear wheels and longer front spindles. Companies in California, Louisiana, and Florida produced items that raised the tractor six inches over standard.

Between November 10, 1938, and January 26, 1939, Karl Schultz produced two small prototype tractors for Henry Ford, incorporating Ferguson's hydraulic system.

Ford experimented in late 1919 with air-cooled four-cylinder engines to propel trolley cars he proposed for Detroit's streets. Afterward, Joe Galamb and Gene Farkas tried some in experimental rear-engined automobiles. Then 20 years later, Karl Schultz adapted them to his tiny prototype tractor. *Henry Ford Museum and Greenfield Village*

pushed Schultz to develop air-cooled engines. These appeared first in flat-four-cylinder form in Ford's gas-engined street cars tested in the early 1920s. Ferdinand Porsche's small air-cooled "pancake" engine for the Volkswagen renewed Ford's interest. Schultz's engine took pistons, valves, and connecting rods from the 85-horsepower V-8.)

Laurence Sheldrick surmised that Schultz's tractors were done solely to show Ford "one type of tractor which could be produced embodying the Ferguson hydraulic system. Henry Ford could absorb principles of the hydraulic system only by watching the building of a tractor which incorporated it." He also guessed Ford may have wanted to "needle" Ferguson on his return from Ireland, however. Ford could make hydraulic-system tractors also, but he could make them better.

Work began on the new Ford tractor the day Ferguson arrived in Michigan. A large team led by Henry Ford himself began not in Dearborn offices but in a corner of the Rouge far from prying eyes, inside Gate Four. Only six experimental engineers remained at Dearborn. The larger group of 28 in all moved in mid-November to an area known as the Blue Room.

"The idea of moving me to the Rouge," Howard Simpson explained, "was because Sorensen wanted tractor design under his control. That was a logical step anyway, because there were no facilities at the airport to make models or do any experimental work. All we could do there was paperwork. . . .

"Mr. Ford and Mr. Sorensen liked to have models right away and they could visualize a part better in model form. . . . I remember the front axle design, the adjustable front axle. Ferguson didn't have that on his tractor. We had to have a tractor that would straddle rows of corn and other crops, and therefore the tread had to be adjustable. I spent considerable time designing adjustable front and rear axles." Simpson devised a rear adjustment by creating reversible disc wheels to change the tread from narrow to wide.

Ferguson quickly supplemented Sands and Chambers with Harold Willey to develop implements for the new tractor. Laurence Sheldrick commandeered Mark Feeley, chief tractor engineer from Cork, who came to Dearborn when Irish operations closed.

"The Ferguson tractor had not been designed for American production," Simpson explained. "The engine and transmission, wheels and axles, didn't fit our ideas of tractor construction or the use to which it would be put on American farms. In England the row crop work is very minor in nature.

"Most experimental work concerned the external parts of the tractor. It was not until the middle of January 1939 that any thought was given to the transmission and engine and hydraulic system." Simpson and others began receiving conflicting directions. Henry Ford, of course, was to be taken at

Karl Schultz's prototypes were garden tractor–size, at just 84 inches overall length on 57-inch wheelbases. Schultz used Ford's English truck 88T four-cylinder engine connected to an ultra-lightweight two-speed transmission to drive the one on the right. Schultz's two-cylinder air-cooled effort is on the left. Henry Ford Museum and Greenfield Village

face value; he was smitten with the Ferguson's size and maneuverability. Sorensen, who was away when Ford and Ferguson agreed, had little respect for the tractor and felt not much could be gained from adapting it. Ferguson, of course, claimed to have final say on everything.

Laurence Sheldrick first met Ferguson, Sands, Chambers, and Willey in late January, after design began in the Blue Room. Ford instructed Sheldrick to "assist Ferguson and his staff in building a tractor to incorporate the hydraulic system and linkage which were on the Ferguson tractor. There was considerable stress placed on making the tractor suit American conditions. . . . During the work in the Blue Room, a Fordson tractor, an Allis-Chalmers Model B tractor, and a Ferguson tractor were physically present in the room."

Howard Simpson saw some benefits to the tractor, but he believed he could have produced something better had Ford left him to his own devices. Having this machine forced on him, under conflicting directions, was too much. He quit in late January. Sheldrick brought up Harold Brock around the first of February to become chief tractor engineer. Brock began to design a three-speed transmission for the tractor, now designated the 9N. (Sheldrick created the alpha-numeric system in mid-1937. The first numeral represented the introductory year; the letter *A* indicated passenger cars; *T* was trucks, and *N* was tractors. Cars and trucks had another numeral after the letter designating engine type.)

Against Ford's dislike of organizational titles at

Ford, Sheldrick grew concerned about responsibilities for tractor and implement development. He created a chart. Once during a meeting, he showed it around, swearing everyone to secrecy about its existence. Henry Ford was listed "in overall charge" with Charles Sorensen "next in line to Mr. Ford, general supervision." Sheldrick labeled himself in charge of the design project.

"Ferguson worked with us in the 'Blue Room' almost as much as Sorensen while I was there," Simp-

Laurence Sheldrick's engineering log recorded that on Thursday, March 30, 1939, they "drove new Ferguson tractor around floor this A.M. Got sheet metal on, this being temporary." The next day, Ford's Styling chief Eugene Gregorie looked over this tractor to prepare final design sketches. Henry Ford Museum and Greenfield Village

engine [was] in giving preliminary data regarding power output desired." Brock completed the transmission, based on speeds defined for various farm operations by Ferguson, Sands, and Chambers.

Hydraulics were Sands' and Chambers' work, with Sheldrick's assistance on "the relationship of top and bottom links to ensure that the geometry was not upset." (Sheldrick maintained that "the hydraulic system and the linkage were the only contributions to the tractor of any importance made by Ferguson and the others.")

Chief of styling Eugene Gregorie at Dearborn did early work on the 9N's appearance, which was completed by Ed Scott at the Rouge Plant. This was common procedure with automobile and truck styling. Ford told them to make clear the "family heritage." Gregorie created the hood and radiator shell resemblance to the 1939 Mercury and the already-approved 1940 commercial truck. Scott did detail finish work.

"All Ferguson did here was to state criticism or approval after work was done," Sheldrick said. "However, both Ferguson and Henry Ford wanted the tractor a dull gray color with the apparent view of keeping it a 'dignified job.' Edsel and I thought it would be better to make it a bright color which would show up in the field, but we were overruled."

According to the Dearborn Engineering Laboratories Log, 9N development proceeded in fits and starts. Ferguson was in daily. Sorensen stopped by almost as often, and Ford routinely visited them two or three times a week.

On Monday, April 24, the Rouge delivered the second tractor to Experimental Engineering. Eugene Gregorie designed the hood and grille. *Henry Ford Museum and Greenfield Village*

From November through April, Harry Ferguson proposed the tractor be called the "Ferguson." Henry Ford knew it was a Ford but, acknowledging Ferguson's System, felt it should be called "Ford-Ferguson." In late April, Eber Sherman convinced Ferguson that without Ford, there would be no tractor or plow. New badges were completed in early June. *Henry Ford Museum and Greenfield Village*

son recalled. "Ferguson was very dictatorial and had extreme views and nothing could vary an iota from what he said. Sorensen just ignored him. He finally dropped by the wayside and let the Ford engineers go ahead with design.

"I think Ferguson had some good ideas, but some were extreme. He wanted all nuts and bolts in two sizes so he could use one wrench for the whole tractor, plow, and other implements. He had extreme ideas about suitability of different materials and, of course, that didn't get very far in Ford where they were tops on metallurgy. Ferguson didn't engineer the tractor."

Once broken down by assignments, responsibilities fell mostly to Ford engineering and to Ford's outside suppliers. Front wheels, for example, were produced with Kelsey-Hayes, using standard Ford hubs, bearings, and bearing races.

Adolph Eckert designed the engine, "incorporating as many standard Mercury parts as possible. The only part Ferguson people played in design of the

"Ford engineers could have designed and built the 9N faster," Sheldrick said, "and with less headaches had it not been for Ferguson's presence. A considerable amount of time that I spent in the Blue Room was devoted to keeping peace between Harry Ferguson and the various Ford engineers.

"One of the basic policies governing design of the 9N was of using as many high-production standard parts as possible. Ferguson was opposed to standard parts on the grounds they were not good enough for the tractor, especially differential gears for Ford trucks."

The tractor engine was devised, essentially, by slicing the new Mercury 95-horsepower V-8 engine in half. Adolph Eckert completed drawings, referred to as "9C," by mid-December 1938. On December 28, foundry men at the Rouge cast the first engine, and the next day Sheldrick, Eckert, and Karl Schultz saw it. Holley designers arrived the same day with sample carburetors.

For the next two months, discussions, designs, and development continued over transmissions (Ferguson wanted three cases built of aluminum for tests; he was overruled), brake and clutch pedals place-

ment, and dozens of other things. Harvey Firestone came to Dearborn to show Ford and Sorensen rubber tires for the tractor. By late February, engineering had a completed drivetrain with a small worm-gear rear end. Harold Brock began a "life test" to determine gear- and running-life potential of his prototype.

In mid-March, Sheldrick, Sands, and George Sherman settled on the tire size. Sheldrick wrote: "Arrived at 32 rear and 4.75 x 15 rib front to give proper rolling radius. Went to Tool Room to see first tractor backbone. Oil leak in pan. Will fix tonight."

A week later, Charles Balough of Hercules came in with his company's new 113-cubic-inch kerosene engine for an evaluation loan.

"Tuesday, March 28, 1939: We now have Ferguson tractor complete with exception of radiator, gas tank, and battery mounting. Steering gear assembled this A.M. and seems to be quite satisfactory. Spent considerable time with Mr. Ferguson standardizing bolts and nuts for tractor."

The rest of the log read like, well, a log. It summarized and abbreviated five fast months into brief lines that revealed mostly highlights, many facts, and little drama.

Even as production began, Ford continued testing and developing the new 9N tractors. A great deal of work was performed at Ford's Richmond Hills Plantation farm at Ways Station, Georgia. Here the operator cultivates cabbage. *Henry Ford Museum and Greenfield Village*

"Thursday, March 30: Drove new Ferguson tractor around floor this A.M. Got sheet metal on, this being temporary." Sorensen met Ferguson and Sherman to discuss tread widths, whereupon Sorensen decided on a 76-inch maximum width, adjustable inward in 2-inch increments.

"Friday, March 31: Had Gregorie to Rouge to look over tractor with sheet metal assembled so that he might prepare some design sketches." At this point,

the tractor wore cobbled-together sheet metal resembling an unadorned Allis-Chalmers. In that guise, it successfully performed its first field trials on Saturday, April 1, at Fair Lane. It was cleaned up and photographed on Monday. Over lunch on Tuesday, Ford, Sorensen, Sheldrick, and Ferguson discussed manufacturing the tractor in England and Germany. They saw Farkas' design for a 2.6-inch-bore four-cylinder overhead-valve engine Karl Schultz would build at

Ford's request. Monday, April 10, Sorensen advised Engineering that Henry Ford wanted 50 prototypes completed right away. On April 19, Ford came in to see Ed Scott's 9N clay model. He told Sheldrick to ask Edsel Ford to come make suggestions.

Throughout the process, Ferguson proposed the tractor be named "Ferguson." Henry Ford, naturally, knew it was a Ford; however, he readily accepted that it should be called the Ford-Ferguson, giving Harry Ferguson credit for his "system." As it got nearer the time Engineering would release the tractor to production, Ferguson became more insistent on sole, or at least top, billing. This annoyed Sheldrick and infuriated Sorensen, sentiments that Eber Sherman understood clearly. On Sunday, April 23, Sherman called on Ferguson at the Dearborn Inn, took him for a walk, and explained that without Ford, there would be no tractor. Ford's name would sell the tractor. Without a tractor there would be no plow and nothing for Harry Ferguson to market worldwide. Sherman proposed a compromise: Ford Tractor with Ferguson System. Harry Ferguson was mollified.

"Monday, April 24: To Tractor Room: Mr. Ferguson, CES [Sorensen] and myself together on clay model for finish job and for first time arrived at some conclusion which will enable us to proceed with sheet metal drafts and hammer blocks. Mr. Ferguson seems to be satisfied in using the name 'FORD' on the machine, apparently this was settled by Mr. Sherman last week. Have #2 tractor in garage. South end of 'B' Bldg, second floor, being cleared out for tractor offices."

During the last week of April and all of May, the log continued with daily entries reconsidering things long-thought settled and other issues arising in more

logical sequence. Sheldrick noted that all the 9N assembly drawings had to be released at once, on Friday, May 26. A week later, he received from Eugene Gregorie a temporary outline of the tractor medallion.

"Monday, June 5: Ed Scott shipped clay model of tractor back to Dearborn. Began making stamping of final design tractor hood.

Tractor production began. Invitations sent to 400 dignitaries, politicians, and journalists to a luncheon Thursday, June 29." Time was getting short. As workers hurried, the pressure built.

"Thursday, June 8: J. E. Clickner made drawing of tractor wrench, open at both ends, and having scale in inches forged on. Gave drawing to Feeley. Ed Scott received first cast aluminum tractor grille and hood side panels. They were rushed through and are not correct in size due to wrong shrinkage.

"Thursday, June 15: Ed Scott received instructions from Mr. Sorensen to design a cast aluminum tractor grille for permanent production. Stopped work on the stamping design." (Design approval delays left insufficient time to produce stamping dies for a steel hood, radiator shell, and grille, and get them cast for series production. Sorensen's son owned an aluminum casting plant. He produced pieces for early production models. More than 700 tractors were delivered with aluminum hoods and

From the start, both Ford and Ferguson made it clear their tractor must be operable by women and children. Ford Motor Company made great use of this photo of 72-year-old Mrs. McMillan of Kansas at work plowing with her new 9N tractor. Henry Ford Museum and Greenfield Village

"The Ford-Ferguson set the pattern for all tractor design," its chief engineer Harold Brock said nearly 60 years after its introduction. "Mr. Ford said to us, 'Don't look at what anyone else is producing. This has to be different.' In the past ten years, every tractor maker has come back to this configuration." Henry Ford Museum and Greenfield Village

Assembly-line workers manufactured Ford-Ferguson 9N tractors in the Rouge Plant, Building B. Assemblers used lightweight templates to perform chassis and axle alignment in this photograph made in mid-November 1939. From this point, tractors went to the paint shop. *Henry Ford Museum and Greenfield Village*

Ford created a new paint facility just for the 9N tractors inside Building B at the Rouge. Tractors moved along a chain conveyor system beneath down-flowing air vents over rapidly running water. This eliminated dust and worked well to contain overspray. Paint was dried in ovens similar to those used for automobiles. *Henry Ford Museum and Greenfield Village*

grilles before there were enough steel stampings for production needs.) Everywhere, everyone was cutting it close.

On Monday, June 26, Ed Scott received a complaint from the tractor assembly line that the radiator ornament vibrated on the hood top. He hurriedly designed a rubber pad to separate them.

On Thursday, June 29, Harry Ferguson rose from his seat at the speaker's table in the Dearborn Inn. Beside him, Henry and Edsel Ford sat quietly, taking no part in the presentation, which they sponsored. Before him, 460 newspaper, farming, and technical journal reporters, business leaders, agricultural officials, and envoys from 18 foreign governments waited, sipping their coffee after lunch. His remarks, atypically, were brief. Typically, before he would invite them out to Fair Lane, he would make them skeptical.

"History is going to be made here today," he began. Some of them had heard it before. Some of them had made history themselves. They left Fair Lane after three hours of plowing and field tests, seeing 15 new Ford-Ferguson 9Ns at work. The tractor's

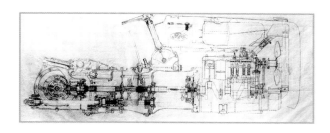

deeds, some of them best demonstrated by eight-year old David McLaren, convinced them Harry Ferguson was right.

Precedents Set

"The Ford-Ferguson set the pattern for all tractor design. The reason was Mr. Ford said to us, 'Don't look at what anyone else is producing. This has to be different.' "

The speaker was Harold Brock, 9N chief engineer, designer of its transmission and eventually Ford

Motor Company's chief engineer for all tractor development.

"We didn't stick to standards. Not even with power take-off. He said, 'IH and Case and Allis and Deere and Massey all produce the same types of row crop tractors. Don't look at those!'

"Mr. Ford was trying to find the tractor that would do for agriculture what the Model T did for transportation," Brock went on. "He felt the Ferguson System and their tractor would really satisfy their market. And of course, the poor old man died. He never did realize that he was absolutely right on target."

Production started slowly. Just as with Fordsons, the process moved cautiously while employees felt their way around pieces and procedures. Just 77 were completed between June 5, 1939, the production start date, and the end of the month. By December 1, 6,849 had been produced and, by the next December 1, 90,000 tractors were completed.

*P*roblems with hydraulics in Ferguson's three-point hitch appeared soon after Ford introduced the 9N. Harold Brock created a longer taper on the hydraulic inlet valve. To show off the new system's strength and reliability, Ford Photographic stood five men on the plow in the yard of the Rouge. *Henry Ford Museum and Greenfield Village*

*B*y the time this drawing was completed on November 22, 1939, the first changes were already in effect. This second series 9N for 1940 placed the Safety Starter button on the transmission housing and added a hinge to the battery cover. *Henry Ford Museum and Greenfield Village*

*B*y late April 1940, daily 9N production reached 300 tractors. The day's entire output was parked along the rail yard beside the Rouge plant. Ford told Howard Simpson and Laurence Sheldrick he wanted the tractor scaled so 14 tractors would fit in each box car. *Henry Ford Museum and Greenfield Village*

1939 Ford-Ferguson 9N
*W*ithout enough time to make casting patterns for steel grilles, hoods, dashes, and other pieces, Laurence Sheldrick and Charles Sorensen substituted cast aluminum. Records are inexact; between 700 and 800 tractors were produced before steel castings replaced the aluminum in mid-September.

*B*efore the end of March 1939, Ford, Sorensen, and Ferguson discussed tread widths, Ferguson arguing in favor of a 76-inch width, Ford of Europe representatives wanting 84. Sorensen, Ferguson, and Eber Sherman settled on 76 inches maximum, adjustable in 2-inch increments. This very early example is the 16th 9N produced.

"The unfortunate thing was that Mr. Ford priced the tractor without ever knowing the cost of it," Brock said.

"He asked us, 'What's the cheapest tractor on the market?' It was the little Allis-Chalmers. It sold for about five hundred dollars. So he said, 'Well, that's what we'll sell ours for.'

"He sold it to Ferguson for probably three-hundred-fifty dollars, something like that." The tractor came out at $585 with another $85 for the two-bottom Ferguson-Sherman plow. It was striking, even if its gray color wasn't inspiring.

Meanwhile, Back in Europe . . .

Soon after production started, Willie Sands, after his six months in Dearborn, returned home. Brock felt that Sands was an unsung hero.

"Willie Sands didn't get along with Ferguson," Brock said. "He was really the brains behind it. Ferguson was the marketing guy, the guy who'd have an idea: 'We ought to have a hitch that would automatically work on the back of a tractor.' But executing the idea, that was Willie Sands."

Ferguson expected that Sands, Chambers, and Willey would be relocated to Dagenham after the plant was reorganized to produce the new tractor there. Ferguson expected a seat on the board of directors of Ford Motor Company Ltd. Whether these expectations were realistic will never be known, as World War II spoiled Ferguson's plans.

By March 1935, France, Italy, and Britain recognized Adolf Hitler as a threat to world peace and took the first steps to respond. Hitler, named supreme commander of Germany in March 1938, invaded Austria in April. The rest of Europe knew it was just a matter of time.

In England, Lord Percival Perry had watched Europe. He remembered difficulties getting tractors during World War I. Production delays and shipping blockades held them up months. Perry and Patrick Hennessey, now manager of Dagenham works, approached Sir Reginald Smith, the minister of agriculture and fisheries (MoA), early in 1939 with an idea. According to Michael Williams, in his *Ford & Fordson Tractors* (Blandford Press, 1985), the Ford executives proposed increasing Fordson N production to

Henry Ford wanted to use production materials and parts wherever possible. Adolph Eckert sliced Ford's new 1939 Mercury V-8 95-horsepower engine down the middle to create the 9N engine, known as the 9C. He finished designs by mid-December. Foundrymen cast the first prototype before the new year. Eckert also did the front axle, support, and cooling system.

Harry Ferguson insisted that Ford round off all bolts, leaving only one thread exposed so they wouldn't catch on clothing. He had Ford buy contour grinders to finely polish the joint between the plowshare and the moldboard. He had cultivators set up on a table, their shanks set to exactly the same length.

create a 3,000-tractor surplus. They offered this excess to the government at 27.5 percent below list price. The government would distribute these around Britain where they would be stored at Ford dealers against the day when they might be needed. If war came, the MoA would have tractors on hand, ready to distribute as the Ministry of Munitions had done in 1917 and 1918. If there was no armed conflict, Ford Motor Company Ltd. would buy them back. Ford would pay its dealers to service the tractors in storage. The MoA liked the plan, until it learned a new, modern tractor was to be introduced in Dearborn.

Harry Ferguson had written to the MoA. His agreement with Ford included manufacturing his tractor in the United Kingdom. Ferguson proposed the government get involved in building it in England. According to Fraser, Ferguson had obtained backing from the Bank of England. MoA officials assumed this meant Ford's plant at Dagenham would be converting production; the Fordson Ns they'd been offered in the Perry/Hennessey proposal were obsolete machines. Perry and Hennessey were unaware of this new tractor and of any joint participation on such a project

between Ford and Ferguson. Hennessey had endured hours of fieldwork assisting Ferguson and Archie Greer in 1921 when they perfected the unit plow and its depth-control system. Hennessey recalled Ferguson's ego and temper. Notwithstanding Hennessey's unpleasant memories, the larger issue was availability of raw materials to produce tractors. Perry personally assured the MoA that Dagenham had no plans to switch from the English to a new American model. The MoA approved the Perry/Hennessey plan on Thursday, May 18, 1939. On Sunday, September 3, when Britain and France declared war on Germany, nearly all of the MoA Fordsons were ready for work.

The MoA tractors were finished in orange paint as regular production models; however, responding to concerns over visibility of bright tractors against the fields of England, Dagenham changed the color to solid green, which they remained until Fordson N production ended in 1945. The huge factory, which already was geared up for nearly double-time

1939 Ford-Ferguson 9N

*O*n June 15, 1939, Edwin D. Scott, who designed 9N sheet metal for production from Eugene Gregorie's sketches, got word from Charles Sorensen to design a cast-aluminum tractor grille for permanent production. Two weeks later Ford and Ferguson introduced the 9N to 460 journalists and members of the tractor industry.

*T*his Model 9N was the 504th built, and it rides on the original tires. Production of the 9N began on June 5, 1939. By the end of June, only 77 were completed. By year end, 10,310 had rolled out of B Building.

production for the MoA run, reaped a large benefit from its advance planning. With a highly productive work force running smoothly, Dagenham never let up during the war; 12-hour days, 72-hour work weeks were normal by 1941. Between the declaration of war and D-Day in June 1944, the factory produced 136,811 Fordson Ns. By D-Day, according to Allan Nevins, Ford claimed 85 percent of the 140,000 tractors in use throughout Britain. The factory produced engines (a quarter million new and reconditioned ones) and more than 200,000 vehicles for the British war effort, in the process suffering from half a dozen bomb raids. Henry and Edsel Ford personally underwrote 450 emergency food

vans to provide help to bombing victims during the Battle of Britain.

Back in 1937, Dagenham introduced tractors to run on distillate fuel, tractor vaporizing oil (TVO), a substance just introduced. This operated at higher compression than did kerosene and yielded higher horsepower. To take advantage of this fuel in the United States and England, Ford produced first the 9NAN and later a 2NAN, whose engines used a Holley Vaporizer similar to what was fitted on Fordson Fs. While these were produced at the Rouge, nearly all of them were shipped to Great Britain and distributed through Dagenham's dealer network during the war.

1940 Ford-Ferguson 9N

From the start of its development life, the Ford-Ferguson tractor would bob up and down as it struggled to maintain a constant plow depth. The plow's depth sensor would react to soil conditions and engine load, raising or lowering the plow on its own. Willie Sands nearly eliminated the problem by using steel wheels for English farming. Ford, however, wanted 9Ns sold on pneumatic rubber. The compressible tires confused the depth sensor.

133

In its Nebraska tests, a 1940 9N developed 12.61 horsepower on the drawbar at 1,400 rpm and 23.1 horsepower PTO maximum at 2,000 rpm. Even with 300 pounds of wheel weights and dual rear wheels, the test tractor weighed only 3,375 pounds.

Dagenham took responsibility for operator training and stocking service parts.

As with farming efforts during World War I, women were drafted into tractor operation during this period as well. Known throughout England as "Land Girls," these women, wearing green and brown, took training classes on farming and tractor operation and repair at Ford's facility at Boreham in Essex, near Dagenham. Many of them farmed days and worked in Ford's factories on night shifts. Throughout the war, Dagenham, which was in a constant state of expansion and growth, provided green tractors for agriculture, beige ones for North African campaigns by the British Army, and others (painted with undercoating only) for the Royal Air Force to finish in blue, or in camouflage brown-and-green for the Royal Army.

Recognizing that, just as with World War I, government demand would not last forever and afterwards farmers would want something new, Dagenham engineers began to design a Fordson replacement. In 1944, they started to develop a new engine as well.

During all this time, despite Dagenham's com-

plete independence from Dearborn, there was much thought given to adapting the Ford-Ferguson tractor for English production. It was a problem larger than personalities, but Harry Ferguson blamed Lord Perry and Patrick Hennessey. Changeover from Fordson to Ford-Ferguson tractors would have shut down Dagenham, laying off a large labor force for months. Duplicating machinery, tools, and dies to make the 9N in England required large quantities of money and steel, both precious rarities in England. Importing assembled tractors from the United States involved the same labor unrest as a factory retool. Perry and Hennessey worked steadily for two years, appealing to ministries of labor, customs, agriculture, raw materials, and to Chancellor of the Exchequer, trying for rules waivers. It was an immense, unsolvable problem. Still, Ferguson blamed Dagenham's management for never producing "his" tractor.

Working with Ferguson

"Harry Ferguson was a very detail-oriented person," Harold Brock recalled. "He could sit for an hour

The earliest criticisms of the 9N tractors—aside from the plow bobbing—were placement of both the tractor brakes on the operator's left side and that the levers felt the same. This was remedied for 1941. The three-forward-gear transmission provided a top road speed of 7.5 miles per hour.

Ford submitted the 9N to the University of Nebraska for testing in April 1940. Ferguson's unit-plow system relied not on tractor weight, or even high drawbar-pull, but on physics. In its first attempts, it ran without wheel weights. With 300 pounds of weight and mounted dual rear wheels, the 9N achieved a 1,568-pound pull.

and discuss the serration on the little handle that shut off the fuel feed. He was really very fussy. We had to round off all the bolts so they wouldn't catch on clothing, to end with only one thread exposed.

"And we did that. We did all that. He was very detail conscious, but he had no idea what this all cost.

"I had a lot of fun with him. The rest of management disliked him terribly. That was because he could always go to Mr. Ford where a lot of them didn't dare to. . . . So Ferguson would always say, 'We decided to do this.' The management didn't know whether they had or not. Nobody had the courage to go to Mr. Ford and ask him.

"His people were supposed to furnish implements for the tractor. When we got done with it, we found that he didn't have a plow suitable for U.S. conditions. We had to design the plow. We designed the cultivators. The planter, the whole bit. He didn't know how to do any of that.

"We made the first plow in the foundry out of cast steel, the first time anybody made a cast steel plow instead of cast-iron beams. And we got a

contour grinder because Mr. Ferguson said, 'When you put the share against the moldboard, you're not supposed to see a crease between the two. Soil will stick if there's a crease.'

"We didn't know any better. We bought a contour grinder and those things fit with perfect precision. Cultivators had to be set up on a table! And adjusted so the shanks were the same distance. We believed what he was telling us, and he got his way, because we didn't want to go to Mr. Ford and say, 'Hey, this guy's crazy!' "

Making the Ferguson System Work

Ford went outside for implement production. Ferguson-Sherman marketed and distributed them and the tractor. Within a few months, however, Ford engineers began to hear about a condition afflicting the Ferguson system: bobbing had come to America.

The Ferguson tractor and its hydraulic system were designed to operate on steel wheels. David Brown's frustration with Ferguson was as much a result of his perception that the tractor was too small as that

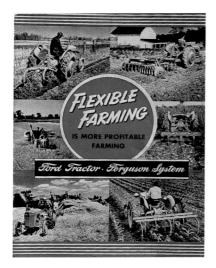

1939 Ford Tractor with Ferguson System sales brochure. *Duane and Carolyn Helman collection*

1941 Ford-Ferguson 9N
*T*his all-steel-wheeled 9N is equipped with a Model N Swan Rapidigger post-hole driller, made by the Modern Machine Company of Minneapolis, operated off the optional rear-mounted belt pulley.

the hydraulic system was not foolproof. It failed, leaving plows up or down. Brown had ideas to fix it, but Ferguson would not accept changes to his system.

As Ford brought the tractor and Ferguson's system to its specifications, Ford made many changes. It fitted 9N tractors with modern pneumatic rubber tires, affecting the way the tractor reacted to soil changes and how the depth-control system acted on the tractor.

"The tractor was done in very short order," Brock explained, "because the 'project engineer' was the Old Man. It was a project we started in January of 1939, and we went into production in June. Normally you have a three-year cycle."

"We didn't have too many complaints, except I had trouble getting the hydraulics to work. Ferguson's draft-sensing mechanism tried to maintain a constant load up and down on that top link. When we got our first experimental tractor in the field, well, the plow would come up out of the ground.

"We had a governor on the engine. As the plow went deeper, the hydraulic would say, 'Correct it! It's too deep!' It would try to raise it, the governor would

kick in, and the thing would come completely out of the ground. It was on rubber tires, which made things even worse. The tires would change the depth as they squashed. Then the depth sensor would over-correct. We had a heck of a time."

Brock solved the problem through hydraulic valving. The small suction pump had a square valve on the end with two ports, one to let hydraulic oil in to raise the implements, the other to let oil out. The square valve moved back and forth as the sensing mechanism told it to raise or lower the implement. It responded extremely quickly. Brock put a long taper on the valve. This modulated oil flow in and out, slowing response time and allowing for rapid, insignificant, soil condition changes to no longer upset the balance.

"We ran it through all kinds of soils, with different kinds of tools and implements with different suction characteristics," Brock explained. The bobbing condition was not universal, ever decreasing until late in 1941. Soil conditions had much to do with it. Dry, hard clay was the worst, causing the plow-tractor combination to ride porpoise-like over the field. Fer-

Ford offered both 9N and 2N tractors as industrials, fitted with either pneumatic or solid rubber tires. Headlights and front bumpers—in either painted steel or chrome—were often part of the industrial equipment, as on this Rouge plant tractor. *Henry Ford Museum and Greenfield Village*

After a great deal of trial and tribulation, Harold Brock in Dearborn and Willie Sands in Belfast devised a cure for the Ford-Ferguson plow bobbing. Sand's quick-reaction hydraulics were slowed down by a tapered valve that Brock designed. *Henry Ford Museum and Greenfield Village*

Inside the foundry at the Rouge, hundreds of rear-axle castings each hour were completed to keep pace with tractor production reaching 300 every day. *Henry Ford Museum and Greenfield Village*

137

The onset of World War II brought women back into Ford's factories, as it had done during World War I in Dearborn and in England. Women performed virtually every task from heaviest assembly to finest adjustments on automobiles, trucks, and 2N Ford-Ferguson tractors. *Henry Ford Museum and Greenfield Village*

While 300 tractors a day rolled out of the Rouge Plant's B Building, inside the building hundreds of Ferguson-Sherman one- and two-bottom plows awaited completion of the tractors to use them. Plow storage covered more than an acre on each of four levels. *Henry Ford Museum and Greenfield Village*

W. A. Riddell Company of Bucyrus, Ohio, updated the Fordson-powered Wehr One-Man Grader with its Warco application for Ford-Ferguson 9N, 2N, and, later, 8N tractors. Illinois Steel produced the same arched beams for Riddell as it had for Wehr and the other makers. *Henry Ford Museum and Greenfield Village*

There were as many aftermarket creations for Ford-Ferguson tractors as there were for Fordsons. American Marsh Pump Inc. and Barton Fire Pump, both of Battle Creek, Michigan, produced the three-seat fire pumper rig for farm, ranch, and brush fire applications. *Henry Ford Museum and Greenfield Village*

guson served as liaison between Belfast and Dearborn, working not as engineer but as one-man pep squad and cheerleader. He wrote to Sands and Greer often.

Ferguson's encouragement to Willie Sands and Archie Greer often went ignored as they struggled to find answers, as did his entreaties to Brock and John Chambers to not let up. When Belfast or Dearborn had solid information to report, Ferguson worked rapidly and got quick responses. He meant well, but it was self-interest he was serving: his name was on

the plow and the system. Brock's tapered hydraulic valve alleviated the problem, freeing up engineering minds on both sides of the Atlantic for new ideas.

Ferguson's 9N Engine Ideas

Ferguson wrote Sands in late August 1942: "For a long time I have been thinking of a new engine for our tractor. The present one is durable but has hot spots and is rough. I have always been determined to make a hemispherical head and work out best possi-

ble economical ways of operating the valves.

"In talking this over here with the boys a few days ago . . . [they are] of the opinion that, of course, a blower [supercharger] would make all the difference to a hemispherical head at speeds of 3,000 rpms because the blower would give necessary turbulence. . . ."

Ferguson ordered Sands and Greer to drop everything and begin developing plans for a new engine with, at least, overhead valves. It took Sands months to answer this one. Finally, in mid-January 1943, he responded.

"We cannot see the idea of making a big change like fitting overhead valves [now] as all we would gain so little in fuel consumption that it would not be

Another industrial use of Ford-Ferguson 2N tractors was the B-NO-25 Moto-Tug, here towing a Ford-built B-24-E Liberator outside the Willow Run bomber plant in mid-March 1943. The 80-acre factory and 850-acre airfield employed more than 42,000 and turned out 8,685 bombers. The number of airport tugs built is uncertain. Henry Ford Museum and Greenfield Village

worthwhile altering the engine, fuel tank, and other parts necessary to provide for the increased height of the engine. . . ." He ignored Ferguson's wilder ideas.

Wartime U.S. Production

Just as Ford engineering sorted out the last problems with the 9N, World War II invaded American consciousness. In anticipation, President Franklin Roosevelt created a War Resources Board (WRB) in August 1939. He named William S. Knudsen (president of GM at the time and Ford's former production manager at Highland Park) commissioner for industrial production in late May 1940. Roosevelt established an Office of Price Administration and Civilian Supply (OPA) in mid-April 1941. Eight months later, on December 11, four days after Pearl Harbor was bombed by Japan, Roosevelt declared war on Germany and Italy. Critical materials, aluminum, copper, and rubber particularly, were needed by the government for production of aircraft, weapons, and vehicles.

Feeding the country was still deemed a critical national interest. Tractor manufacturers got supplies of steel yet had to work around other limits. Ford responded with its 2N, manufactured without

1943 Ford-Ferguson 2N
After the United States entered World War II, the War Production Board (WPB) restricted supplies of copper and rubber for civilian applications. WPB also reduced tractor production, but less so than autos since agriculture was still a national priority. Ford and other makers responded by introducing tractors on steel wheels without copper-laden electrical systems.

Magneto ignition systems and steel wheels were only sold for six to eight months during late 1942 and 1943. Manufacturers replaced copper radiator cores with steel and aluminum. Effective September 22, 1942, the Ford-Ferguson was designated the 2N. By the end of 1942, restrictions were relaxed; copper and rubber began to reappear.

starter, generator, or electric lights, and delivered on steel wheels.

"This is to advise you," John Chambers wrote from Dearborn on April 7, 1942, to Roger Kyes, Ferguson-Sherman's executive vice-president and sales manager, "that owing to the numerous changes which have been made to the tractor since it was designed in 1939, and because of the fact that steel wheels are now being fitted, the Ford Motor Company is now changing the model number from 9N to 2N."

Laurence Sheldrick defined nomenclature further as of September 22, in a memo to Kyes, identifying all farm tractors as 2N and all industrial tractors as 2NBN. Motor numbers would continue in the 9N series, however.

The OPA froze all retail prices during the war. The only way a manufacturer could increase these was to introduce a new model incorporating changes. Ford's 2N was such an example, and Ford raised the price $60 to Ferguson-Sherman, who passed on $30 to the farmer.

About this time, late September 1942, J. L. Meyers of the Eastern Idaho Equipment Company in Idaho Falls, a Ford-Ferguson dealer, dashed off a short

Subtle cosmetic differences marked the change from 9N to 2N. A tiny 2N was stamped into the Ford oval logo. The Ferguson System badge grew deeper, and the grille center bar added a pair of slots. These changes continued into 1947. Front cranks were first installed by the factory in late 1942 and disappeared before the fall of 1943.

Wartime shortages caused Ford to replace chrome trim, such as the radiator cap, with black-painted steel pieces until materials restrictions were eased beginning in late 1942. These supply limits caused the elimination of much of the underhood wiring on Ford-Ferguson 2N tractors, revealing how simple the machine was.

note to his colleagues in Salt Lake City at Arnold Machinery Company. While the war in Europe was in full fury, tractor wars had been resumed at home between the other makers and Ford.

"One of our customers just came back from the CW&M Company after purchasing a couple of sprockets and chain to convert his potato digger attachment to fit the Ford. [When] he mentioned Ford to them, they launched a tirade against Ford and everything connected to it. 'Why the dirty so-and-so's are trying to put over the idea with the government that they should be permitted to make all the tractors until the war is over!' They informed our customer then that they were doing all they could to block the idea."

The competition had good cause to worry. Ford had approached the OPA with such a proposal. The agency listened, but declined, in part because of the other wartime contracts Ford had undertaken.

Henry II Steps Up

The war marked the winding down of Henry Ford's career, though his temperament and energy level remained high. Ford suffered a minor stroke in 1938, at age 75, but it caused no lasting damage. In 1941, however, his second stroke had more effect. His attention span lapsed, his temper shortened, and his opinions hardened.

Ford's age left the door open for the will of others to prevail. One of those who strongly influenced Ford was Harry Bennett, a man who had served as Ford's "eyes and ears" in the Rouge. By the time Ford suffered his second stroke, Bennett nearly ran the company. For the past decade, Bennett had locked horns with Sorensen, who was perhaps Ford's most loyal—if ambitious—employee. Countless talented executives and engineers left, fired or terrorized by Bennett, over the previous five years.

Early in 1943, Edsel Ford's longstanding stomach ulcers became terminal cancer. In the predawn of May 26, 1943, Henry Ford's only son and the president of Ford Motor Company died at age 49. His father had always thought him too soft, misunderstanding his sensitivity, and he had tried to toughen him up through relentless challenges. Edsel swallowed them. It was not in his nature to fight back, especially against his father whom he adored and understood.

The morning before the funeral, Ford told Sorensen that he would resume the presidency he

1944 Ford-Ferguson 2N High-Crop

Aftermarket kits added crop clearance to N-Series Fords. A spacer raised rear fenders four inches to accommodate 11.00-40 rear tires. The extra ground clearance gave farmers one more chance with the cultivator, two weeks closer to harvest, without bruising leaves, fruit, or vegetables. This Model 2N is equipped with such a kit.

abdicated 24 years before. He was 80. Sorensen was stunned, but he recognized that this meant Bennett would be in charge, to the probable detriment of the company, its name, and its products.

The power at that moment rested with Edsel's widow, Eleanor, and his mother, Clara. Together, they argued that Henry II, not Henry I, should take charge. They represented 45 percent of the family-held company. Any threat they made, selling stock to the public, for example, had to be given attention.

In August 1943, Henry II was released from the Navy. During his training in suburban Chicago, he kept up on production and company business matters through Ford's former secretary, Ernest Kanzler. While Edsel had despaired that little could be done to save the company, Henry II knew otherwise. He loved auto production and was concerned about the company approaching the end of the war. Hearing that Eugene Gregorie had new car drawings, he told Sorensen to get busy. Henry Ford II was not quite 26, and while he was not yet in charge, he was very close.

Bennett's tyranny eventually cost him. When he orchestrated the dismissal of Sheldrick and Eugene Gregorie, and after Sorensen resigned, young Henry stepped into place.

During 1943 production, Ford introduced pressurized cooling systems on 2N models. Starting in 1944, the company offered sealed beam headlights. In midmodel year, tractors were available with helical transmission gears.

Starting in the 1950s, aftermarket manufacturers created kits to increase ground clearance of Ford tractors and other makes by using larger rear wheels and longer front spindles. Companies in California, Louisiana and Florida produced items that raised the tractor another six inches over standard.

143

144

Ten

FUNK CONVERSIONS

Hot-Rodding the N-Series

Henry Ford I probably would have appreciated Quinton Nilson. Anytime Ford got his hands on a new machine or invention, he worked at improving it. Nilson, farming near Spink, South Dakota, did the same thing with a 9N tractor. He felt it needed more power, which led him to install a Ford flathead V-8. When it came time on Tuesday morning, September 20, 1949, for the National Plow Terrace Contest at West Point, Nebraska, every manufacturer was there with new tractors and expert operators. But Quinton knew he had a chance.

The Nilson farm near the Big Sioux River demanded terracing, and he was good at it. He and his father just completed a 12-year conservation program on their 250-acre farm, creating 10 miles of terraces and two big dams. To work faster, he replaced the 9N engine with the Mercury V-8 95. At the contest, before 12,000 spectators, he won hands down.

"He wasn't plowing," recalled Delbert Heusinkveldt, who was among those 12,000 spectators watching, "he was throwing dirt. It took him just twenty minutes to do the job. The second place took an hour."

Wednesday's Omaha *World-Herald* commented: "Mr. Nilson's souped-up machine isn't just a freak he devised to win the contest. He uses it on his farm. It pulls a two-bottom plow at 13 miles an hour, considerably better than a conventional tractor. The more powerful motor and

1952 Ford 8N with Funk V-8 Conversion
Funk Brothers Aviation sold about 225 V-8 conversion kits while 8Ns were produced.

1948 Ford 8N with Heusinkveldt V-8 Conversion
*D*elbert Heusinkveldt won't take full credit for inventing the V-8 installation in 8N tractors. Besides the help he got from brothers Marion, Glenn, and Garrett, there was also Quinton Nilson, a South Dakota farmer who completed his V-8-powered Model 8N while the Heusinkveldt brothers were finishing their machine.

double set of rear wheels were his own ideas.

"Maybe souped-up engines and jet propulsion won't power the tractor of the future. But who knows? Ingenious fellows like Mr. Nilson start other people thinking about [doing] things faster and better. Then anything can happen."

Heusinkveldt and his brothers farmed in Springfield, Nebraska, with their dad and his 9N. They also felt their tractor lacked power. Delbert and his brothers, Marion, Glenn, and Garrett, each had studied the V-8 engine in the family's 1935 Ford. Delbert even measured it. It was two inches too long. When the 1948 pickup trucks appeared with removable bell-housings and side-mounted distributors, Delbert figured that might work without changing the tractor frame.

Heusinkveldt located a shop in Sioux City, Iowa, to fabricate an adapter. While that was being made, the brothers went to the contest, watched Quinton, and later, got to know him. When Delbert went back to pick up his adapter, the shop owner mentioned Funk Aircraft in Coffeyville, Kansas. Funk produced kits to install Ford industrial six-cylinder engines in the tractors.

Delbert and his brothers finished their conversion, with help from cousins who did bodywork, splitting the hood to accommodate the wider engine and widening the grille by two inches.

"I had to widen the hood," Heusinkveldt explained, "to fit in a bigger radiator and the six-bladed truck fan. The minute we went that route, cooling became a dream. Before, the temperature gauge just kept creeping up." Delbert exchanged other ideas with Quinton, and when Heusinkveldt's second V-8 was done, he and Nilson together hauled it down to Coffeyville to show Joe and Howard Funk.

"When they saw it, they just loved it," Heusinkveldt recalled recently. "They wanted to build tractors just like it. But when we got into widening the hood, they debated for a while. They were sensible guys. They decided widening the hood was not something that every farmer or dealer wanted to fool with.

"So they raised the hood about six inches, left the gas tank there, and put a long, narrow radiator in, sped the fan up, things like that. I never liked the looks of theirs, but they worked. We never thought

The forward-tipping hood made sense to service the 1948 pickup truck V-8 the four Heusinkveldts installed. Before 1948, they measured the V-8 in their family's 1935 Ford sedan several times, but the 1948 truck engine with its removable bell-housing and side-mounted distributor made a perfect fit. They fabricated a box frame to support the engine.

about anybody but Funks. They made the six cylinders. Sixes did everything the V-eight would do. You didn't need a V-eight. That was just a crazy thing of us guys. Sixes had as much power. Oh, it was a homelier outfit, longer. But that was a good engine . . . and later, in [nineteen] fifty-two, Funks used the overhead-valve engine."

The Funks introduced V-8 kits quickly. Heusinkveldt remembered getting promotional brochures in the fall of 1950, a few months after they'd visited the brothers. Neither Quinton nor Delbert ever intended to mass produce V-8 tractors. Nilson was a farmer; after winning the 1949 contest he never returned. Heusinkveldt was a trucker, and, while he ultimately produced seven completed V-8 tractors, it took too much time from his real work.

"Funk sold only kits. They made cast-iron oil pans. That's how it came about. I tried talking Sioux City Foundry into making one. The old guy who ran it really liked the idea. He thought about it and

finally sat me down. The only problem is for the first one, somebody has to come up with about ten grand. After that, they'll be cheap.' Pattern making cost was unreal," Heusinkveldt said.

"Down at Coffeyville, an old pattern maker got interested in the idea. He told me he was going to try it, for the challenge. He got drawings from Ford archives, made a pattern. When he was done, it bolted up nicely. After that, Funk had him make one for the six cylinder as well, and they got rid of those frame rails they had to add at first."

The Heusinkveldt-Nilson V-8 kit became a popular item. Its big appeal was the dual exhaust pipes sprouting from below the rear axle. It wasn't until years later that younger farmers reversed exhaust manifolds and ran pipes up. Funk produced about 225 kits. When more powerful tractors were introduced, production slowed. Another 80 leftover kits lined the shelves until recent years when fascination with the power and glory of flathead V-8s brought

**1952 Ford 8N with Funk
Six-Cylinder Conversion**
Early Funk six-cylinder
conversions required a subframe to
support the long, heavy industrial
engine. Joe Funk readily credited
origination of this idea to Olaf E.
Glover, a Ford tractor dealer and
mechanic in Millford, Illinois. He
showed Joe Funk a 9N in which he
fitted the long six. Glover
encouraged Funk Brothers to
produce kits.

them out of hiding. Heusinkveldt believes there may be more than 315 of the original 225 left.

Funk Brothers Beginnings

Howard and Joe Funk had worked with Ford for decades, beginning with adapting extensively modified four-cylinder Model B water-cooled engines to their own aircraft in Akron, Ohio. After building 110, the Funks went broke. They moved to Coffeyville, working with a pump maker who loved their airplanes. Immediately after World War II, Joe and Howard returned to airplanes, building 350 before bankruptcy stopped them again.

The machine shop they'd developed to fabricate their planes became their savior, and they quit aircraft for earthbound machines. They began producing Harold Brock's transmissions for Ford tractors in the early 1950s. Their catalog contained hundreds of gears, adapters, mounting systems, and converters.

One day in 1950, calling on Olaf Glover, the Ford tractor dealer in tiny Millford, Illinois, Glover

showed them a 9N tractor in which he had just fitted Ford's industrial in-line six-cylinder engine. Glover, a repairman and mechanic, not a machinist, crudely welded an adapter and side-support frame rails from the radiator to the transmission housing to support the longer, heavier engine. This framework provided a bearing on the front to attach the front axle.

He applied for a patent in March 1950, describing his invention: "I have found that by increasing power in a Ford-Ferguson and Ford tractor according to my invention, the well-known advantages of this type of tractor's hydraulic system are preserved, and this type of tractor and its implements do not have to be replaced to fill the need of more power. . . . The converted tractor will handle three 14-inch plows and other implements accordingly." Ollie Glover's invention was rough, but it provided 100 smooth horsepower to farmers. Joe Funk loved it.

"He had done it with welding," Funk recalled. "Glover was the first spark. Did it first. Gosh, we came back down here and made fancy patterns and

castings, machined it up, and worked all the details out and had tremendous instruction books. It was all dealt through Ford tractor dealers.

"We made some six-cylinder conversions for that old boy, Glover. By the time we were done, we made more than five thousand. Got into a few incidents with them, too.

"We got into trouble, associated with a night shift foreman they'd put on Ford tractor assembly. He was the dude that thought heat treatment of the pinion and ring gear in the differential was kind of like polishing. You didn't have to do that.

"So he put un-heat-treated gears in there.

"What happened was a ghastly epidemic of failures around the country. Guys all just thought, 'It's those darned guys in Kansas putting that six-cylinder in there that's doing it.'

"I went up there to Dearborn. Joe Bachman who was head of Ford Industrial Engine Division, used to sell me industrial engines. He was cursing me out to high heaven.

"I went to see the president of the company. Gave the girl my card. We still had the name Funk Aircraft then. She called upstairs and, 'No

This converted 8N has a pickup truck 227-cid, in-line six-cylinder engine installed from an early Funk Brothers kit. The Kansas pattern maker whom Delbert Heusinkveldt located to fabricate a cast-iron sump for the V-8, turned his attention to the Ford Industrial six as well.

The Dearborn One-Way 18in plow
*I*n addition to the one-way plow's automatic reset feature, it could be used as a ditcher as well.

The Funk kit raised the hood six inches. This allowed farmers not only to retain original gas tanks but also for Funks to include larger radiators than original. They used one that was taller and narrower. They also increased fan speed by about 25 percent. This 1952 8N has a 1953 V-8 engine under the hood.

1952 Ford 8N with Funk V-8 Conversion
Original Funk conversion kits used the stock Ford exhaust manifolds, which routed exhaust down and, through pipes, back under the rear axle. Few of the original kits still appear with low exhaust pipes, as collectors favor flipping the manifolds and pointing the exhaust pipes skyward.

thank you, we don't want to buy an airplane.' So I leaned over and said, 'No, ma'am, we're the folks that put six-cylinder industrial engines in the Ford tractor.

"That gal upstairs screamed like she was stabbed. Two tall young boys came down that big marble stairway, got me underneath the armpits, carried me into the board of directors meeting and sat me down at the end of the table. There were about two dozen guys there.

" 'Mr. Funk, would you believe that this meeting was called for the purpose of setting up to sue Funk Aircraft?' " Joe Funk, now 87 years old, laughed hard at his own story. It wasn't funny then.

"That day, they had five tractors delivered on a flat car. Two made it to the agency, the other three failed. Gears in back of the differential broke and broke the case. We went down there, reached in, and we filed the ring gear. It was like working with soft plastic. It hadn't been heat treated. I called them up, but they'd already heard it. They shut down production, sent guys around the country to make sure gears were heat treated, replacing everyone that wasn't. They honored every complaint.

"And then they fell in love with us," Funk laughed again. "See, we sold five *thousand* industrial engines for them. Through dealers! Not through industrial wholesalers at factory price. *Five thousand!*"

1953 Ford NAA Golden Jubilee with Funk Six-Cylinder Conversion

This Golden Jubilee has one of the early Funk Ford Industrial six-cylinder conversions, still using a steel subframe to support the long, heavy engine. Later versions eliminated the framework, and still-later models used Ford's overhead-valve engine. The Funks sold about 5,000 of the six-cylinder conversion kits.

Eleven

FORD AND FERGUSON SPLIT

The Slap Felt Around the World

Considering Harry Ferguson's disposition and will, it was perhaps inevitable that he and the Ford Motor Company would part ways. When Henry Ford I passed away in 1947, Ferguson lost his best ally at the Motor Company; tolerance for Ferguson's antics faded. The fact that Ferguson made money on tractors while Ford revenues went into the red didn't help matters. The differences were aggravated by their attempt to build a larger tractor, dubbed the 4P. When Henry shopped around Ford technical drawings in an attempt to build tractors independently, the bond that created the Ford-Ferguson tractor frayed irreparably. When the split came, both parties were glad to be rid of the other.

Throughout 1942, correspondence between Harry Ferguson and Willie Sands related to tractor improvements and small problems Ferguson perceived with Ford's tractor. Sands offered solutions, such as they could be, to the problems, such as they were. In early 1943, a new message arrived in the mail. Ferguson still felt betrayed by Ford's unwillingness to force their tractor on Dagenham. Conceiving alternatives to dealing with Henry Ford, whom he still referred to as "Black," he wrote on February 19, 1943, to Sands, concerning a major revision of the steering gear, which had caused a problem.

"We do not know the minute we might break with Black's and we have had unbelievable anxiety. If

Patrick Hennessey took the Ministry of Agriculture's (MoA) postwar tractor requirements and in late 1943 began updating the Fordson. He felt Ford's 9N had features worth adopting, but Ferguson's dedicated implements were an economic hardship to farmers with sheds full of tow-behind implements. Few of these tractors made it to the United States.

Harry Ferguson became convinced that American farmers wanted larger tractors. Through mid-1943, Ferguson, his own chief engineer, Daniel Cromer Heitshu, and Harold Brock of Ford, considered, created, and designed a four-plow Ford-Ferguson tractor. In November 1943, they completed the first prototype 4P tractor. *Henry Ford Museum and Greenfield Village*

we did break with them we would have to design a new steering immediately and that might delay us for months because we cannot find another company to make the present steering. . . .

"Our vital interest now is to work on things which will keep the tractor on the market, or, if we break with Black's, will enable us to get going quickly again." Ferguson's alternative was a future without Ford.

By year end, Harry Ferguson Inc. had fielded complaints from dealers over broken parts, warranty repair costs, and improvements they wanted made in tractors and implements. As frustrated as Ferguson was with Ford, so was Sands with Ferguson. He threatened to quit several times and finally did. Sands had money in the bank, his wife was ill, and he wanted to care for her.

Ferguson wrote a rambling, downbeat good-bye letter on November 18, 1943. His style in correspondence to anyone was to label various sections. This time he titled one, "My One Mistake":

"I have often said to you that if only we could work out something good enough and far ahead of

anything else, there would be manufacturers who would jump at the chance of taking it up. . . .

"I have vastly changed my mind. . . . I know [now] that the years we spent together were nothing more than fun and interest compared with the work and anxieties of manufacture and distribution.

"I took risks of my own finances and career which [I] do not think any other man in the world would have done. . . . If I [had] foreseen the hell that I have been through I would never have gone on. You know what it was at David Brown's and how they ruined everything. The Shermans created a mass of ruin here. . . . I did not want to come back to [the United States] . . . but if I hadn't neither of us would have made any money or any future out of the years we worked together in the field—and that was fun compared to manufacture and distribution."

Oddly, by Ferguson's standards, he was in the midst of fun. He had pushed a large tractor on Sands since mid-1943. By late September, Willie Sands could hold his tongue no longer. On September 24 he wrote back to Ferguson: "Is it a good policy to produce a heavier tractor, after all our arguments in favor of the lightweight job? It is an admission that our tractor is failing in some respects. Would it not be better to complete [the] line of implements for our present job? You know we have practically no harvesting equipment, and after all, what good is a crop if you have nothing to harvest it with?

"Would it not be better to fit . . . say . . . a six- or eight-speed gearbox, and if any more weight is required, to add this in the portion that it would be most effective?" Ferguson read these words, but he was listening to other voices.

"Ferguson didn't have an engineering department when we did the 9N," Harold Brock explained. "He had Sands, Greer, and Chambers. It was cut-and-try engineering. When Ferguson saw the effect that Ford engineers had on 'his' tractor, he figured he needed engineers of his own. He hired people from Allis-Chalmers, Minneapolis-Moline, Deere. I mean, these were chief engineers he hired.

"Before the war, these people, the whole industry in fact, laughed: 'All you've got is a toy. Nobody's going to buy that.'

"Now Ferguson had engineers who came in with the same ideas they had in their former companies. They prevailed on Ferguson, 'We ought to have a second size of tractor.'"

Ferguson became convinced by his staff that American farms needed a larger tractor than Ford produced in 1943. After wartime manufacturing projects were under way, Harold Brock began developing and testing a new tractor with Ferguson, known within Ford and Harry Ferguson Inc. as 4P, the four-plow tractor. (Ferguson-Sherman dissolved when Eber Sherman resigned as president in 1941, a year after George Sherman left. Eber disagreed with Ferguson over engineering, marketing, and the general direction they would follow after the war.)

By March 1944, Ferguson and Brock, each heading up separate engineering staffs (Ferguson had about 30 people; Ford's tractor group had 50), agreed on performance and physical characteristics of the 4P. Daniel Cromer Heitshu, Ferguson's chief engineer, outlined for Brock and the tractor group features his boss felt necessary.

Ferguson argued that because hauling wagons would be practical with the 4P, he wanted easier shifts between third and fourth gear, incorporating a "syn-

chro-mesh" mechanism. He proposed keeping 48-inch tread on a longer 84-inch wheelbase for adequate front weight to balance equipment used on the tractor.

When the front end was under load and the tractor was backing up, 9Ns could become difficult to control. Harry Ferguson wanted those complaints remedied. He wanted to add the continuous-running power take-off (PTO) system Ford engineering already had developed. He also wanted to investigate larger diameter front tires, up from 5.50x16s to 5.25x21s. Heitshu ordered full-size drawings of the 84-inch wheelbase tractor on 21-inch front rubber so Ferguson could see the changes. Once the tractor was approved by both sides, Chambers ordered a full-size wood mock-up. It was completed in late August 1943, but no one liked its hood or grille. Brock asked Clare Kramer of Ford Body Design, the stylist for the jeep, to improve the appearance. Kramer made drawings and another model, and in early November 1943, Ferguson approved it. Brock ordered one running prototype hurried through. He, Chambers, and Heitshu accompanied it to Richmond Hill for winter testing. It was so good that Brock had two more built. Through July 1944, Engineering thoroughly tested them at Fair Lane.

Heitshu and Brock's groups developed 4P plows, cultivators, and other tools. Another three 4Ps were authorized, six in all; however, Engineering stopped after the fifth prototype.

Clare Kramer from Ford Body Design styled the appearance of the Ford-Ferguson 4P tractor. Brock, Ferguson's John Chambers, and Heitshu thoroughly tested the 4P at Ford's Richmond Hill Plantation at Ways Station, Georgia. It was so good Brock ordered two more built, and testing of the three moved to Fair Lane Farm. *Henry Ford Museum and Greenfield Village*

"Ferguson approached Edsel," Brock continued, "because the Old Man was occupied with so much wartime production. Ferguson proposed making this a second size tractor: 'We've done so well on the smaller size that if we had a second size we would do much better.'

"Edsel said, 'If we lose as much money on the second one as we are on the first one, we can't afford it.' So they were just put aside. . . . With Mr. Ford backing out, there went Ferguson's only friend. . . .'"

Development costs for the entire project, about $938,000 from concept to field testing five prototypes, eventually were split equally between Harry Ferguson Inc. and Ford Motor Company. On July 27, the project ended. Two work orders, KX-524 and KX-633, creating two of the five prototypes, were closed out. Brock delivered them to Ferguson.

G. H. Van Husen in Tractor Engineering produced a postmortem for Brock, "Engineering Report Number 7: Study of Model 4P Tractor" on April 17, 1946. Using Continental in-line four-cylinder 162.4-cubic-inch conventional L-head, wet-sleeve engines,

4Ps provided 45 percent more horsepower with 42 percent more weight than the 2Ns." Van Husen recommended, primarily, that Ford and Ferguson consider a large tractor similar to the 2N, which would benefit from interchangeable parts. Without support from Henry Ford, despite successful tests in Georgia and Dearborn, the project died. A tiny type-written memo, FEH/INO 135614, dated February 26, 1946, served as their obituary. Of the five built, one was sent to England for evaluation at Dagenham, two were delivered to Ferguson, one was left at Ford's Cherry Hill farm, and the fifth burned while filling with gasoline at Ford Dearborn Farms.

On September 30, 1946, Harry Ferguson, now back in England, wrote to Willie Sands at his home in Ireland to discuss the "Large Model Tractor."

"I am sure we should view the subject with a long distance vision, but why should we not very quickly design a larger model of the present tractor and get into big production on it in America and here? There is a vast market waiting for us and it might take us years to develop the tractor of the

1950 Ford E27N
*H*arold Brock devised hydraulics for the updated Fordson and replaced the original worm gear with spiral bevel gear final drive, providing higher ground clearance. Hennessey's engineers increased the N's engine output to 27 horsepower.

1953 Fordson Power Major
*T*he American import of the E27N was dubbed the Fordson Major. In 1952, its successor appeared, named the New Major.

*H*ennessey hoped to introduce a three-plow tractor, but lack of raw materials and funds limited him to improving his two-row Fordson. Ford offered it in three versions: Land Utility, Standard Agricultural, and Row Crop models. Although the 1950 model pictured is equipped with a gasoline engine, the E27N introduced Perkins diesels to Ford farmers.

1958 Fordson Power Major on Leeford Rotaped Tracks

*T*his series of Ford engines was coded E1ADN for gasoline, E1ADKN for tractor vaporizing oil (TVO), and E1ADDN for diesel fuel. TVO engines had to start on gasoline, a practice that added complexity and cost. Cheaper, more readily available diesel fuel eventually won the day and displaced TVO. By the early 1960s, 98 percent of English Fordsons were sold with diesel engines.

*F*ord introduced the Power Major in 1958. Modifications to the diesel engine with the Simms Minimec injection pump provided farmers with 53.7 gross horsepower, the highest output ever in a Fordson. Optional live PTO, introduced on Majors in February 1957, was carried over.

future. . . . I say all this with the feeling that we have no practical solution for all the problems that face us for all the future. . . ."

Separation Tactics

Ferguson's problem for the future was his eminent separation from Ford. Losses from the tractor division were huge. Henry Ford had grown restive over the tractor. He, Edsel, and Sorensen considered buying out Ferguson. While Henry hated distribution, his losses were insupportable. Ferguson, despite his complaints, had made a good profit. They knew he'd never sell, preferring to keep his Golden Goose alive.

Sensing the endgame, Harry Ferguson offered to research cost reductions. He antagonized enough people at Ford that they encouraged him. They knew no one on earth could mass-produce products cheaper than Ford. Yet assigning this to Ferguson got him out of their hair.

158

Ferguson hired Ford, Bacon and Thomas Inc., an industrial management consultant, to assist him in his quest for more economical suppliers. They would shop suppliers to obtain unit prices on the various components using 9N blueprints, something Ferguson never before had required, nor been given. Edsel authorized the release of the drawings, probably with a bit of trepidation.

Starting in early 1944, Ferguson sent the drawings, and staff members led by his new chief engineer, Albert W. Lavers, out to visit suppliers and jobbers around the United States. They arrived at engine manufacturers such as Buda and Continental with blueprints, power curves, metallurgy specifications, manufacturing quantities, and proposed delivery dates. They modified the drawings, obscuring Ford's name, a common treatment if one seeks honest bids unaffected by the client's size or significance.

But Ferguson had Lavers do more than just shop. Several suppliers became suspicious of the project after recognizing plans and quantities requested as decidedly Ford-like. One of those was Ernest R. Breech, president of Bendix Aviation Company, a GM subsidiary that provided parts to Ford. Breech liked Henry II, then company president, and had considered becoming vice-president of Ford Motor Company.

Lavers raised Breech's suspicions with part of a Ferguson proposal that suggested Bendix and Ferguson team up to manufacture the entire tractor, at a 51–49 split in costs and profits. Breech contacted Henry II, who made a few discrete inquiries that revealed other improprieties. Henry II reacted decisively, immediately attempting to purchase part of the Ferguson company. Henry II notified Roger Kyes that since his grandfather had loaned Ferguson $60,000 to set up the tractor distribution firm (which was repaid), Henry II felt it would be beneficial to his family to acquire 30 percent of Harry Ferguson Inc. Henry II let that idea settle, knowing from his grandfather that Ferguson might agree to release some control to Ford's family but none to the company.

On July 1, Ernie Breech became Ford vice-president. He had seen Ford's books and did quick math on the 9N and 2N tractors delivered and what Ferguson's profit had been. He concluded that Ferguson had made around $9 million, while Ford had lost about $15 million. He quickly outlined Ford's next idea to Kyes and another Ferguson board member, Horace D'Angelo. Owing to a new inter-

pretation of the "Handshake Agreement," Breech felt they should establish a new tractor distribution firm, which Ford would control with 51 percent, split between family and company. Ferguson would keep 49 percent.

Critical business reasons demanded a new company. Breech, recognizing Ford's fiscal condition was grave, knew he needed help. Top salaries were taxed at 85 percent; few executives at the level he needed would leave current positions without stock options as deferred income. The Ford Family and the Ford Foundation, created in January 1936, controlled all shares of Ford Motor Company. Stock in a new tractor and implement company cautiously managed, rather than one just thoughtfully aimed as Ford and Ferguson had done, would be an attractive perk. Breech gave Kyes and D'Angelo months to consider this proposal.

Then in November, Henry II went to see his grandfather. He outlined what happened and what was necessary. Henry II, quoted in Allan Nevins' and Frank Hill's *Ford: Decline and Rebirth 1933–1962*, replied, "Use your judgment. Ferguson is a hog anyway and just keep on building the tractor."

On November 11, Breech presented to Kyes their next plan: Ford Motor Company would take 70 percent equity of a new company no longer bearing

Leeford's Rotaped track system is a simple and clever adaptation. Leeford replaced the traditional crawler configuration of idler and track wheels with a chain and pulley system.

159

Harry Ferguson's name but of which he would receive 30 percent. They would pay no royalties to Ferguson for his patents either. At the same time, they announced formation of Dearborn Motors Company as the marketing, sales, and service arm of Ford Motor Company to handle farm tractors and implements. In essence, Breech exercised a "clause" of the verbal compact, the one that permitted ending it for any reason at any time by either party.

Kyes took the news with equanimity. Inside he was smiling. He wrote Ferguson later that day. "I have never been so relaxed, so happy, so relieved in my life." When Ferguson heard, he replied, "Glory be. We're free."

On New Year's Eve, Breech notified Kyes formally that as of that date, Ford no longer would manufacture machines for Ferguson under the previous agreement. So as to not summarily put them out of business, Ford would provide them tractors through June 30, 1947. The Handshake Heard Around the World echoed as a slap in the face.

Back on June 30, before Breech offered Roger Kyes the 51–49 percent reorganization, E. C. McRae in Ford's Patent Department at Dearborn put final touches on a three-and-a-half page memo to engineering and management. It was an infringement avoidance guide:

"Our examination of the Ferguson patents shows that some of the features of the Ford tractor and Ferguson system, and some of the implements used therewith, are still covered by claims in active patents. However, the patents on the basic features of the Ferguson system have expired and it is our opinion that a tractor almost identical in appearance and operation to our present tractor, and one which employs a hydraulic lift and implement control, can be made by us without infringing on Ferguson's patents." Pages that followed dictated precise and specific changes to make on objects still under Ferguson patents to avoid problems.

When Ernie Breech started at Ford, he brought additional talent in with him, among them Harold Youngren, who left the top engineer spot at Borg-Warner transmissions to become chief engineer of Ford. He took Sheldrick's job, left open since the war. Youngren sized things up and put Harold Brock to work quickly revising the 2N tractor into something they could introduce that year without risking any Ferguson claims.

Revising Fordsons

Brock knew tractor revision. From 1943 through mid-1946, he visited England twice on such projects, having only just returned from Dagenham. Sent in April 1946, he stayed through mid-August doing designs and layouts, supervising creation of a full-size wood mockup of Dagenham's replacement E87N tractor, introduced in two engine and frame sizes as the Dexta and Power Major in 1957 and 1958, respectively.

Dagenham earlier renewed its vows with the Fordson in 1945 with the Major. This was known internally as E27N (English 27-horsepower tractor). Work on this update began in late 1943 when Patrick Hennessey suggested producing something new. The Ministry of Agriculture defined its needs for postwar tractors: light two-plow, medium three-plow, and heavy Caterpillar-type crawler. Seeing that resources existed to do only updates on their "light two-plow" Fordson, Lord Perry worried that Dearborn might force on them the Ford-Ferguson tractor. He wrote Edsel in April 1943, asking pointedly for an answer. Assured Dearborn would not, Hennessey then asked Edsel for help doing a new three-plow machine, referred to as the Improved No. 3 Fordson, to introduce after the war. Laurence Sheldrick, in his last days at Ford, sent Brock to England.

"The English factory produced their big, simple, heavy machine with low clearance that still used a drawbar for pulling," Brock explained. "There was huge worldwide demand for this tractor from which they derived great profit. It was rugged . . . you pulled these big, heavy pieces of equipment—double the weight and more—without abusing the tractor. If you pull double the weight with the 9N, it would break."

Hennessey recognized that some 9N improvements were worth adapting. However, by not adopting the 9N, buyers could still use their own implements. This was important to Dagenham. While 80 percent of the tractors operating in the United Kingdom were Fordsons, Ford Motor Company Ltd. sold £1,000,000 worth of Fordsons in Europe the year before the war. Continuity in implements was critical in many countries after the war, which had no money for new "systems."

"They sent me right after the war, in 1943. I stayed at the Picadilly Hotel in London, on rations, one egg a week." Brock was perfect for the

assignment. Dagenham mainly wanted hydraulics and to eliminate the worm-gear rear end. Brock had devised the spiral bevel gear final drive for the 9N, and he had tamed the troubling hydraulics with his tapered valve. Their third desire was a new engine to improve fuel economy yet offer better performance. (That would await the arrival of Perkins' diesels.)

Dagenham's designers restyled the radiator grille and recast the radiator-top tank, gaining maximum effect for minimum expense. They introduced changes gradually, not in one dramatic unveiling. They restored the dark blue with orange color scheme. Production started in June 1945; however, there were vast stores of Fordson N parts, which lingered until replacements were needed. Clearly there were not resources enough to produce a new tractor. The 87N waited.

The Improved Fordson No. 3, the Fordson Major, brought 12-volt systems with electric starting and lights. In 1948, Perkins six-cylinder diesel P6TA engines appeared. A four-cylinder model, the P4TA, was introduced in 1953. Hydraulic power lift did not arrive until 1948, on a system that did not carry over Ferguson's automatic draft control. Standard Agricultural models and Row Crop versions came on steel wheels, the Standard with a single driveshaft brake, the Row Crop fitted with two rear wheel brakes, and adjustable rear track. The Land Utility model was carried over, on rubber tires. In addition, Dagenham shipped chassis to several outside suppliers. County Commercial Cars in Fleet produced industrial models, and Roadless Traction Ltd. in Hounslow, Middlesex, developed crawlers around the Major.

After Harold Brock returned from his second trip in 1946 with the rudiments of the Power Major and Dexta in his briefcase, his new boss, Harold Youngren, set him quickly back to work with Dale Roeder, the commercial vehicles chief engineer, on the Ford Tractor without Ferguson System, coded the 7N, for planned introduction by Dearborn Motors in 1947.

Twelve

MODEL 8N AND NAA JUBILEE

War and Peace

The partnership between Ford Motor Company and Harry Ferguson may have ended, but they continued to trade blows. Like feuding relatives living in the same small town, they couldn't stand to leave each other alone. Things would get much worse before they would get any better.

Yet, until the separation, both sides put on game faces and made the best of growing tensions. Engineering, insulated from boardroom dramas, began work on the next Ford tractor, the 7N, and its experimental prototype, the 7NX.

"The 7NX tractor—there was more than one 7NX tractor assembled—was an experimental model on which [we] incorporated changes over the 2N." Dale Roeder, the speaker, was chief engineer of the commercial vehicle department during the 1940s. Working with Harold Brock and the tractor engineering group, they completed the first prototypes in late 1945, between Brock's journeys to Dagenham, and before the breakup of Ford and Ferguson. That was because originally it was to be the next Ford-Ferguson, with the improvements, corrections, and updates they had wished to make during war years.

"The first 7NX tractor was assembled sometime in the fall of 1945. The others were completed shortly thereafter. Some of them were delivered to the Snow Road Farm, where Ferguson had a lot of his equipment, where tests were conducted."

First production 8N tractors used radiator grilles drilled with holes for mounting the Ferguson System identification plates. Originally intended as a 7N Ford Tractor with Ferguson System, the names and numbers were changed at the last minute when Ford and Ferguson parted bitterly. *Henry Ford Museum and Greenfield Village*

On April 19, 1946, a Ford film crew shot an instructional film on operating the new 7N tractor, set for introduction toward the end of the summer. While the cameraman shot tight close-ups of the hydraulic system controls, actors explained how operation differed from the previous versions on 2N and 9N tractors. *Henry Ford Museum and Greenfield Village*

An engineer reached for a fuel-feed switch during fuel-economy and drawbar power tests on the 1953 Golden Jubilee tractors on May 4, 1953. Tractor engineering constantly experimented to improve performance, reliability, strength, and economy, not only on future models but also for those in production. *Henry Ford Museum and Greenfield Village*

With the onset of winter, these experimental prototypes were shipped to Georgia. Some tested with the new four-speed transmission.

With these, engineering began finding ways to improve strength, reliability, and even the gear ratios of the four speeds to make better use of engine performance, provide better fuel economy, and to farm better. At the same time, management was in the midst of testing Harry Ferguson's resolve. In the end, Breech, Youngren, Roeder, and Brock concluded the 7N should become an 8N, a Ford Tractor with no mention of a Ferguson System, postponed until late 1947. So in January, five new experimental tractors, 8Ns, were begun.

As work continued on these, and as the first two prototypes neared completion, Henry Ford died on April 7, 1947. He was three months shy of his 84th birthday. In his long lifetime, he had seen 1.7 million farm tractors go out, all but a few thousand Ministry of Munitions and prototype models with some variation of his name on them. Ironically, the 8N tractors finally bore his name alone.

Dearborn Motors Corporation (DMC), the new farm equipment division of Ford Motor Company, had few facilities of its own at this stage. Roeder asked Brock to supervise 8N development on the prototypes completed between April 15 and May 5, 1947.

Number 1 went to Ford's Cherry Hill farm for a month photographing it for brochures and advertising. Then it and number 2, both born April 15, were centerpieces of DMC's dealer show May 14 and 15 at Highland Park. Number 3, finished April 28, went to Highland Park "for preparation of repair, operator's and time schedule manuals," for DMC. Number 4, assembled May 1, became Brock's real test and evaluation unit for converging hydraulic links in rigorous tests in Kentucky. Number 5, completed May 5, was the converging links hydraulic system demonstration rig at the distributor's meeting with an electric motor running the hydraulic pump. Brock and his tractor group devised these new links to further stabilize the implement. This mainly held the implement more rigidly in place against sideways movement.

At the end of their testing, modeling, and demonstrating careers, Dearborn Motors kept the first three prototypes while Ford Engineering retained numbers 4 and 5, used as ongoing test tractors on future developments and projects.

The Color Contest

"Battleship gray was the color of the old Fordson," Brock recalled, "That was also our 9N and 2N. It was the color of the machine tools at the factories. Rust used to bleed through. Castings rusted over the years. I suggested that International Harvester had red tractors that wouldn't show rust. They said, 'We want something flashier!' The Dearborn Motors group were from General Motors Frigidaire Division. Real marketers. They said, 'We ought to do something different!'

"I said we ought to have a light color on the hood so it doesn't show dirt. We don't want all red like International Harvester. Chickens roost on the tractor. The top gets white, dirty. So, use a light color on top.

"They couldn't decide the color to paint them. 'We'll take a vote!' They all voted for their own school colors, whatever those were. I was the one who collected the ballots.

"My wife had a pretty dress. Red and silver gray. I thought it was really attractive. I told them the vote came out that the tractor was going to be red and gray. Spruced up the look of the tractor. And the rust wouldn't show through the red. . . ."

Dearborn Motors Corporation was incorporated two days before Thanksgiving 1946 as the new tractor and implement division. Breech hired Frank Pierce, a GM marketing manager, to run DMC. Ford executives were immediately offered stock in the new company. DMC opened its doors on Monday, January 6. As word of the dissolution of the Handshake spread among Ferguson's tractor and implement dealers, many of them quickly signed up with Dearborn Motors to handle the new Ford products after June 30.

Ferguson and the Lawsuit

In England Harry Ferguson gave up hoping Dagenham would produce the Ford-Ferguson tractor. Lord Perry and Sir Patrick Hennessey, knighted after Dagenham's role in wartime production, had legitimate excuses for not manufacturing it. Still, Ferguson sought British production.

Ferguson learned of a 1-million-square-foot factory in Coventry that Standard Motor Company

1947 Ferguson TE-20

Harry Ferguson first produced his TE-20 (Tractor, England, 20 horsepower) in 1946 with Sir John Black of Standard Motor Company at Coventry, England. While its model name was well known, its nickname among competing tractor sales staffs was the Grey Menace, because no one could compete with it. American versions were designated TO-20 (Tractor, Overseas). Ferguson first manufactured TE and TO models in Coventry. He began production in Detroit on November 11, 1948, but tractors were still called overseas versions. In Dearborn by now, Ferguson himself was known as a menace.

instructed Sir John Black, managing director of Standard, to do it in the national interest. On September 18, Sir John announced that Standard would produce the tractor called, simply, the "Ferguson."

(Ferguson's correspondence while this came together got confusing. Maintaining secrecy in case his mail fell into the wrong hands, he now had a real Black to refer to as well as his Dearborn partner, Mr. Black [Ford]. For a time, Sir John remained Black, but Ford became "White." Soon, even Ferguson got confused. He referred to both of them as "Black," relying on the context in which they were referred to be sufficient to identify which was the subject.)

Quoted in the *Coventry Daily Telegraph* a month later, Ferguson announced that "I am sure the time is not far distant when the Standard Motor Company will be employing 50,000 men in building tractors." He planned daily production of 200 tractors starting just after the 1947 New Year, offering 10 separate implements. In the *Coventry Daily Herald* in late October, Ferguson called his tractor "the peace-time jeep [that] can handle any farm job."

Production began just before the new year, 1946, in Coventry, as Ferguson was freed from Henry Ford. Ferguson named the new tractor the Ferguson TE-20, for "Tractor, England, 20 horsepower." He provided a full electrical system. His engines had overhead valves and four-speed gearboxes, items he wanted in the 2N. For Ferguson, the days were stressful but uplifting. Seven years before, he'd borrowed $60,000 from Ford to set up his distribution company, but he used some of that to pay his hotel bill at the Dearborn Inn. He had done well, ending the Handshake agreement with $6 million in the bank. In July 1947, that could buy him a factory in the United States to manufacture his tractors.

Kyes found the former Pneumatic Aerol war

used making wartime aircraft engines. Leased to Standard, it still belonged to the government, in what was referred to as a "shadow factory" arrangement. It was virtually abandoned. In London in July 1945, Harry Ferguson planned to present his case to the government itself: his tractor was needed in the United Kingdom and in Europe. He met Sir Stafford Cripps, England's chancellor of the Exchequer, who, after some verbal sparring, agreed to provide Ferguson steel to build 200 tractors a day. Cripps

1956 Ferguson TO-35 Diesel

*F*erguson introduced the TO-35 in 1954. He was never enthusiastic about diesel engines or fuel, but his sales staff and the competition forced him to adapt as early as 1951 with the TEF-20. Just as with all the Detroit-built Fergusons, the larger 35 used six-volt electrics. The 35s had a six-speed transmission and an improved hydraulic pump.

plant in Cleveland and acquired the large empty factory for $1.9 million; however, they needed $8 million more to get it into operation. Initial support slipped away, and they sold the Cleveland facility but at a slight profit.

Ferguson took his show to every major manufacturer in the United States, raising serious interest at General Motors (still watching Ford), Willys Overland, and Kaiser-Frazer. Willys wanted control, GM disagreed on what type of tractor Ferguson should produce, and Kaiser-Frazer, hearing from the other two, backed out. Ferguson and Kyes' relationship unraveled and Roger left. Harry was under great pressure, but he threw up a bold attack. He filed a lawsuit against Ford Motor Company.

"It'll be a grand fight," he said as he accused his former partner of patent infringement, conspiracy to restrain fair trade, to destroy his business, and to control the tractor and implement industry. This went beyond patents into questions of monopolistic behavior. As such, Ferguson could seek three times the actual damages plus patent royalties. The total came to $251 million.

"My God! The Marshall Plan," Allan Nevins quoted a stunned Ernie Breech after reading the 26-page complaint. Filed in January 1948 in U.S. District Court in New York as Civil Action Case 44-482, preparations and the trial itself dragged on until April 1952. Harry Ferguson's own deposition numbered 10,312 pages, an unfathomable, impenetrable obfuscation of his history with Ford.

Ferguson's suit brought his company attention and sympathy from those who cheered underdogs. Sales abroad increased. But in America Ferguson had no time to establish a plant to make tractors. Sir John shipped 25,000 Coventry-built Fergusons to Detroit. Called the TO-20 (Tractor, Overseas), these let Harry renew dealer networks and his name. (It worked; gross sales exceeded $312 million in 1947, his first year independent of Ford.) In January 1948, Harry Ferguson Inc. purchased a 72-acre site in Detroit, and in mid-February, broke ground for a factory. Contractors finished hurried construction in July, and on October 11, 1948, Ferguson drove his first Detroit-built TO-20 tractor off the line. At Christmas, production was 100 tractors a

Capper's Farmer magazine carried this ad in its September 1951 issue announcing Harry Ferguson's new, more powerful TO-30 models.

1951 Ferguson TED-20 with Reekie Conversion

G. Reekie Engineering Group in Scotland performed 28 separate operations to modify Ferguson TEs as "berry tractors" for vineyards and some vegetable and fruit applications. Reekie narrowed the tractor to work in 40-inch rows. They were so popular that Ferguson sent his staff to Reekie and began producing his own Vineyard TEs. The Ferguson S-LE low-volume sprayer on the rear would put out 3.5 gallons per minute driven off the PTO.

day; he recorded profits of $500,000 in the United States alone.

Both companies worked at producing tractors and depositions. Ford, calling Ferguson's bluff, countersued in July 1949, charging Ferguson with conspiring to dominate the world's tractor markets, running Ford Motor Company, and stealing Willie Sands' patent ideas. Ford hoped to wear Ferguson down.

In March 1951, both sides waived a trial by jury and Judge Gregory F. Noonan gaveled the case to order, but not before Harry Ferguson added another $90 million to his claim as additional patent infringement royalties since the suit had been filed. Three and a half months later, Harry Ferguson asked his lawyers to accept a settlement if Ford offered something. Judge Noonan was notified and the trial continued in the courtroom while negotiations began outside. On April 9, 1952, Ferguson accepted Judge Noonan's carefully worked out terms of $9.25 million, for patent infringements only. (DMC wrote the check.) The trial cost Harry Ferguson $3.5 million in

1956 Ferguson 40 High Arch
Massey-Harris-Ferguson took Ferguson's gray-and-gold TO-35, stretched its wheelbase four inches to make a cultivating tractor, and called it the Massey-Harris 50. Ferguson decided he needed a cultivating tractor, so he took the stretched red MH-50, straightened the front axle, and rebadged it in beige and green as the Ferguson 40. These were sold only in 1956 and 1957.

1948 Ford 8N
The 8N tractor introduced the Clare Kramer-Harold Brock-designed flip-down grille for easier cleaning. Brock's engineers also replaced the sector-gear steering system from the 9N and 2N models with a recirculating ball-type steering. Tractor engineering gave the 8N tractors a slightly higher steering wheel, a flip-up seat, and running boards to facilitate stand-up operation of the tractor.

1947 Ford-Ferguson 2N and 1947 Ford 8N
This 1947 2N (serial number 305295) and 8N (serial number 637) both have engine blocks cast June 6, 1947. Superficial differences between the two models are obvious: paint colors, air intake, grille badges, and front and rear wheel hubs. Of course, a fourth gear was added to the 8N's transmission.

1948 Ford 8N with Wood Brothers Dearborn Harvester
Dearborn Motors opened its doors in January 1947, finding suppliers willing to provide implements. Among them, Wood Brothers of Des Moines, Iowa, stepped up with a full line of picking and harvesting equipment.

legal fees and fed 200 lawyers on both sides. Attorneys gathered nearly 1 million pages of documents. Corporations throughout the United States watched everything with interest; it was *the* case study in implied agreements and understandings. For Ford and Ferguson, it was a nightmarish experience in inferences, disagreements, and misunderstandings.

Ferguson tractors in the United Kingdom became successful, counting more than half of new tractors sold. In the United States, the familiar shape with its familiar name—if not because of the Ferguson System on 9N and 2N tractors, then certainly because of underdog status—steadily increased in sales. In 1949, Ferguson produced 1,808 tractors and 72,680 TO-20 and TO-30 tractors in 1952. Ford had produced 37,900 8Ns in 1947 (although DMC that year sold 80,092 tractors, most being 2Ns); peaking at 108,442 in 1951 and then 82,041 its final year, 1952.

"The 8N came out of the separation," Harold Brock recalled 50 years afterward. "Management knew Ferguson was talking to other manufacturers about building Ford's little tractor himself, and so when Breech came, we did the 8N tractor without Ferguson knowing it."

*H*igh-clearance tractors often spent most of their lives in cotton and sugarcane fields in Florida and south Georgia. As a result, many worked until they died, not of engine fatigue but of terminal rust. High-clearance N-series Fords were all produced by aftermarket suppliers.

1949 Ford 8N Hi-Crop

*A*ftermarket specialists continued offering high-clearance conversions when Ford replaced the 2N with the improved 8N. For the aftermarket shops, there were few differences between tractors.

1951 Ford 8N Hi-Crop

*O*ne feature consistent among the various aftermarket high-clearance Ford conversion kit makers was adjustable rear wheels. Ford's innovative front axle allowed track adjustment and these rear wheels permitted mounting inside or outside of the hub.

"It was quite a task. It became the highest volume tractor ever produced, twenty-five percent of the total market of tractors with [that] one model. No options. My friends at Deere, and IH and Case then said, 'My goodness. I guess you have got the right idea, haven't you?'

"They still had cultivators in front. The contention was farmers would never accept a cultivator on the rear. Part of that, of course, was because you had to cultivate the weeds out. They didn't have herbicides back in those days." Brock's tractor engineering group mounted cultivators off the rear to utilize the hydraulic lift. With the converging lower links perfected, it trailed the steering. Ford's rear-mounted cultivator would go around curves and track a row.

NAA Jubilee

"The NAA Jubilee was the Fiftieth Anniversary tractor," Harold Brock explained. "It was Henry II's idea. Ford, when they reorganized, they brought 'product planning groups' in; that was a big thing. The planners felt they ought to have a Jubilee model. It was pretty stylish."

Work on the NAA began in 1951. The NAA was to be Ford's first new tractor since Ferguson. The

4P had provided Brock and Roeder some valuable information. They stretched the 8N wheelbase and overall length four inches. Brock's engine designers produced a new "Red Tiger" in-line four-cylinder with overhead valves. This engine (and relocating the muffler alongside the top of it) increased the height of the tractor four inches as well.

They heavily revised the hydraulics. Buyers could add optional remote hydraulic cylinders for front-mounted implements. Engineering made live PTO an option, operated by hydraulic clutch with its own pump. They replaced the governor and the rear-axle brakes and seals. Improvements, upgrades, new

1952 Ford 8N Road Maintainer

Meili-Blumberg Company of New Holstein, Wisconsin, produced its model 19-35 road maintainer for Ford's Dearborn Motors Corporation. It stretched out the 8N to a 14-foot wheelbase, giving it a 39-foot turning radius. Total weight with the tractor was 6,900 pounds.

1952 Ford 8NAN

Kerosene-burning 8Ns used Holley vaporizing carburetors beneath their special manifolds. Most kerosene tractors were shipped to England, where gasoline was in tight supply even several years after World War II. Few kerosene-burning Fords remained in the United States.

standard equipment, and its slightly larger size added only 100 pounds to total weight. Ford wrapped this in handsome sheet metal that turned Eugene Gregorie's "streamline era" 9N styling into the industrial look identifying machines of the 1950s. Production began in September 1952, and the first new tractors were delivered before Thanksgiving.

"I was involved in the development and testing of the NAA," Eddie Pinardi recalled. Pinardi and his brother, Charles, worked for Harold Brock in tractor engineering for more than 20 years. Eddie began in 1937 as a draftsman and retired 50 years later as the last one who signed engineering drawings before they went to production. "I was the one who made the Jubilee nameplate . . . the drawing for that, with the gold and the wheat. In those days, you made a design and sent it to Dearborn, to the stylists. They'd do their idea, and it would come back.

"The stylists thought the wheats were too narrow. Should have been wider. The proportion wasn't right. Came down too fast to a point; it should have come down slower and been wider at the bottom. The word 'Ford' wasn't right, letters weren't right. They had comments, ideas, suggestions about everything.

1953 Ford NAA Jubilee
*T*he Jubilee carries a two-bottom Ford Model 101 plow, and the tractor was equipped with live PTO, Sherman over/under transmission, and remote hydraulic valve.

*I*n anticipation of settling Ferguson's lawsuit against Ford, Harold Brock's staff began developing the Ford-Ferguson tractor replacement soon after the introduction of the 8N. Engineers incorporated numerous changes, including a new independent hydraulic pump and PTO (patented by Brock and Leon Smith in 1952), which were distinctly different than Ferguson's hydraulics.

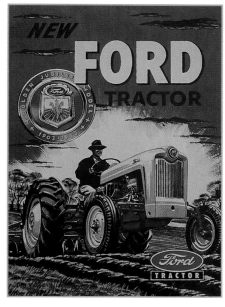

Ford Motor Company produced a lavish brochure introducing its Golden Jubilee NAA tractor. *Dwight and Katy Emstrom collection*

"If styling at Dearborn said it was not right, there was not much you could do about it. Finally, we agreed to it."

Don Horner, a Ford tractor dealer in Geneva, Ohio, remembered being invited to Columbus to see the new Jubilee.

"In late October 1952, we went to Columbus to the Ohio Theater for the introduction of the Jubilee. It was a real show. After they rolled out the tractor on the stage and we got to admire it from a distance, they took it by bus back to Tom Hayward's distributorship to touch the metal.

"This was a tractor a lot of people were waiting for. This was an area [northeast Ohio] and a time where there were a lot of fifty-, sixty-acre farms, and people were making a good living off these small farms. For these people, the Jubilee tractor was the next step up from the 9N they had for ten years now or from the 8N they bought a year before.

"The Jubilee engine was called the Red Tiger, but it was really nothing but the I-block six with two cylinders cut off. It was the first overhead-valve six-cylinder that Ford made for civilian use.

"Right after our introduction at Columbus, we

got our first Jubilees, right away. We had an open house at our dealership. Coffee and sandwiches. And boy, the people came. They came from all over. And they bought 'em, right off the floor." Horner recognized the work that went into the new tractors, and he admired the appearance. He knew it helped sell the tractors.

"The Jubilee was the [nineteen] fifty-three," Eddie Pinardi explained. "The one with the wheat medallion, the NAA, the work tractor, like a utility, an industrial, but you could put plows on it. The NBA was agricultural. There were too many changes. They added on, changed the letters going up one in the alphabet each year, NAA, NBA, NCA, like that, until they got to the big ones, the Hundreds series."

Pinardi's boss, Harold Brock, remembered the nomenclature. He is sometimes amused by tractor collectors and historians looking for significance in every detail.

"The letters NAA didn't stand for anything," he said. "They were just the next letters available. The 9N, 2N, and 8N were the years they were brought out. Then they got into more planning and . . ."

The Golden Jubilee, produced only for the 1953 model year, introduced Ford's new Red Tiger overhead-valve, four-cylinder 134-cid engine producing 30 horsepower. Jubilees were introduced to dealers before Thanksgiving 1952, and customer deliveries began immediately after.

Thirteen

TRACTORS BY THE HUNDREDS

The Whiz Kids Expand the Tractor Lineup

"**W**hen Dearborn Motors got organized," Harold Brock explained, "they brought in outside guys from our competition. 'We need to have a product planning group.' We'd done pretty well with our small group: twenty-five percent of the business. We need to make a tricycle tractor. Like IH or Case. If we did that, we'd get more market.'

"They persevered. I said, 'Show me the advantages of these tricycle tractors.' They'd get out their cultivators, and by the time they found all the parts to bolt on the front and the rear, we'd have been in the field and out.

" 'What's the advantage,' I asked them, 'if you're still looking for the parts to bolt on?'

"The advantage was that we'd be more like all our competitors and that would make all of *them* more comfortable. What they really did was changed something fundamental. Instead of shipping fourteen tractors, all the same, in a box car, now you ship them on trucks or flat cars. Cost us more. Confused dealers with more products, spare parts, and replacement pieces. You had the classic design and then . . ."

Even before Ford introduced the Golden Jubilee in late 1952, Harold Brock's tractor engineering group began designing, engineering, testing, and proving a wide range of new machines. In the United States Ford would offer tricycle tractors.

1955 Ford 740
Ford introduced its 740s in late 1954 as 1955 models. These were essentially Model 640s reconfigured as row-crop tricycles. This 1955 Model 740 has a Sherman over/under transmission to supplement its standard four-speed Ford gearbox and PTO. The 3,390-pound tricycle configuration sold new for $2,670.

In 1957, Ford's Tractor Division product planners and marketing staffs renumbered the tractor series introduced in 1955 and added names reflecting performance: 134-cid Red Tiger engines introduced in the 1953 NAA were now named Workmasters, while the larger 172-cid engines went in tractors called the Powermasters. *Henry Ford Museum and Greenfield Village*

County Commercial Cars of Fleet, Hampshire, England, continued producing four-wheel-drive and tracklaying versions of Ford's tractors even after American and European production was unified under Ford Tractor Division. This Model 1164 used Ford's 120-horsepower TW engine, coupled to a dual-range 16-speed forward, four-speed reverse gearbox. *Henry Ford Museum and Greenfield Village*

"The evolution from the NAA series to the Hundreds . . . ohhh boy." Eddie Pinardi whistled. "From the earliest, with the little Ford-Ferguson, we had a tractor that would pull two plows. Then came the NAA, and we had a tractor that would pull three plows. . . .

"Then they wanted a tractor to pull five plows. So we increased everything to pull five plows. Three or four years later, they wanted a tractor that could pull six plows. Everything again had to be increased.

"We knew one thing. We had a tractor that could pull three plows and they wanted one that would pull six. We couldn't just double everything and figure it would work. The more we pulled, the bigger we had to make it. And there was the model year change. Like cars, they wanted a new tractor every fall."

Mechanized farming was changing. The numbers of farm tractors on U.S. farms grew explosively in the late 1910s, swelling from 15, 525 in 1917 to 246,083 by the end of 1920. The numbers continued to grow through 1950, when the U.S. Department of Agriculture counted more than 3 million tractors on domestic farms. Average farm acreage increased

as well at that time, which drove demands for greater numbers of larger, more powerful tractors.

"In 1953," Eddie Pinardi continued, "we had an NAA tractor that only held ten gallons of gas. You send a man out and he could only work two hours before he had to come back and gas up. Now, with four plows, or five or six, we had to design the tractor to hold much more gas, as much as possible. We already had optional lights on those tractors so they could work later or go back out after supper. . . .

"But once you got the operator out there, they're in the hot sun. Before they were in every two hours, take a break, cool off, have something to drink before they went back out. When we got to doing the big tractors, we developed machines where you

sent an operator out at six o'clock in the morning, and he came back at eight o'clock at night on one fuel fill up. You're the farm owner; you go fill him up instead of him coming in.

"I can't use a seat made out of steel like on the 8N. So I give them a padded seat, but it's not enough. You have one operator who weighs one hundred-fifty pounds and another weighs two-fifty, one six-feet-three tall, the other five-feet-five. You make adjustment. Fit a shock absorber to soften the ride, add a spring.

"You put a cab on those tractors. Operator out there twelve, fifteen hours. Make it dustless, air-conditioned. Give them a radio. That's how everything developed."

1955 Ford 660

Ford's new Tractor and Implement Division created a wide range of machines it introduced in 1954. First came the 600-series, using the NAAs Red Tiger four-cylinder engine. Its top-of-the-line model, the 660, introduced Ford's new five-speed transmission, and the live PTO and hydraulic pump. Ford introduced the 660 at $2,265 in 1954 and continued production through 1957. Power steering was optional. The 3,095-pound tractors developed 32.3 gross horsepower.

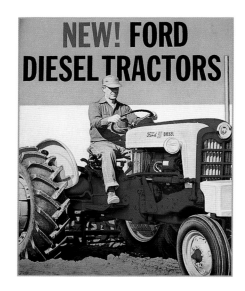

Ford Tractor and Implement Division announced its new diesel engines beginning with its 1957 model year line-up from the 600 through 900 series with the 500 series joining in 1959.

1956 Ford 950 High Crop
Extended front spindles and oversize B. F. Goodrich tires on 40-inch reversible rear wheels added about 7 inches of ground clearance to the 950 standard front tractor. The 950s and 960s came standard with Ford's 172-cid engine, independent PTO, power steering, and five-speed transmission.

At this point, Ford tractors had drifted some distance from Henry Ford's simple, lightweight machine to take the burden off the backs of man and animal. Tractors were market-driven. Ford's tractor division was a survivor, one of nine full-line companies left after a tumultuous half-century of tractor making. Full-line manufacturers were those who produced not only tractors but a complete assortment of implements, wagons, accessories, and harvesting equipment under the same logo. In 1955, these nine were supplemented by 13 companies producing crawlers and 35 other firms manufacturing wheel-type tractors.

The leader was still International Harvester, enjoying the position it regained from Ford in 1927. Second was Deere and Co., followed by J. I. Case, and then Massey-Harris-Ferguson. (This ranking was not in terms of tractor production but revenues from all implement and harvesting equipment sales.) Ford ranked ninth. Product planners and marketing staff were scrambling. Expanding the product line seemed a sensible way to broaden the appeal of the red-and-gray tractors.

The Quiz Kids
The other reason for the tractor line expansion was purely business: In late 1954, Henry Ford II took Ford Motor Company public, offering on the New York Stock Exchange shares of Ford for the first time since 1919. This resulted from seven years of hard work from Ernie Breech and Ford Division's new president, Robert S. McNamara. McNamara arrived in 1948 with nine former U.S. Army Air Force statistical control systems managers. They could quantify everything from shells to soldiers. This group, directed by a 32-year-old former colonel, Charles "Tex" Thornton, was hired en masse. Stock in Dearborn Motors made it worth their while; it was for them that DMC was created. From the start, they asked so many questions of other executives that they were dubbed Thornton's Quiz Kids. That name stuck until they began providing answers themselves. They pulled Ford back from the edge of bankruptcy, and their name changed to the Whiz Kids.

Going Public
Before Edsel Ford's death in 1943, Henry Ford held 55 percent of the company stock, Edsel had

The Sherman Forklift worked off the tractor's on-board hydraulics and PTO to provide as much as 4,000 pounds of lift. *Dwight and Katy Emstrom collection*

41.5, and Clara Ford controlled 3.5 percent. Before Henry's death in 1947, the family turned over nearly all the nonvoting stock to the Ford Foundation, keeping control and decision making in family hands yet avoiding colossal inheritance taxes.

Eight years after his grandfather's death, Henry II was ready to let the public in, announcing that 10.2 million shares would be offered starting January 26, 1956, opening at $64.50 per share. Within weeks, the offering sold out to 350,000 buyers, many of them farmers wanting to buy "some shares of Ford for the grandkids." The effect was more than a massive infusion of cash. From 1919 until 1956 Henry and Edsel answered to their own consciences for their decisions, good and bad. Now, 350,000 scrutineers watched and wondered. Before this, 10 Whiz Kids asked questions. Now Ford management had to satisfy 350,000 inquisitors. This meant Ford's Tractor and Implement Division had to pull its own weight.

Competition was fierce, but not only from domestic makers. Ford's Dagenham works came within 5,000 tractors of matching U.S. production. If Dagenham offered a variety of tractors, domestic operations had better learn something. Brock's trac-tor engineering group responded to Thorton's Quiz group with several new tractors offered in late fall 1954 as 1955 models.

New Hundred Series

First came the Model 600, which carried over the NAA's Red Tiger four-cylinder engine with 134-cubic-inch displacement. Product planning set three levels of features: the 640 with the NAA four-speed transmission and dependent PTO, the 650 with a fresh new five-speed gearbox and the same PTO, and the 660, which used the new five-speed and introduced Ford's live PTO.

Brock's group gave marketing a three-plow tractor in the 800 series, the 850 configuration with dependent PTO and 860 with live-PTO, both with five-speed transmissions. Engineering bored out the Red Tiger to 172 cubic inches. Each of these five models offered three-point hitches, but each of these was a four-wheel tractor of the Ford-Ferguson utility-type.

In the fall of 1955, the Tractor Division unveiled the first tricycles, the 700 and 900 series. As a 740, it mirrored 640 specifications while the 950 and 960 matched equipment available on the 850 and 860,

1957 Ford 840 with Sherman Forklift

Ford 840s came standard with the 172-cid in-line four-cylinder engine and five-speed transmission. In this case, the forklift also had the Sherman reversing transmission, which, with the flip of a lever, provided full transmission range in either forward or reverse.

1959 Ford 541 Offset

From the rear, the advantages of Ford's limited production offset high crop tractors are obvious. Besides high clearance available to work over banked vegetable and fruit crops, the narrow track made the machine practical for small farms and single-row cultivation.

Model 541 tractors were the Workmaster series, with the 134-cid gasoline or 144-cid diesel engines. This sparsely equipped model had a standard four-speed transmission and a PTO. Steering power came from the operator's arms.

introducing power steering for the top two. Styling of each of these four models and their variations came from the NAA, keeping Eddie Pinardi's shock of wheat within the radiator grille badge.

For 1957, the Tractor Division performed cosmetic surgery on the entire line-up, adding a bold grid motif to the grille. These tractors, with a "1" added to their numbering systems, got names from product planning and marketing staffs, eager to provide obvious product identity. They called the small-engined tractors the Workmaster series, while they tagged the larger ones the Powermasters. Ford introduced liquefied petroleum gas, LPG, as a fuel option in mid-1957 across its entire range of tractors. The 19.2-gallon (working capacity) fuel tank replaced the gas tank; it and the other equipment necessary added about 100 pounds to the tractor weight.

The Typhoon

Harold Brock's work was not simply following the lead of product planners. In its experiments, the division led the industry in the late-1950s. Where the 1930s and 1940s were the "streamline age," the 1950s were the Jet age.

In July 1957, Ford unveiled its "Typhoon," a free-piston turbine engine installed in an extended 961 tractor chassis. Engineering built three. Its complicated name masked the fact that it was two engines, not just one.

Ford's free-piston diesel engine used two pistons sliding to and from each other in a single cylinder. This engine needed only to produce exhaust gas, not reciprocal or rotary motion to move the machine. The pistons had no connecting rods. Ignition shoved them into "bounce cylinders" of compressed air at opposite ends of the combustion chamber. This bounced them back toward each other, compressing new diesel fuel into ignition.

Exhaust ran turbine driving double-reduction gears to which engineers Oscar Noren and Robert Erwin connected main and auxiliary drives. The auxiliary operated the hydraulic pump and PTO while the main drive, reduced 5,600:1 in first gear, moved the tractor. The turbine, running at 15 to 25 psi of pressure, idled at 10,000 rpm, and under load, reached 43,000 rpm. Capable of 100 horsepower, Noren and Erwin limited output to 50. They lengthened the 961 wheelbase 14.0 inches beyond the normal 85.3 inches to accommodate hardware necessary to create this system. At 4,200

1958 Ford 861 with Model 711 Front Loader
Ford Tractor and Implement Division's unusual "one-arm loader" offered operators the benefit of much greater visibility than more usual two-arm varieties. The 711 used hydraulics only to raise and lower the arm; the bucket operated mechanically.

1959 Ford 621

The 621 was the natural successor to the Fordson. With neither PTO nor hydraulics, this tractor was ordered with nothing more than a drawbar. The simple option list was chosen with a specific task in mind, in this case, to pull a gang of lawnmowers around a golf course. The bottom-of-the-line tractor did without tachometer or lights.

pounds, it weighed 900 pounds more than a gasoline-engined 961. It stood 4.0 inches taller and 11.0 inches longer overall. Noren and Erwin obtained fuel economy equal to other tractor engines. The benefit was that fewer moving parts cost less to replace, and the entire engine experienced much less wear per hour.

Ladysmith, Wisconsin, Ford tractor dealer Harold Ypma recalled the Typhoon passing through a neighboring village in far northern Wisconsin in late spring 1958.

"A truck and trailer from Ford Tractor Division stopped in for fuel and on it was a prototype, a turbine-powered tractor going to the Minnesota State Fair in [St. Paul]. When I went to the fair at Machinery Hill, they had a big roped off circle and a guy was driving it around. You had to start it with compressed air. It had quite a sound.

"But even more than the sound was the gearshift wand, the Select-O-Speed. They never said a thing about that, just the guy was changing gears while it was moving by sliding that wand up and down. Of course, that didn't come out until the next year. I was watching them shift the gears on the go. . . ."

Select-O-Speed

In reports on the Typhoon published by Ford in Society of Automotive Engineer journals in July 1957, the transmission was described only as a "full power shift, 10 speeds forward—2 reverse."

For Ford Tractor and Implement Division, the introduction of the Select-O-Speed was as exciting as bringing into the world the Ford-Ferguson 9N with its three-point hitch and hydraulic system. Almost as quickly, it proved as frustrating.

The first tractor assembled with the Select-O-Speed, serial numbered 60949, was manufactured on January 16, 1959. It was part of a fleet of 861 introduction tractors painted gold and provided to Ford's distributors. Not an automatic transmission, the S-O-S was a system of four planetary gearsets in series, one behind the other, shifted hydraulically. There was no longer a clutch although an "inching" control allowed the tractor forward or backward movement with critical accuracy. The operator shifted the tractor while moving and engineers conceived gear ratios to apply engine power most efficiently. Downshifting from sixth to fourth gear doubled the drawbar pulling power while coming down from tenth to

fourth increased pull eight times.

It facilitated PTO use over uneven terrain; the operator could shift down or up while maintaining steady engine speed. This meant less risk of a PTO-driven implement jamming. Top road speed was 18 miles per hour at 2,200 rpm in tenth gear, yet without varying engine speed, it was possible to gear down continuously to as slow as 1.2 miles per hour in first gear.

"Engineering the tractor is different from an automobile," Harold Brock said, "because the tractor is under more sustained load. On the transmission for an automobile, you can test it in low gear under full power, and if it lasts forty-five minutes, it's a good transmission. In a tractor you put it in low gear and run it thousands of hours. Because that's how it's going to work. So the durability and testing of tractors is more severe than cars. Of course, you're off the road, running into ditches or fences.

"There's more real engineering that goes into tractors. Today we have computers and finite analysis. We do a lot of design and testing in computers before we ever build a prototype. Whereas with the little tractor, the 9N, most of the people working on

1959 Ford 871 Gold Select-O-Matic

Dealers and customers remembered the gold Select-O-Matic tractors because each dealer used one to introduce the new shift-on-the-fly transmission to farmers and customers. Unfortunately, the transmissions were not ready for production, and the 100 or so gold tractors spent more time in the shop than in the fields. Only a handful of these gold tractors still exist.

it were master mechanics back then, what we'd call technicians today; they were the engineering people doing the design work of those days.

"We designed some by proportion and some by experience. We did a lot of testing. We didn't have [the] sophisticated testing procedures and equipment we have today. We just overdesigned things. We didn't know. So we added more metal than we

1959 Ford 971 Select-O-Speed High Crop
Ford's top-of-the-line tractor series, the 971s, were offered from 1957 through 1962, available with gas or diesel 172-cid engines.

needed. Today you can nearly calculate how much metal you need. Because of the expertise, engineers sometimes make things too light. They get too close to the edge and they get in trouble."

The Select-O-Speed got in trouble. Early production models would not run very long before they failed. It was attributed to several causes, but in the end, the Tractor and Implement Division warranted a huge number of tractors.

"It wasn't ready," Eddie Pinardi recalled, "it just wasn't ready. We'd say, 'Well, maybe its this end, here.' We'd fix that to what we thought it should be and then something else popped up over there. It wasn't one of those products you could look at, fig-

ure out what the problem was, fix it, and afterward it's a fine product. This was a case where we couldn't find the problem.

"We brought in different engineers, they last a while and go back. The next set would come. Finally nobody wanted the job. Solve one problem and something else would go. Why? Because a hole was too small for the oil to go through. We'd fix that, but something else would fail. It wasn't just simply gears overheating. We finally redesigned the whole thing, based on everything we learned from all the fixes that didn't quite do the job. We redesigned the whole thing, and it went on to be a fine product."

1959 Ford 961 Row Crop
Ford introduced a 700 and 900 series of narrow front row crop tractors for 1955. Equipped with the 10-speed forward, 2-speed reverse Select-O-Speed transmission, this gas-engined tricycle relied on the Powermaster 172-cid in-line four-cylinder engine to produce its 46 gross horsepower. The tractor sold for $3,880 new.

1961 Ford 741 Workmaster
Both Ford's 700 and 900 series tractors were available as row-crop narrow front tractors as well as standard configuration machines. This gas-engined version used the straight four-speed transmission and was equipped with the remote hydraulic valve and power steering.

Auto-Pilot

One other project kept Ford engineers challenged, but pleasantly, through the mid-to-late 1950s. As with the Typhoon, C. B. Richey's tractor auto-pilot was not meant for production but simply to test the limits of imagination and technology at the time. Guided by a small wire imbedded in a concrete test track at Ford's Engineering Research Center in Birmingham, Michigan, Richey showed off an 841 Powermaster nicknamed the "Sniffer," equipped with a small antenna set between the front wheels. Signals on one channel provided directional information. A second channel instructed the driverless tractor to operate brakes, clutch, or implement lift. Practical applications for this system were limited. Submerging a guide wire in a field that would be plowed or disked presented obvious complications. Richey's tractor system proved of great benefit for engine and transmission durability tests, evaluations that could be performed on a hard surface. By the time journalists and invited guests saw it in late May 1958, Richey had used it testing tractors at Birmingham for three years.

Fourteen

REQUIEM

At the end of the 1950s, Ford Tractor and Implement Division at Birmingham and the tractor operations at Dagenham took steps toward unification. Dagenham introduced its Dexta series in 1957, with a three-cylinder Perkins Diesel. A year later it brought out the Fordson Power Major to replace the New Major, and it carried on the same three engine options: gasoline, diesel, and tractor vaporizing oil (TVO or distillates). The Power Major remained in production into early 1961 when Dagenham unveiled the Super Major. Supplanting the Dexta was the Super Dexta in 1962, imported to the United States as the Ford 2000 Diesel from 1962 through 1964.

In the fall of 1961, Ford Tractor Operations announced its new Model 6000. This six-cylinder machine represented the top of the line by replacing existing machines and issuing new numbers to fit the Thousands series nomenclature. Plagued with problems, Tractor Operations ended up replacing every 6000 at no charge. The new Model 4000 replaced 801 models, and the smaller 2000 tractors came in for the 601 series. Tractor Operations served as the umbrella organization within Ford to manage consolidation of Ford Tractor and Implement Division with tractor production from Dagenham. A year later the combination was renamed Ford Tractor Division. Dagenham's Fordson Super Major became the Ford 5000 in the United

In March 1961, Ford consolidated international Tractor Operations—both the Tractor and Implement Division in Michigan and the Ford Motor Company Ltd. in England—to produce a line of worldwide tractors. Ford then introduced its new Model 2000, replacing the 601 series. The red paint used on tractors sold in America was replaced with Dagenham blue. This model is a 1963 Model 2000.

1966 Ford 4000

*I*ntroduced in 1962, Model 4000 tractors replaced the 801 series. Like the former Powermaster series, these tractors operated with Ford 172-cid four-cylinder engines, grossing 50 PTO horsepower. Weighing 2,976 pounds, this would have sold new for $3,415. Ford donated this tractor to a college in Minnesota for its agricultural engineering program. The donation was part of Ford's Educational Tractor program, which provided machines at no cost to colleges and trade schools for use in the mechanics and mechanical engineering classes.

1967 Ford 6000 LPG

*W*ith Select-O-Speed transmission, full hydraulics, PTO, and the LPG fuel system, the Commander 6000s weighed in at nearly 7,000 pounds and sold for almost $5,600. The 6000s were not part of the World Tractor program, being sold only in the United States, Canada, and Australia with gas, diesel, or LPG fuel choices. Ford's Model 6000 tractors were plagued with problems from their introduction in 1961, ultimately causing Ford to replace them under warranty.

States, and the Super Dexta was renamed the 2000 Diesel. All of this fell under the concept of "World Tractor," an idea created by the Whiz Kids. To provide a unified identity, the product planners married Dagenham blue with U.S. gray as the color scheme for the new production.

"World Tractor" put into effect other changes to unify production and styles. The Tractor Division ended manufacture at Dagenham in 1964, moving United Kingdom production to the new facility at Basildon. Tractor Division took over Ford of Europe's plant in Antwerp, Belgium, to make tractors there. U.S. manufacture remained at Highland Park where it had been since the 9N. For 1965, the range of 2000 through 5000 tractors was replaced; Ford dropped row-crop and offset models. Smaller tractors used three-cylinder diesels; the 5000 got a new four-cylinder, while the 6000, renamed the Commander 6000, was essentially unchanged.

In 1966 the Tractor Division joined many other makers producing lawn and garden tractors as well as agriculture and industrial machines. Ford had climbed into second place in worldwide tractor pro-

duction, behind, ironically, Massey-Ferguson. (The Harris family withdrew from Massey-Harris-Ferguson activities in 1958.) During 1992 and 1993, the AGCO conglomerate acquired Massey-Ferguson.

In 1977, Ford introduced its first articulated four-wheel drive tractors. These were manufactured in Ford blue and gray by Steiger Tractor Company in Fargo, North Dakota. It typified a trend among leading industrial producers to acquire outside engineering, rebadged in appropriate color schemes rather than invest the funds to develop a similar product or machine themselves. A decade later, Ford acquired Versatile Manufacturing Company of Winnipeg, Manitoba. Versatile had incorporated in 1963 and introduced its first articulated four-wheel-drive tractors, the D-100 series, using Ford industrial V-8 engines in 1966. By 1977, Versatile switched to Cummins diesels, which continued to be used in Ford Versatile tractors.

About the same time that Versatile came into Ford, so did the Sperry New Holland Company, the New Holland, Pennsylvania–based manufacturer of harvesting equipment. This represented an effort on

the Tractor Division's part to resume its identity as a full-line company in agriculture. The Tractor Division disappeared into the organization called Ford-New Holland. New Holland implements retained their characteristic golden color with red trim while the tractors remained blue and gray. Tractors were manufactured in Winnipeg, Canada; Basildon, England; Michigan; and in Georgia.

In 1991, after years of effort to enter the American tractor market, Fiat Agri acquired 80 percent of Ford-New Holland, and then increased its share to 88 percent in 1992. In 1993, Fiat Agri purchased the remaining 12 percent from Ford under terms of an agreement in which the Ford name will disappear completely from the tractors by January 1, 2000. In fact, the Genesis and Gemini series tractors as well as the Versatile articulated models produced in late 1997 no longer bore any Ford identification.

1995 Ford 9280

*O*ffered in 1994 and 1995, this Versatile-built articulated four-wheel drive sold new for nearly $108,000. With dual wheels and extension hubs, it weighed nearly 24,700 pounds. To the top of the cab, these tractors stood 11 feet, 7 inches tall and 13 feet, 9 inches wide. The 9280 was powered by a Cummins LT10A in-line six-cylinder diesel, 611-cid engine that produced 250 horsepower. A 12-speed Quadra-Sync transmission was synchronized in the first four gears.

1990 Ford 976

*P*roduced from 1987 through 1993, the Versatile-produced 976 used the 855-cid Cummins in-line six-cylinder engine producing 325 horsepower. The transmission provided 12 speeds forward and four reverse, and the 22,000-pound articulated four-wheel-drive tractors sold new for $99,000.

After 80 years of interrupted Ford tractor production, world economics, stockholder priorities, and board member sensibilities no longer saw agricultural implement and tractor production as a prudent use of corporate resources. It is a decision that is impossible to dispute. In its last days, Ford-New Holland represented something like 3.5 percent of Ford Motor Company's worldwide activities. Ford is governed now by few individuals who were born into the family. The long emotional tie that tugged at Henry II, making him produce a 1953 NAA—even introducing it within months of the end of a costly and time-consuming lawsuit over tractors—is completely severed.

That 1953 tractor was named the "Golden Jubilee," both words connoting 50 years of time passage. It was Henry II's homage to his grandfather's devotion to these machines above all others he produced. That his grandson recognized this fact is certain; there were no Golden Jubilee cars or 50th anniversary trucks.

The concept of "World Tractor" probably would have pleased Henry Ford greatly. He envisioned one make of tractor operating on farms throughout the world as the foundation of universal understanding and peace. It allowed farmers everywhere, no matter their ethnic background, to have one thing in common, provoking in them the need to examine what else they might share with the farmer across the fence or over the border.

Even though the familiar blue oval no longer appears on new production tractors, Ford's legacy is industrywide. Harold Brock, former chief tractor engineer, who worked side-by-side with Henry Ford on the 9N tractor, explained: "When Dearborn Motors got organized they brought in outside guys. They said, 'We ought to have a tricycle tractor, like IH, like Case.' Then Dearborn Motors went from tricycle to the single wheel. They had to go to adjustable axles. . . .

"Eventually, after all these years, every tractor in the world has gone back and copied the basic design of the 9N."

INDEX

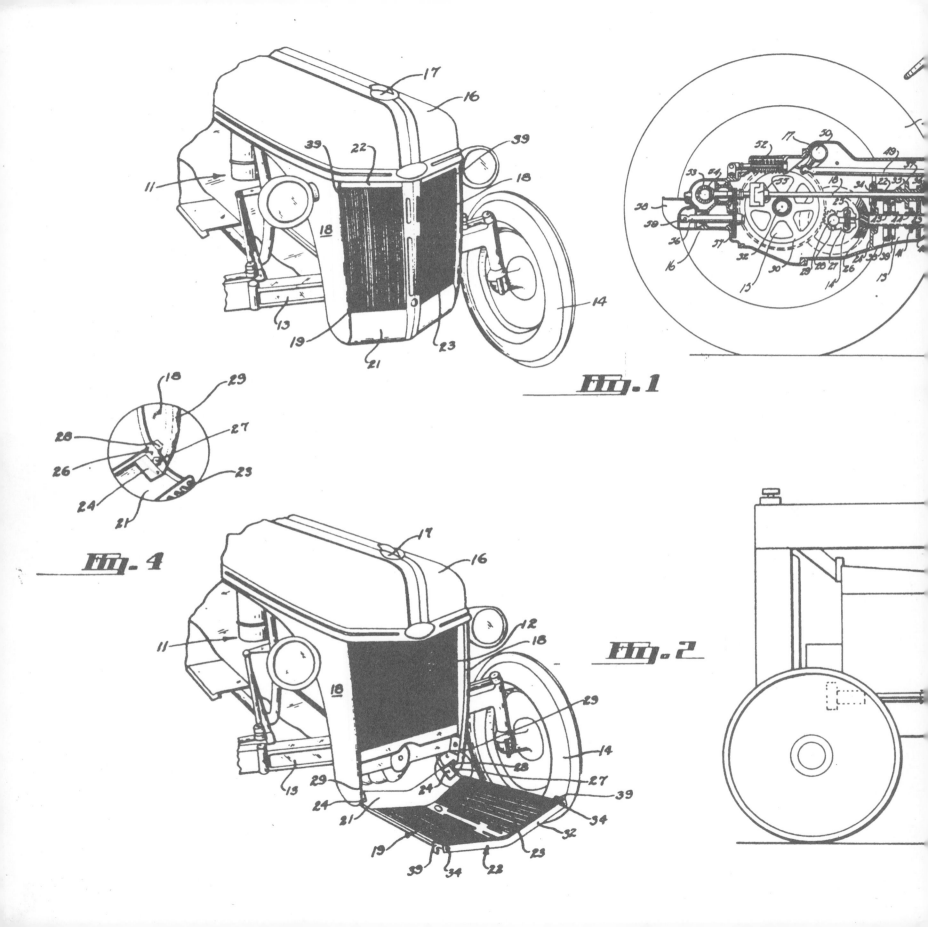

Fig.1

Fig.4

Fig.2